SUPERMAN
TALES OF THE
BIZARRO
WORLD

writer
JERRY SIEGEL

artisits
JOHN FORTE
WAYNE BORING
CURT SWAN

SUPERMAN CREATED BY JERRY SIEGEL AND JOE SHUSTER

ME NOT BE SATISFIED WITH MERELY PUTTING FAKE MAKE-UP ON ACTOR! ME WILL CREATE **REAL, LIVE** AUTHENTICALLY REVOLTING MONSTER!

BIZARRO No.1

Jenette Kahn
President & Editor-in-Chief

Paul Levitz
Executive Vice President & Publisher

Mike Carlin
Executive Editor

Mort Weisinger
Editor-original series

Dale Crain
Editor-collected edition

Nick J. Napolitano
Associate Editor-collected edition

Georg Brewer
Design Director

Robbin Brosterman
Art Director

Richard Bruning
VP-Creative Director

Patrick Caldon
VP-Finance & Operations

Dorothy Crouch
VP-Licensed Publishing

Terri Cunningham
VP-Managing Editor

Joel Ehrlich
Senior VP-Advertising & Promotions

Alison Gill
Exec. Director-Manufacturing

Lillian Laserson
VP & General Counsel

Jim Lee
Editorial Director-WildStorm

John Nee
VP & General Manager-WildStorm

Bob Wayne
VP-Direct Sales

Published by DC Comics. Cover, introduction and compilation copyright © 2000 DC Comics. All Rights Reserved.

Originally published in single magazine form in Adventure Comics #285-299. Copyright © 1961, 1962 DC Comics. All Rights Reserved.
All characters, their distinctive likenesses and related indicia featured in this publication are trademarks of DC Comics.
The stories, characters, and incidents featured in this publication are entirely fictional.

DC Comics, 1700 Broadway, New York, NY 10019 A division of Warner Bros. - A Time Warner Entertainment Company Printed in Canada. First Printing. ISBN: 1-56389-624-9

Cover illustration by Jaime Hernandez. Cover color by Lee Loughridge. Interior color reconstruction by Digital Chameleon. Publication design by Kris Ruotolo.

TABLE OF CONTENTS

All stories by Jerry Siegel, all art by John Forte, unless otherwise noted.

SUPERMAN
DC
NATIONAL COMICS

Bizarro Superman made me rich.

Very rich. Yes, you read that correctly.

As I write this, I am very, very rich, thanks mostly

to Bizarro Superman. Let me tell you how.

A couple of years ago, I was working as a television writer on the hit comedy show of the late twentieth century, *Seinfeld*. Perhaps you recall it. It was that show sandwiched between *The Single Guy* and *Madman of the People*. It was my second season on the show and I was working on my episode and stuck a little bit on the Elaine story—Elaine stories were always tough because she was kind of a girl and I am not. Anyway, I was playing around with the idea of a boyfriend for Elaine who, after she breaks up with him, wants to remain friends with her just like Jerry. The twist was that this ex-boyfriend would actually end up being a much better friend than Jerry ever was. This ex-boyfriend, Kevin, would be kind and compassionate. He would be the exact opposite of Jerry. He would be Bizarro Jerry.

ELAINE: I had to ask Kevin to leave his office and come and pick me up.

JERRY: Well, what are friends for?

ELAINE: Yes, and he is a friend, Jerry. He's reliable, he's considerate. He's like your exact opposite.

JERRY: So he's Bizarro Jerry.

ELAINE: Bizarro Jerry?

JERRY: Yeah, like Bizarro Superman. Superman's exact opposite who lives in the backwards Bizarro World. Up is down. Down is up. He says "hello" when he leaves, "goodbye" when he arrives.

ELAINE: Shouldn't he say "badbye"? Isn't that the opposite of goodbye?

JERRY: No, it's still "goodbye."

ELAINE: Does he live under-water?

JERRY: No.

ELAINE: Is he black?

JERRY: Look, just forget about the whole thing, all right?

That's right, I wrote the Bizarro Jerry episode of *Seinfeld*. As you probably know, the real-life Jerry Seinfeld is a big fan of Superman and comics in general. During the 9-year run of the show, there were numerous mentions of both DC and Marvel characters—e.g., Jerry and George discussing what Iron Man wears under his armor. But in the end, Superman was Jerry's guy. Longtime fans of the show probably noticed the Superman magnet on the fridge and the cool Randy Bowen Superman statue in the living room. There was the episode where Jerry dated a girl named "Lois," and the one where we found out his ATM code was "Jor-el." Mr. Seinfeld, which he let us call him, liked the idea of Elaine dating "Bizarro Jerry" and he liked the idea of taking it further. That's when we turned to the Bizarro Code.

The Bizarro Code is the mantra by which the Bizarro World existed. Soon after his creation, Bizarro Superman went off with

Bizarro Lois to found his own square-shaped world, and the code defined how they lived. "Us do opposite of all Earthly things!" Sure there was more, but this was the basic tenet, and throughout the "Tales of the Bizarro World" that were the backup stories in ADVENTURE COMICS, that code appeared in every issue. Usually on the first or second page. It was a formula but it was a good one.

So if the Bizarro World did the opposite of Earth, then Bizarro Jerry might have his own world that did the opposite of Jerry's Earth. That would be the Bizarro Jerry Code. What if Bizarro Jerry had his own opposite versions of George and Kramer? Bizarro George would be quiet-spoken and honest. Bizarro Kramer would knock before he entered, and come up with useful inventions that he never actually bothered to make. What if Bizarro Jerry had an apartment the exact opposite of Jerry's? The layout was the exact opposite: instead of a bike on the wall there was a unicycle; instead of cereal in the kitchen, there was pasta. And in the living room, if you hit your freeze frame button you'll even see a statue of Bizarro Jerry. The episode was jammed with "Bizarro Jokes" right down to the last moment of the show that featured the Bizarro gang. As Bizarro Jerry, Bizarro George and Bizarro Kramer hug—something that the regular Jerry, George and Kramer would never do—Bizarro Jerry cries out, "Oh. Me so happy me want to cry." We really did that on national television. We had a character talk like Bizarro.

God it was a lot of fun. We would sit around for hours arguing and joking about what the opposite of something was. Jerry has race cars on his walls, so should Bizarro Jerry have regular cars or how about people walking or what about horses? Was pasta really the opposite of cereal? Why not have Bizarro Kramer bring groceries over? If Newman is a post man, what does Bizarro Newman do? Answer: Fed Ex. It was kind of a game, and kind of a puzzle. And I'd like to think that it was probably a bit like it was to write the Tales from the Bizarro World stories. It's not so much that those comics were so wonderful, but it was how inventive they could be when it came to the Bizarro world. And how funny they were.

Every story started the same. Besides the Bizarro Code, each story would usually retell who Bizarro was and how he came to occupy the square Bizarro world. But then the writers would go to town, Bizarro style. For a couple of pages, we would get to see the Bizarro code in action in little vignettes of life on the Bizarro world, such as a Bizarro birthday where the candles are blown up, or Bizarro people sleeping with their feet on the pillows. Every issue had new aspects of the Bizarro world, as if the writers were working from some kind of wonderful master Bizarro list of comedy bits. And then the story, whatever it was, would unfold. Some good stories, some bad, but it didn't matter. The key to a great Tales from the Bizarro World story was really how many great Bizarro bits could be squeezed in. If there was a chase in the story, let's have them fly by an office where we could see Bizarro workers firing their boss. If a giant Bizarro Ape was going to run rampant, then it was used as an excuse to see... a giant Bizarro Ape as well as a crooked Bizarro wrestling ring. And heck, the Bizarro Ape was funny, as were the Bizarro versions of the Daily Planet, Lex Luthor and even Mr. Mxyzptlk. They did a Bizarro version of anything and everything they could.

Anyway, the episode aired and people liked it. Hell, they loved it. More important, I signed a big TV deal with Disney. Like I said, Bizarro Superman made me very, very, very, very rich. But a funny thing happened besides my getting stinking rich. All of a sudden, every-

NOW ME STUCK WITH YOU... FOREVER! ME SO *HAPPY*, ME SORRY ME EVER WAS BORNED!

where I went, people were outing themselves as comic-book readers and as Bizarro lovers. It seemed that no matter how long it had been since they had read a comic, people never forgot Bizarro Superman. He made an impression.

What started as a one-shot Superboy story was quickly brought into the mainstream Superman books, and it just kind of took off. Bizarro had a life of its own. The backup stories in ADVENTURE COMICS were just a natural offshoot of the character's popularity. Perry White never got his own recurring backup story. Neither did Lana Lang. Nor did any of Superman's other villains. There was no "Adventures of Lex Luthor" or "Tales of Brainiac." Not that Bizarro was really a villain. He just kind of seemed confused. That's all. Like Fredo in *The Godfather*. You felt a little bit sorry for him. He didn't know any better. I'll never forget the time Metropolis was celebrating Superman Day—it was reprinted in that great Superman hardcover with stories from the '30s, '40s, '50s and '60s. Superman is getting all these great gifts and along comes Bizarro with his gift: Kryptonite. I laughed out loud. Hey, at least he brought a gift.

It sounds stupid, but Bizarro was… bizarre. Duh. That was the point. Bizarro was an off-note. He was something different in a world of comics where so often characters were only differentiated by the color of their capes. His individual appearances in the main Superman books and the Tales backups represent some of the most unusual and funniest super-hero stories you will ever see. People even use the word bizarro a lot now. You see it in magazines and on MTV. Was it just because of the episode? No. But as I sit here, writing this in my giant mansion, I like to think that we reminded people what a good word it was. And while I can joke a lot about what that particular episode did for my career, I figure part of what got me into this career in the first place was a desire to be funny. Like Bizarro.

Hello.

—David Mandel

The Bizarro Story...

Bizarro was originally created for the Superman newspaper strip in the 1950s by writer Alvin Schwartz and artist Curt Swan, but its publication was delayed and Bizarro  actually first appeared in SUPERBOY #68, in a story written by Otto Binder and with art by George Papp. Unique about this appearance was the fact that the "first" Bizarro was an "imperfect duplicate" of Superboy. The lifeless animation was produced by a machine invented by a Dr. Dalton (which immedi-  ately afterwards exploded). After several run-ins with Superboy, Bizarro was "disintegrated into the lifeless molecules from which he was formed."

He next appeared as the adult Bizarro Superman that we now most remember in ACTION COMICS #244-245, written by Otto Binder and drawn by Al Plastino. Lex Luthor, having recreated the duplicating machine, trains it on Superman to create the classic Bizarro. At the end of this two-part appearance Bizarro leaves Earth with his newly created wife, Bizarro Lois, looking to find happiness on a distant planet.

In his additional "guest" appearances, it was revealed that Bizarro #1 and Bizarro-Lois #1 had settled on a distant planet and had created even more duplicates of themselves to populate their world—a world that was then reshaped by Superman himself into a cube-shaped planet. Never a true villain, Bizarro was more of a confused nuisance in this, and his subsequent earlier appearances, but in June 1961, in ADVENTURE COMICS #285 Bizarro was given his own regular backup feature and a new tone. Gone was any semblance of seriousness. This Bizarro was played strictly for laughs. And here, our story begins...

Us People

An Interview with Bizarro Superman #1

By David Mandel

The call came from his agent early in the morning. A little before eight. I was still in bed. "He'll meet you. Noon. The Ivy. No photographers." I was very excited. Bizarro Superman #1 had been a childhood favorite of mine. And while he had changed a bit over the years, from Curt Swan to John Byrne to Bruce Timm, he still looked the same as his car dropped him off in front of the fashionable Beverly Hills eatery. A few hours late and a little tired, "#1" had been up all night, working on the new DC Bizarro Trade Paperback. I was thrilled to spend some time with him.

David: Hello, Bizarro.

Bizarro #1: Goodbye.

D: Ha-ha. Right, of course. "Goodbye." How are you doing today?

INTO THE TIME-BARRIER SUPER-SPEEDS *BIZARRO.*

ME WILL TRAVEL JUST FEW YEARS INTO PAST, TO TIME WHEN FIRST *ABOMINABLE SNOWMAN* WAS SEEN ON EARTH!

BIZARRO NO. 1

B: Me am bad. But me very happy, it am raining.

D: Ha-ha. That's funny, because I, of course, am sad it is raining, which is the opposite of what you think. (The waiter approaches) Why don't we order?

B: Yes.

D: Wait. Does that mean you want to order or not order? Are you speaking backwards?

B: Bizarro want to order.

D: How do I know that isn't

Bizarro-backwards-talk also?

B: Bizarro am hungry.

D: Ok, but if you say you are hungry, doesn't that mean you aren't hungry? Because if you were really hungry, wouldn't you say you were not hungry.

B: (Angry) Hungry!!!

D: Gotcha. You're hungry. I guess we should order some delicious ice-cold soup and some cold dogs with mustard. Ha-ha.

B: Look, cut the crap.

D: What?

B: You heard me. Cut the crap. I can't take it anymore.

D: Bizarro, what's going on? You don't sound like yourself.

B: God, do you have any idea how sick and tired "me am" of all this crap?

D: Ok, I get it. Mr. Mxyzptlk is here. He's using some of his 5th Dimensional magic to make you act this way. Right?

B: You are so sad. Mr. Mxyzptlk

isn't here. There is no Mr. Mxyzptlk.

D: The Toyman. He's behind this. No. Lex Luthor! It's got to be.

B: Stop it. You're acting like an ass. (To waiter) Let me get a Stoli, neat. (The waiter leaves.) DC picking up the tab? I'm going to get a steak.

D: I… I don't understand.

B: Then let me explain it to you. Me Bizarro. Me say everything backwards. Me live on a square planet, with ugly women, in crooked house, where have no

grammar and eat-'em gravel. What am I, retarded?

D: You can't say that.

B: What, "retarded"? Oooooh. Call Superman. I'm sorry, but I have had it with being a "Super idiot."

D: No, Bizarro, you're not a "super idiot." The Bizarro planet is an imperfect duplicate of our own world.

B: Imperfect duplicate? Riiiiiight. I'll give you imperfect duplicate. On the Bizarro world, everyone celebrates Valentine's Day on

January 1 and New Year's Day on February 14. What is that?

D: Well. It's kind of imperfect.

B: It's bananas. And how about this? On the Bizarro World, people give tickets to the police. That's not imperfect. It's like some kind of bad Yakov Smirnov routine. [Does bad Yakov Smirnov impression.] "In Russia, magazine reads… you."

D: We don't have to talk about Yakov Smirnov.

B: Yes we do. 'Cause on the Bizarro World, everyone *loves* Yakov Smirnov. He's a friggin'

SUDDENLY, A GIANT, HAIRY PAW CLUTCHES THE SUPER-TALENT SCOUT FROM THE *BIZARRO WORLD*…

HOORAY! GOOD LUCK, AT LAST!

Bizarro World

genius, and all the Bizarros go see him when he comes to our house and then we sit on the stage and watch him in the audience. And he's not Russian. He's Chinese.

D: That doesn't make any sense.

B: I know. That's what I am trying to tell you. And that ain't the half of it. Have you seen how ugly the women are on the Bizarro World?

D: Well…

B: Don't well me. Bizarro Lois #1. Have you seen her?

D: Yes.

B: Is she good-looking?

D: (long pause) No.

B: Bizarro Lois #2. Is she good-looking? How about Bizarro Lois #3. Or #4 or…

D: I get it. But you Bizarros love and appreciate ugly things. It's part of the Bizarro code.

B: I'd like to take that code and-- (The drinks arrive. He wolfs one down.) Where was I? Oh yeah. let me tell you something about the code. OK, sure we love ugly stuff. I laugh when Dracula kills people in the movies, I cheer for robbers to beat the cops, and I am a Red Sox fan, but these Loises are hideous. Hell, I'd rather watch Chinese Yakov Smirnov than make out with one of those rock hounds.

D: I still don't understand why Yakov Smirnov is Chinese.

B: Join the club. Look, I'm sorry to lay all this on you. But it's not my fault that Superman got hit by that stupid duplicator ray and I was created. I didn't ask for all this.

D: But you are beloved. Everyone loves Bizarro.

B: Then how come Superman has four different books a month? Four! What do I have? None! Zero. Zero isn't the opposite of four. The opposite of four is seven. I should have seven books a month.

D: Seven isn't the opposite of four.

B: It could be. If Yakov Smirnov is going to be Chinese, then seven could be the opposite of four. Look, I'm not asking for much. How about one lousy book a month. Maybe a backup story. Something.

D: I'm not really in a position to do anything—

B: Maybe an Elseworlds. What if Bizarro fought in the Civil War, huh? I could kill Lincoln by accident, and unfree the slaves. What if I was hit with the Bizarro ray and an imperfect duplicate of an already imperfect duplicate were made? What if Bizarro got to make out with the real sexy Lois Lane?

D: You've changed.

B: That's what Bizarro Lois said. Just 'cause I don't want to vacation in winter and stay home in the summer, I've changed.

D: I'm leaving.

B: Fine! Leave! That's what Bizarro Lois did too. She took off with my Bizarro Baby #1 and then accused me of not seeing other woman. Now she's so angry, she wants to get married, so we're getting a divorce.

D: Huh?

B: I don't know. This is why I drink so much. I think I am losing my mind.

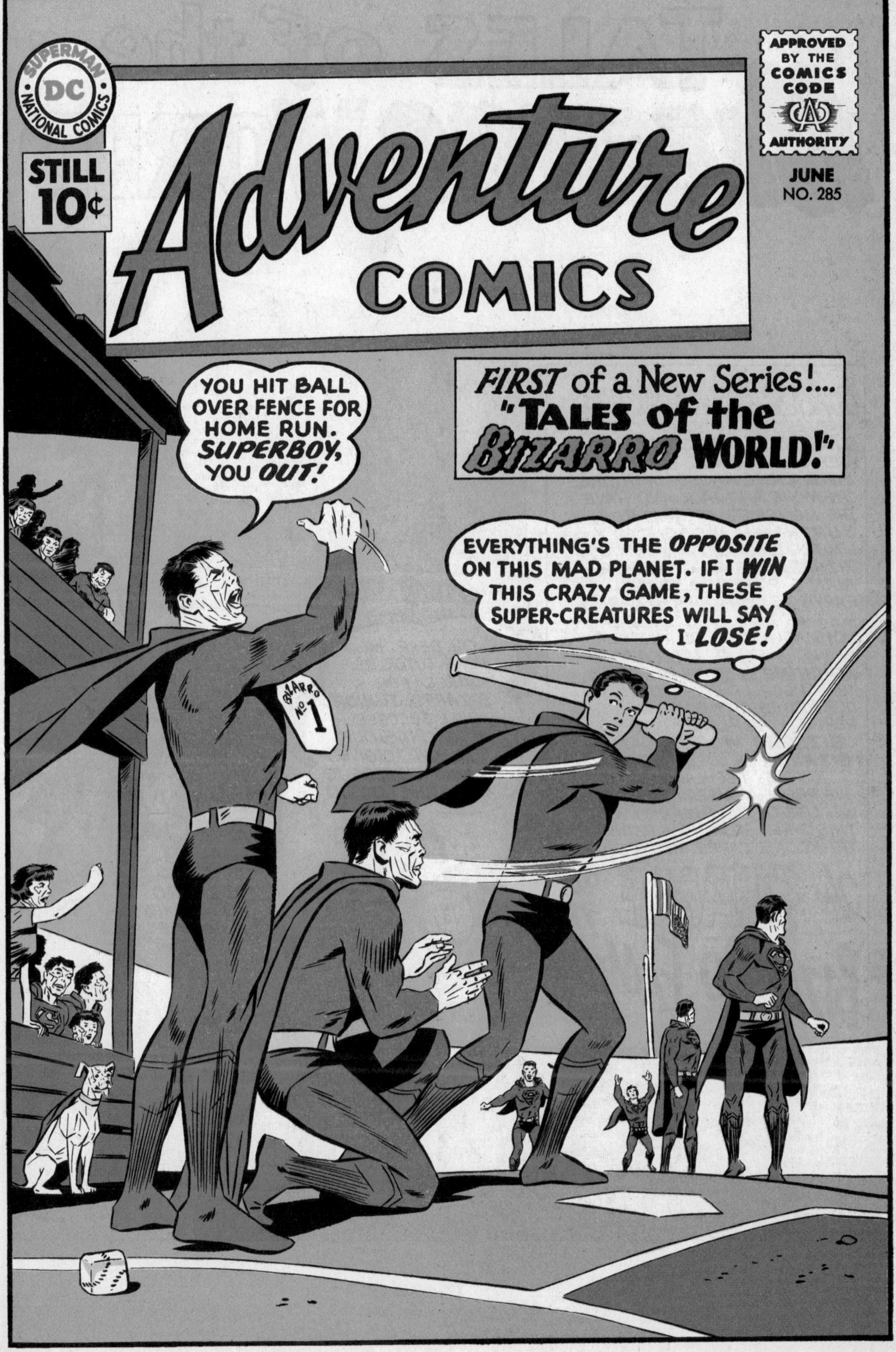
SUPERMAN DC NATIONAL COMICS
STILL 10¢
Adventure COMICS
APPROVED BY THE COMICS CODE AUTHORITY
JUNE NO. 285
FIRST of a New Series!... "TALES of the BIZARRO WORLD!"
YOU HIT BALL OVER FENCE FOR HOME RUN. SUPERBOY, YOU OUT!
EVERYTHING'S THE OPPOSITE ON THIS MAD PLANET. IF I WIN THIS CRAZY GAME, THESE SUPER-CREATURES WILL SAY I LOSE!
BIZARRO No 1

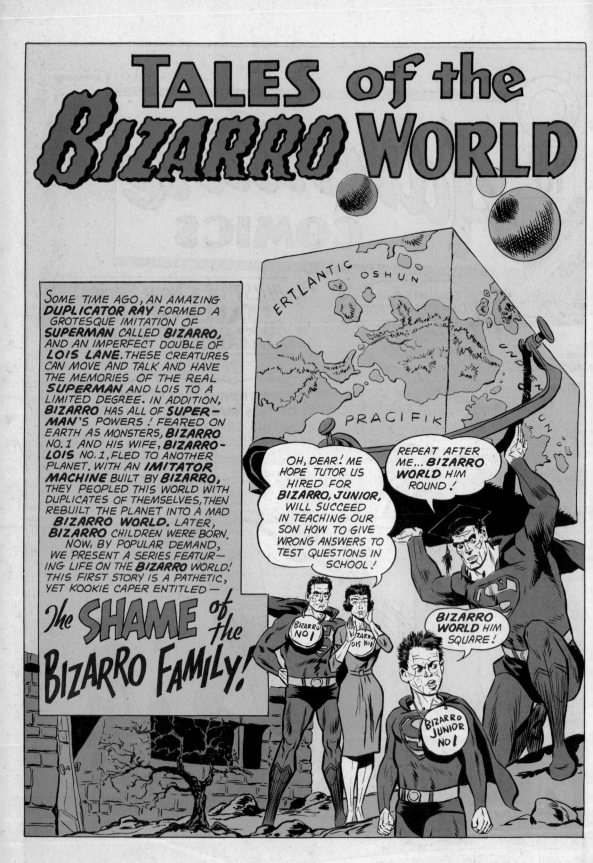

TALES of the BIZARRO WORLD

The SHAME of the BIZARRO FAMILY!

SOME TIME AGO, AN AMAZING **DUPLICATOR RAY** FORMED A GROTESQUE IMITATION OF **SUPERMAN** CALLED **BIZARRO**, AND AN IMPERFECT DOUBLE OF **LOIS LANE**. THESE CREATURES CAN MOVE AND TALK AND HAVE THE MEMORIES OF THE REAL **SUPERMAN** AND LOIS TO A LIMITED DEGREE. IN ADDITION, **BIZARRO** HAS ALL OF **SUPERMAN'S** POWERS! FEARED ON EARTH AS MONSTERS, **BIZARRO NO. 1** AND HIS WIFE, **BIZARRO-LOIS NO. 1**, FLED TO ANOTHER PLANET. WITH AN **IMITATOR MACHINE** BUILT BY **BIZARRO**, THEY PEOPLED THIS WORLD WITH DUPLICATES OF THEMSELVES, THEN REBUILT THE PLANET INTO A MAD **BIZARRO WORLD**. LATER, **BIZARRO** CHILDREN WERE BORN.

NOW, BY POPULAR DEMAND, WE PRESENT A SERIES FEATURING LIFE ON THE **BIZARRO** WORLD! THIS FIRST STORY IS A PATHETIC, YET KOOKIE CAPER ENTITLED—

OH, DEAR! ME HOPE TUTOR US HIRED FOR BIZARRO, JUNIOR, WILL SUCCEED IN TEACHING OUR SON HOW TO GIVE WRONG ANSWERS TO TEST QUESTIONS IN SCHOOL!

REPEAT AFTER ME... BIZARRO WORLD HIM ROUND!

BIZARRO WORLD HIM SQUARE!

FAR OUT IN SPACE EXISTS AN AMAZING MARVEL OF THE COSMOS... A **SQUARE WORLD!** IT IS THE HOME PLANET OF THE **BIZARRO** CREATURES...

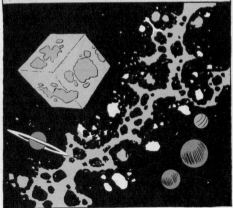

ASTONISHINGLY, EVERYTHING ON THIS CUBE-SHAPED WORLD IS A WHACKY VERSION OF EARTHLY CIVILIZATION! CITY SKYSCRAPERS LEAN CROOKEDLY AT ALL ANGLES! FOR THE PATHETIC **BIZARRO** PEOPLE HATE PERFECTION!

FOLLOWING A CRAZY CALENDAR, ALL EARTHLY HOLIDAYS ARE MISPLACED...

IS JANUARY 1ST! TIME TO GIVE OUT VALENTINES!

FEBRUARY 14TH IS NEW YEAR'S DAY HERE!

6019 JANUSCAREY 9106

6091 FEBROOHAIRY

Valentine Due

New Ears Due

SQUACK!

YES, THIS IS THE **WORLD OF BIZARROS**, WHERE EARTHLY CUSTOMS ARE BACKWARDS... EVEN THE USE OF ALARM CLOCKS WHOSE NUMBERED HOURS ARE CRAZILY SCRAMBLED!

¡YAWN¡... ALARM CLOCK GO OFF! IS TIME FOR US TO GO TO BED!

HA, HA! STUPID EARTH PEOPLE USE IT TO WAKE UP!

BRINGGGG!

AND THE **BIZARRO CODE** IS...

BIZARRO CODE

US DO OPPOSITE OF ALL EARTHLY THINGS!

US HATE **BEAUTY!** US LOVE **UGLINESS!**

IS BIG CRIME TO MAKE ANYTHING PERFECT ON **BIZARRO WORLD!**

LET US LOOK IN ON THE NUMBER ONE **BIZARRO** FAMILY AS **BIZARRO-LOIS LANE** BUSILY "CLEANS HOUSE" WITH HER RUBBISH DISPENSER...

YUM, YUM! BANANA PEEL TASTE DELICIOUS!

BANANA YOU TOSS AWAY MAKING HOUSE DIRTIER! FINE! ME TELL DADDY YOU GOOD BOY LIKE YOUR SISTER!

BIZARRO LOIS No 1

BIZARRO JUNIOR No 1

2

UH... WHERE IS DADDY, MOMMY?

OH, HIM OUT GETTING PRESENTS FOR YOUR BIRTHDAY PARTY, JUNIOR!

AT THAT VERY MOMENT, MILES AWAY, *BIZARRO* NO. 1 SUPER-BORES DOWN INTO THE GROUND...

AH-MY X-RAY VISION SEES VALUABLE *BURIED TREASURE!* MUST HAVE BEEN BURIED HERE BY *BIZARRO*-PIRATES!

INSTANTS LATER, HE TRIUMPHANTLY EMERGES WITH...

WOW!- OLD TIN CANS! WORN-OUT SHOES! NUTS! BOLTS! BOTTLE CAPS! THESE WORTH FORTUNE ON *BIZARRO* WORLD. MORE VALUABLE THAN GOLD OR DIAMONDS ON EARTH!

SOON, AS HE RETURNS HOME...

SEE MARVELOUS *JUNK* ME BROUGHT? *NOW* ARE YOU HAPPY?

GEE! HOW WONDERFUL! NOBODY CAN EVER SAY *MY* PAPA IS *CHEAP!*

PRESENTLY, AS THE PARTY STARTS...

ME GIVE GIFTS TO EVERYBODY!

A B-BROKEN BOTTLE FOR ME? OH, *THANKS!*

YES, ON THE *BIZARRO* WORLD, IT IS THE CUSTOM TO *GIVE* OTHERS PRESENTS ON *YOUR* BIRTHDAY!

③

THEN, AN EAGERLY ANTICIPATED EVENT...!

UH... IS TIME FOR YOU TO BLOW UP CANDLES ON BIRTHDAY CAKE, HONEY!

ME DO IT WITH X-RAY VISION!

However, **BIZARRO** JUNIOR'S X-RAY VISION NOT ONLY LIGHTS THE CANDLES, BUT SETS OFF THE BOMB, TRADITIONALLY HIDDEN INSIDE **BIZARRO** WORLD BIRTHDAY CAKES...

GOODY!

HOW PRETTY!

BWAAMM!

THEN EVERYONE GAILY CHORUSES...

UNHAPPY BIRTHDAY TO YOU, UNHAPPY BIRTHDAY TO YOU, UNHAPPY BIRTHDAY, DEAR **BIZARRO** JUNIOR, UNHAPPY BIRTHDAY TO YOU!

CHUCKLE! - SON HIM HAVING SWELL TIME!

NEXT DAY, AS **BIZARRO'S** CHILD FLIES TO SCHOOL...

HERE COMES **BIZARRO** JUNIOR NO.1! HIM STUPID! HIM ALWAYS GIVE TEACHER THE RIGHT ANSWER!

AND DOES **SHE** GET SORE, HA, HA!

HIM JUST CAN'T UNDERSTAND THAT YOU ONLY PASS IF YOU GET **FAILING** GRADES...

HIM CAN'T THINK OF WRONG ANSWERS, THE GOOF! HA, HA!

SOON, IN THE CLASSROOM...

IS TIME FOR DAY'S LESSONS TO BEGIN, SO EVERYBODY GET NOISY!

ER...ME BROUGHT SOMETHING FOR YOU!

AN APPLE FOR THE TEACHER?

NO, NOT AN APPLE, BUT INSTEAD...

A **SNAKE!** OH, HOW NICE YOU ARE!

ME THOUGHT YOU'D LIKE IT, TEACHER, BECAUSE IT REMINDS ME OF **YOU!**

4

AS THE TEACHER, WHO IS ALSO AN IMPERFECT *BIZARRO* DUPLICATE OF LOIS LANE, BEGINS QUESTIONING HER STUDENTS...

WHO ARE FAMOUS PEOPLE WHOSE FACES ARE CARVED OUT OF STONE ON MOUNT RUSHMORE MEMORIAL ON EARTH?

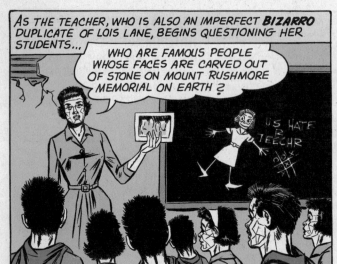

US HATE R TEECHR

THE RIGHT ANSWER, OF COURSE, IS PRESIDENTS WASHINGTON, JEFFERSON LINCOLN AND THEODORE ROOSEVELT... BUT...

ME KNOW! IS JESSE JAMES, JOHN DILLINGER, MACHINE-GUN KELLY AND AL CAPONE!

CLEVER BOY! ME GIVE YOU "D" MARK!

SOK!

FOR GIVING SO MANY WRONG ANSWERS, YOU ARE NOW HONOR STUDENT, AND MAY WEAR DUNCE CAP AS REWARD!

OH, BOY! ME NEVER FORGET THIS GREAT HONOR!

DUNCE

IS YOUR TURN NOW, *BIZARRO*, JUNIOR NO. 1! ME GIVE YOU EASY QUESTION! YOU WRITE DOWN NAMES OF SOME ANIMALS ON BLACKBOARD!

YES, TEACHER!

A MOMENT LATER...

BAH!... FOOL! THIS IS ANSWER YOU SHOULD HAVE WRITTEN!

CAT DOG HORSE

FLOWER TREE PLANT

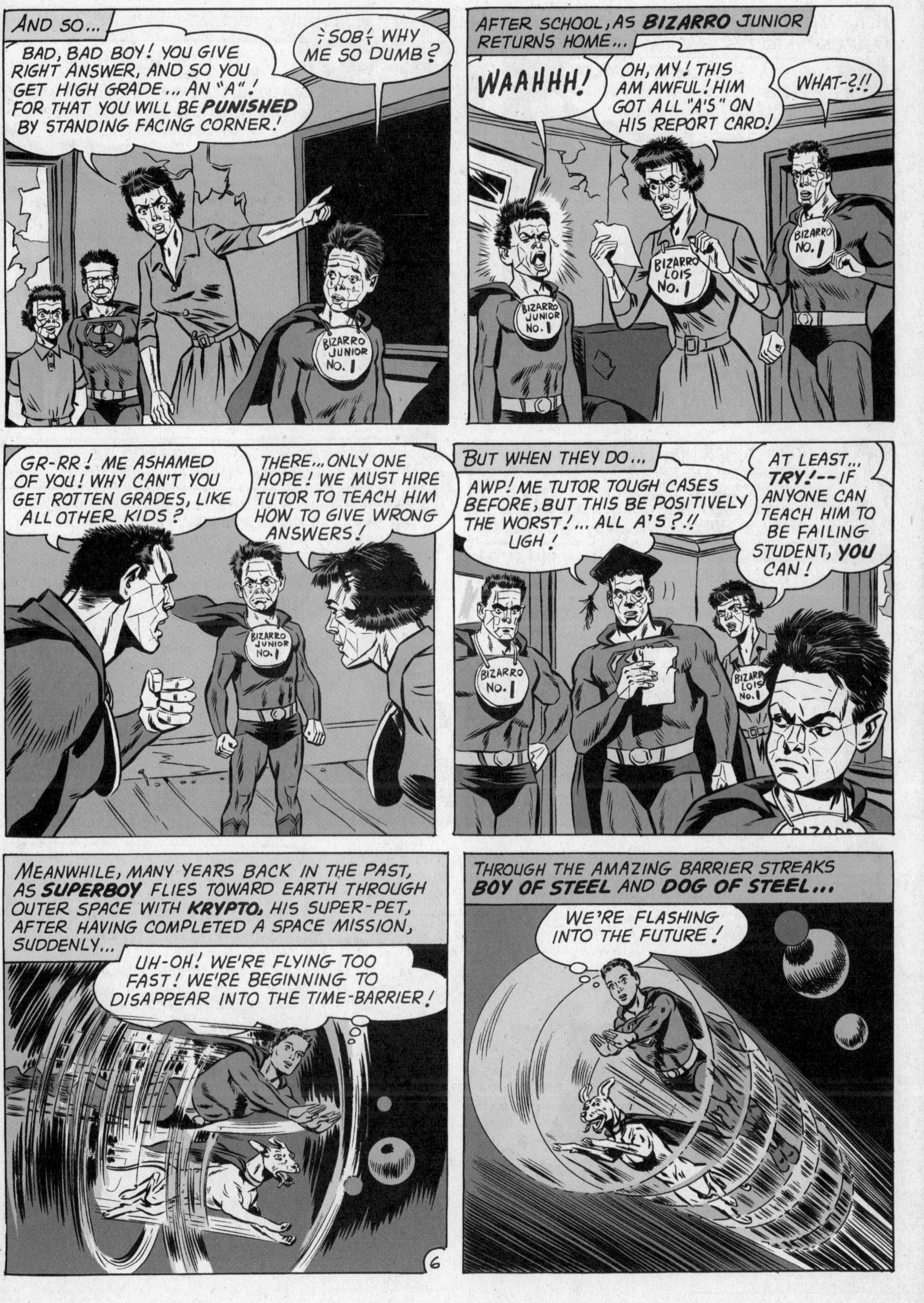
AND SO...
BAD, BAD BOY! YOU GIVE RIGHT ANSWER, AND SO YOU GET HIGH GRADE... AN "A"! FOR THAT YOU WILL BE PUNISHED BY STANDING FACING CORNER!
¡SOB¡ WHY ME SO DUMB?
BIZARRO JUNIOR NO. 1
AFTER SCHOOL, AS BIZARRO JUNIOR RETURNS HOME...
WAAHHH!
OH, MY! THIS AM AWFUL! HIM GOT ALL "A'S" ON HIS REPORT CARD!
WHAT-?!!
BIZARRO JUNIOR NO. 1
BIZARRO LOIS NO. 1
BIZARRO NO. 1
GR-RR! ME ASHAMED OF YOU! WHY CAN'T YOU GET ROTTEN GRADES, LIKE ALL OTHER KIDS?
THERE... ONLY ONE HOPE! WE MUST HIRE TUTOR TO TEACH HIM HOW TO GIVE WRONG ANSWERS!
BIZARRO JUNIOR NO. 1
BUT WHEN THEY DO...
AWP! ME TUTOR TOUGH CASES BEFORE, BUT THIS BE POSITIVELY THE WORST!... ALL A'S?!! UGH!
AT LEAST... TRY!--IF ANYONE CAN TEACH HIM TO BE FAILING STUDENT, YOU CAN!
BIZARRO NO. 1
BIZARRO LOIS NO. 1
MEANWHILE, MANY YEARS BACK IN THE PAST, AS SUPERBOY FLIES TOWARD EARTH THROUGH OUTER SPACE WITH KRYPTO, HIS SUPER-PET, AFTER HAVING COMPLETED A SPACE MISSION, SUDDENLY...
UH-OH! WE'RE FLYING TOO FAST! WE'RE BEGINNING TO DISAPPEAR INTO THE TIME-BARRIER!
6
THROUGH THE AMAZING BARRIER STREAKS BOY OF STEEL AND DOG OF STEEL...
WE'RE FLASHING INTO THE FUTURE!

AND AS THEY EMERGE OUT OF THE BARRIER, INTO THE YEAR 1961, EARTH TIME...

¿GULP!¿--A SQUARE WORLD! HOW UTTERLY FANTASTIC! I MUST INVESTIGATE THIS!

WHEN THEY ALIGHT ON THE CUBE-SHAPED PLANET...

IT'S A WORLD OF BIZARROS! THE MALES ARE IMPERFECT UNLIVING DUPLICATES OF SUPERMAN, THE MAN I'LL BECOME WHEN I GROW UP!

"YEARS AGO, IN SMALLVILLE, A SCIENTIST ACCIDENTALLY SHONE AN IMPERFECT DUPLICATOR RAY ON ME, CREATING AN UNLIVING BIZARRE IMITATION OF ME INSTANTS BEFORE HIS RAY-PROJECTOR EXPLODED..."

IS IT ALIVE, PROFESSOR?

HARDLY, IT'S AN IMPERFECT DUPLICATE OF YOU, SUPERBOY, MADE OF NON-LIVING MATTER! WHAT A BIZARRE CREATURE!

"AFTER THE YOUTHFUL BIZARRO TERRIFIED SMALLVILLE, WE TWO HAD A TERRIFIC BATTLE..."

ME SMASH YOU! GRRR!

HE HAS ALL MY MIGHTY POWERS, AND KRYPTONITE DOESN'T AFFECT HIM! HOW CAN I POSSIBLY DESTROY THIS MENACE!

"FINALLY, I TRIUMPHED, AFTER DISCOVERING THE METAL FROM THE BLOWN-UP DUPLICATOR RAY MACHINE AFFECTED HIM SOMEWHAT AS KRYPTONITE AFFECTS ME..."

HIS SUPER-IMPACT WITH THE METAL, PLUS THE METAL'S RADIATIONS, IS DISINTEGRATING BIZARRO'S LIFELESS MOLECULES!

BLAMM!

SOMEHOW, IMPERFECT DOUBLES OF MYSELF AS THE ADULT SUPERMAN HAVE BEEN CREATED IN THE FUTURE, AND THEY INHABIT THIS COCKEYED WORLD WHERE EVERYTHING IS MAD!...I'LL LOOK ABOUT, WITH MY SUPER-VISION...

7

WITHIN AN OFFICE BUILDING, THE *BOY OF STEEL* SIGHTS...

FIRE IDIOT WHO IS WORKING HARD!—GIVE LAZY, SLEEPING FOOL RAISE!

YES, BOSS!

INCREDIBLE! EVERYTHING'S BACKWARDS ON THIS WHACKY PLANET!

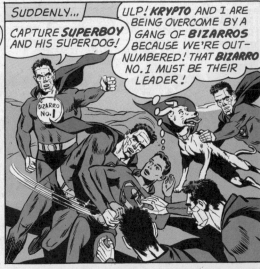

SUDDENLY...

CAPTURE *SUPERBOY* AND HIS SUPERDOG!

ULP! *KRYPTO* AND I ARE BEING OVERCOME BY A GANG OF *BIZARROS* BECAUSE WE'RE OUTNUMBERED! THAT *BIZARRO NO. 1* MUST BE THEIR LEADER!

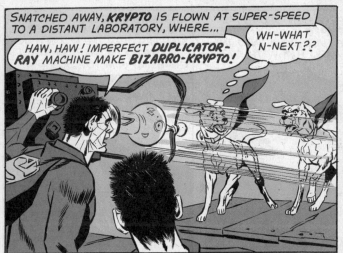

SNATCHED AWAY, *KRYPTO* IS FLOWN AT SUPER-SPEED TO A DISTANT LABORATORY, WHERE...

HAW, HAW! IMPERFECT *DUPLICATOR-RAY* MACHINE MAKE *BIZARRO-KRYPTO!*

WH-WHAT N-NEXT??

PLACED IN A BOX, THE *DOG OF STEEL* IS LOWERED INTO A DEEP FISSURE...

OUCH!...THERE'S JUST ENOUGH *KRYPTONITE* IN THIS BOX TO WEAKEN, BUT NOT KILL ME! I'M TOO... DOG-TIRED... T-TO BREAK OUT!

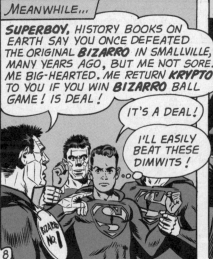

MEANWHILE...

SUPERBOY, HISTORY BOOKS ON EARTH SAY YOU ONCE DEFEATED THE ORIGINAL *BIZARRO* IN SMALLVILLE, MANY YEARS AGO, BUT ME NOT SORE. ME BIG-HEARTED. ME RETURN *KRYPTO* TO YOU IF YOU WIN *BIZARRO* BALL GAME! IS DEAL!

IT'S A DEAL!

I'LL EASILY BEAT THESE DIMWITS!

PRESENTLY...

YOU HIT BALL OVER FENCE FOR HOME RUN, *SUPERBOY*, YOU OUT!

ULP! I FORGOT EVERYTHING'S THE OPPOSITE ON THIS MAD PLANET! IF I WIN THIS CRAZY GAME, THE *BIZARROS* WILL SAY I LOSE!

8

ATTEMPTING TO OUTWIT HIS GROTESQUE OPPONENTS, **SUPERBOY** DELIBERATELY DOESN'T SWING AT THE NEXT BALL PITCHED, AND SO...

STRIKE!

KILL THE PITCHER!

HOLY COW! ON EARTH, SPECTATORS SOMETIMES JEER AT THE UMPIRE, BUT HERE THEY GET INFURIATED AT THE PITCHER IF HE MAKES A **GOOD** PITCH! **KRYPTO** AND I HAD BETTER ESCAPE FROM THIS WHACKY PLANET, PRONTO!

AS THE NEXT SQUARE BALL IS PITCHED...

MY SUPER-VISION SHOWS ME WHERE **KRYPTO** IS HIDDEN! THERE! I'VE HIT THE BALL DOWN INTO THE GROUND, TOWARD HIM WITH SUPER-FORCE!

WHAP!

CRASHING THROUGH THE GROUND, THE EXPERTLY AIMED BASEBALL SMASHES OPEN THE BOX IN WHICH **KRYPTO** IS IMPRISONED, ENABLING HIM TO ESCAPE...

THE FARTHER I GET AWAY FROM **KRYPTONITE**, THE STRONGER MY POWERS RETURN!

SWIFTLY, THE **BOY OF STEEL** AND THE **DOG OF STEEL** FLASH AWAY FROM THE SQUARE WORLD...

QUICK! BACK INTO THE TIME-BARRIER!

AND AS THEY RETURN TO THEIR OWN TIME ERA AND FLY DOWN TOWARD SMALLVILLE...

A **BIZARRO** WORLD THAT DOESN'T EXIST YET! GOSH, LIFE ON THAT WORLD WILL BE UTTERLY INSANE!

YIP, YIP!

IT SURE WILL!

ONLY **BLUE KRYPTONITE** CAN HARM **BIZARROS.**—EDITOR.

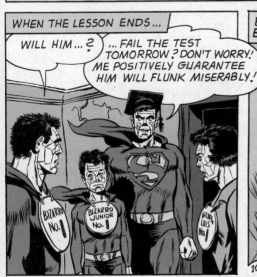

LATER, AFTER THE TEST...

IDIOT! YOU ANSWERED EVERY QUESTION CORRECTLY!

ME C-COULDN'T REMEMBER WRONG ANSWERS!

FAR AWAY, **BIZARRO**, JUNIOR'S TUTOR, WHO HAS BEEN WATCHING WITH HIS SUPER-VISION...

GAAA! WHEN HE SAW THEM HANDSOME SCARECROWS, THE SHOCK SNAPPED HIM OUT OF HYPNOTIC TRANCE! THAT WHY HIM FORGOT ANSWERS!

MEANWHILE...

THERE WILL BE A BIG ART TALENT TEST TOMORROW! IF YOU PASS THE TEST, YOU WILL BE EXPELLED!

¿CHOKE¿... TH-THAT WOULD BREAK MOMMY AND PAPA'S HEART...

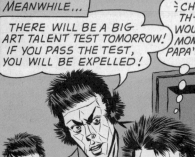

SO UPSET IS YOUNG **BIZARRO**, HE READS A HILARIOUS FAIRY TALE BOOK THAT NIGHT, TO SOOTHE HIS NERVES...

HA, HA! DRACULA, FRANKENSTEIN, WITCH-QUEEN AND WOLF MAN ARE FUNNY!

GRIM FARY TAALZ

OFF TO SLEEP HE DROPS, THEN HAS A FUNNY DREAM...

YOU WANNA FIGHT? OKAY!!

NEXT MORNING, AS **BIZARRO** JUNIOR FEARFULLY FLIES TOWARD SCHOOL...

WILL ME BE THROWN OUT OF SCHOOL TODAY? MY TEACHER AM SO ANGRY WITH ME, M-ME HATE TO FACE HER...

11

BUT WHEN HE ARRIVES...

HERE HIM AM! THREE CHEERS FOR **BIZARRO**, JUNIOR NO. 1! HIM WONDERFUL!

HOORAY! HOORAY! HOORAY!

HUH? TEACHERS... KIDS... EVERYONE ALL CHEER FOR ME! H-HOW COME??

THEN, AN ASTOUNDING SURPRISE...

YOU DARLING, DARLING BOY! HOW MARVELOUS OF YOU TO CARVE THIS MEMORIAL TO FAMOUS EARTH MONSTERS OVERNIGHT! WHAT AN UGLY MASTERPIECE! IT'S MUCH **WORSE** THAN EARTH'S MOUNT RUSHMORE MEMORIAL!

ME DID THAT??!

OF COURSE YOU DID! HERE YOUR NAME... SIGNED ON MONUMENT!

ME DON'T REMEMBER MAKING THIS!...??... W-WAIT!! NOW ME UNDERSTAND!!!

ARTIST BIZARRO JUNIOR NO.

"WHILE ME DREAMED ABOUT FIGHTING FUNNY EARTH HEROES, ME MUST HAVE **SLEEP-FLOWN** TO THIS MOUNTAIN AND CARVED THEIR FACES OUT OF ROCK WITH MY FISTS!"

NO.1 **BIZARRO**-JUNIOR'S PARENTS ARE IMMEDIATELY SUMMONED...

YOU BE PROUD TO KNOW THAT BECAUSE THEM GIANT FACES YOUR SON CARVED ARE SO UGLY, HIM HAVE FLUNKED ART TEST!

FLUNKED? HOW UTTERLY **MARVELOUS!**

ME NOT ASHAMED OF YOU NO MORE, SON! KEEP UP BAD WORK AND SOME DAY YOU WILL BE WORST STUDENT ON WHOLE PLANET!!! WHAT AN HONOR!!!

NEXT MONTH--ANOTHER MAD STORY OF THE **BIZARRO** WORLD!

THE END

23

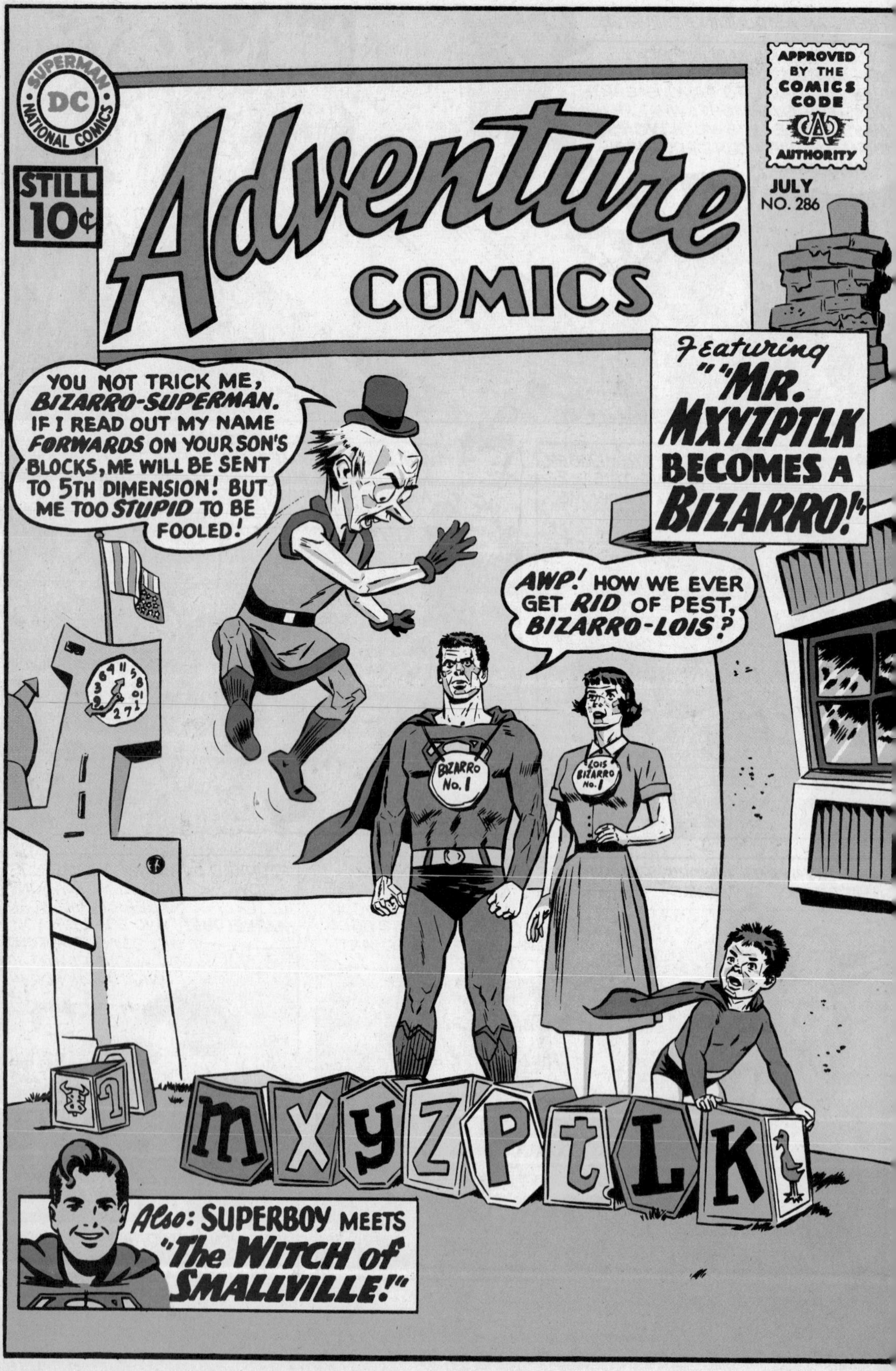
SUPERMAN DC NATIONAL COMICS
STILL 10¢
Adventure COMICS
APPROVED BY THE COMICS CODE AUTHORITY
JULY NO. 286
Featuring "MR. MXYZPTLK BECOMES A BIZARRO!"
YOU NOT TRICK ME, BIZARRO-SUPERMAN. IF I READ OUT MY NAME FORWARDS ON YOUR SON'S BLOCKS, ME WILL BE SENT TO 5TH DIMENSION! BUT ME TOO STUPID TO BE FOOLED!
AWP! HOW WE EVER GET RID OF PEST, BIZARRO-LOIS?
BIZARRO No. 1
LOIS BIZARRO No. 1
mxyzptlK
Also: SUPERBOY MEETS "The WITCH of SMALLVILLE!"

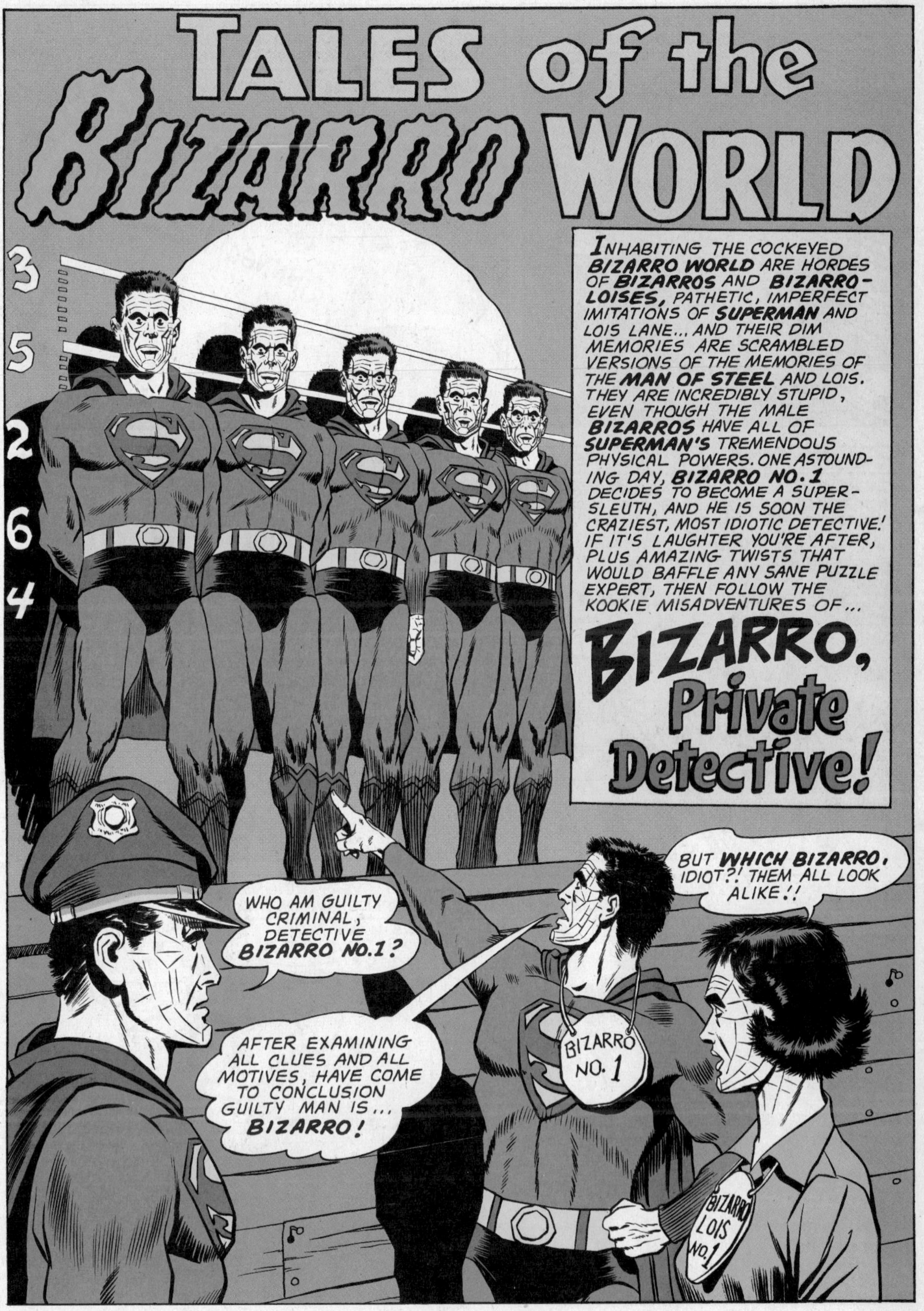
TALES of the BIZARRO WORLD
INHABITING THE COCKEYED BIZARRO WORLD ARE HORDES OF BIZARROS AND BIZARRO-LOISES, PATHETIC, IMPERFECT IMITATIONS OF SUPERMAN AND LOIS LANE... AND THEIR DIM MEMORIES ARE SCRAMBLED VERSIONS OF THE MEMORIES OF THE MAN OF STEEL AND LOIS. THEY ARE INCREDIBLY STUPID, EVEN THOUGH THE MALE BIZARROS HAVE ALL OF SUPERMAN'S TREMENDOUS PHYSICAL POWERS. ONE ASTOUNDING DAY, BIZARRO NO. 1 DECIDES TO BECOME A SUPER-SLEUTH, AND HE IS SOON THE CRAZIEST, MOST IDIOTIC DETECTIVE! IF IT'S LAUGHTER YOU'RE AFTER, PLUS AMAZING TWISTS THAT WOULD BAFFLE ANY SANE PUZZLE EXPERT, THEN FOLLOW THE KOOKIE MISADVENTURES OF...
BIZARRO, Private Detective!
3
5
2
6
4
WHO AM GUILTY CRIMINAL, DETECTIVE BIZARRO NO.1?
AFTER EXAMINING ALL CLUES AND ALL MOTIVES, HAVE COME TO CONCLUSION GUILTY MAN IS... BIZARRO!
BUT WHICH BIZARRO, IDIOT?! THEM ALL LOOK ALIKE!!
BIZARRO NO. 1
BIZARRO LOIS NO. 1

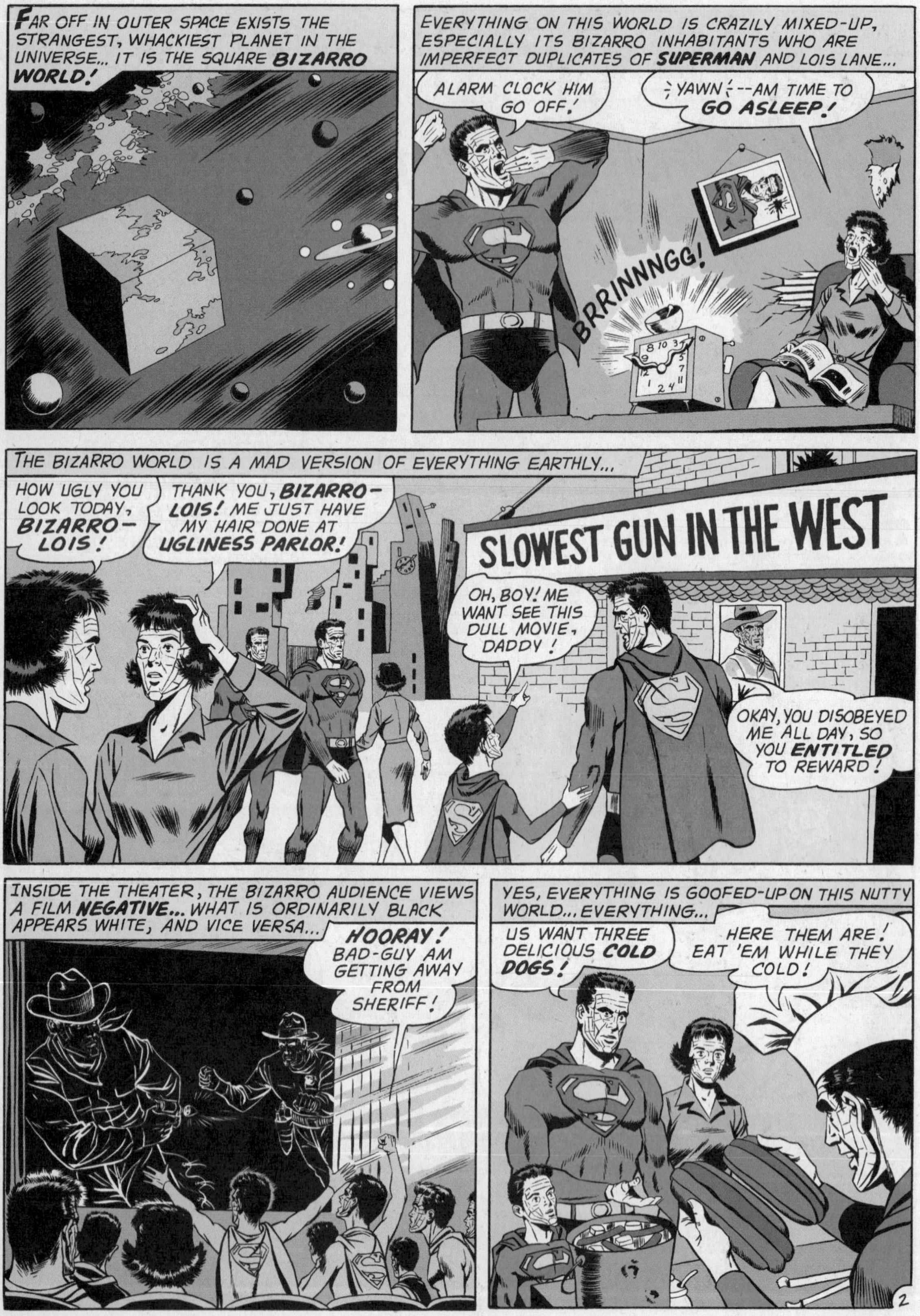
FAR OFF IN OUTER SPACE EXISTS THE STRANGEST, WHACKIEST PLANET IN THE UNIVERSE... IT IS THE SQUARE BIZARRO WORLD!
EVERYTHING ON THIS WORLD IS CRAZILY MIXED-UP, ESPECIALLY ITS BIZARRO INHABITANTS WHO ARE IMPERFECT DUPLICATES OF SUPERMAN AND LOIS LANE...
ALARM CLOCK HIM GO OFF!
YAWN --AM TIME TO GO ASLEEP!
BRRINNNGG!
THE BIZARRO WORLD IS A MAD VERSION OF EVERYTHING EARTHLY...
HOW UGLY YOU LOOK TODAY, BIZARRO-LOIS!
THANK YOU, BIZARRO-LOIS! ME JUST HAVE MY HAIR DONE AT UGLINESS PARLOR!
SLOWEST GUN IN THE WEST
OH, BOY! ME WANT SEE THIS DULL MOVIE, DADDY!
OKAY, YOU DISOBEYED ME ALL DAY, SO YOU ENTITLED TO REWARD!
INSIDE THE THEATER, THE BIZARRO AUDIENCE VIEWS A FILM NEGATIVE... WHAT IS ORDINARILY BLACK APPEARS WHITE, AND VICE VERSA...
HOORAY! BAD-GUY AM GETTING AWAY FROM SHERIFF!
YES, EVERYTHING IS GOOFED-UP ON THIS NUTTY WORLD... EVERYTHING...
US WANT THREE DELICIOUS COLD DOGS!
HERE THEM ARE! EAT 'EM WHILE THEY COLD!
2

THE *BIZARRO WORLD* PEOPLE'S BEHAVIOR IS GOVERNED BY THEIR *BIZARRO CODE*...

BIZARRO CODE
US DO OPPOSITE OF ALL EARTHLY THINGS! US HATE BEAUTY! US LOVE UGLINESS! IS BIG CRIME TO MAKE ANYTHING PERFECT ON *BIZARRO WORLD!*

AND NOW LET'S LOOK IN ON *BIZARRO NO.1*, THE IMPERFECT, ARTIFICIAL IMITATION OF *SUPERMAN*...

BUY *BIZARRO* BONDS! GUARANTEED TO LOSE MONEY FOR YOU!

ME TAKE 5! WHAT A BARGAIN!

;CHOKE!...

BIZARRO NO. 1

ON THE *BIZARRO WORLD*, COAL IS USED FOR CASH...

THIS TINY LUMP OF COAL IS ALL THE MONEY ME GOT LEFT, SO ME CAN'T BUY THEM WONDER- FUL BONDS! ME FLY TO MY FORTRESS AND FORGET TROUBLES!

BIZARRO NO. 1

DIM-WITTED *BIZARRO NO.1* DOESN'T REALIZE HE COULD GET ALL THE COAL HE WANTS BY BURROWING INTO THE GROUND!--SOON...

SUPERMAN'S FORTRESS IS IN *COLD ARCTIC*... SO ME MADE MINE IN *HOT DESERT!*

FOURTRISS UV BIZARRO

ENTERING, HE SPEEDS PAST HIS *WORTHLESS JUNK* "TROPHIES" TOWARD HIS SON, WHO IS PLAYING WITH THE *DUPLICATOR-RAY* MACHINE WHICH MAKES IMPERFECT DOUBLES...

JUNIOR! HOW MANY TIMES MUST ME TELL YOU *NOT* TO FOOL WITH THAT MACHINE?!

CEILING OPENER LEVER

AWP!... M-ME WON'T DO IT NO MORE, DADDY!

3)

SOON, EN ROUTE HOME...

ME OUGHT TO SPANK YOU!

WOULD DO NO GOOD, DADDY! ME INVULNERABLE, REMEMBER?

PRESENTLY, IN THE HOME OF THE **NO. 1 BIZARRO** FAMILY, **BIZARRO-LOIS NO. 1** SPEAKS TO HER HUSBAND...

BIZARRO, US GOT SO LITTLE MONEY LEFT, YOU **GOT** TO GET JOB!

RIGHT! UH... BUT **WHAT** JOB??

SHORTLY, IN HIS LIBRARY OF DETECTIVE FICTION...

ME GOT IT!! ME BECOME FAMOUS PRIVATE DETECTIVE, LIKE HEROES IN THEM MYSTERY BOOKS!

WONDERFUL!

THE NEXT DAY, HE OPENS AN OFFICE...

ME READY TO SOLVE **ANYTHING! BIZARRO** CROOKS, WATCH OUT! ME FAST ON TRIGGER WITH **NON-SUPER RAY-GUN!** TANGLE WITH ME, AND... **ZZ-ZAPP**... MY GUN TAKE AWAY YOUR SUPER-POWERS!

HA! SNEAKING UP ON ME, EH, YOU NO-GOOD CROOK! ME WILL...

WAIT! ME NOT CROOK! ME GOT CASE FOR YOU! ME CURATOR OF **PALACE OF JUNK!** GOT MYSTERY FOR YOU TO SOLVE!

A FEW MINUTES LATER...

INVESTIGATING CLASSY JOINT LIKE THIS AM RIGHT UP MY ALLEY!

INSIDE, AS THEY WADE THROUGH PILES OF TRASH...

OOOOO, WHAT VALUABLE TREASURES! FABULOUS!

STOP DROOLING! WAIT 'TIL YOU SEE WHAT AM... ¡UGH!¡...IN NEXT ROOM!

AN INSTANT LATER...

¡GASP!¡--HUGE D-DIAMONDS! HOW THEM GET HERE?!

THAT AM WHAT I HIRED YOU TO FIND OUT! AN UNKNOWN VANDAL AM SPOILING THIS PALACE BY SMUGGLING IN WORTHLESS DIAMONDS!

SWIFTLY, BIZARRO NO. 1 USES HIS DIM WITS...

AH-HA!...MY SUPER-VISION SEES BABY BEHIND FENCE OF NEARBY ESTATE AND HIM GOT BLACK-SMUDGED HANDS! IS CLUE!!

FOLLOW ME QUICKLY, CURATOR! ME TRACK DOWN HOT CLUE AT SUPER-SPEED BEFORE IT GET COLD!

EGAD! HOW RAPIDLY YOU DETECT!

KRAKK

OH, HO! ME CATCH YOU BLACK-HANDED!!...WITH SUPER-PRESSURE OF HANDS, YOU ARE SQUEEZING VALUABLE COAL INTO WORTHLESS DIAMONDS, WHILE PLAYING! WHEN TOSSED AWAY, THEY FALL IN PALACE OF JUNK!...WHERE YOU GET COAL?

AS THE TODDLER LEADS BIZARRO NO. 1 TO THE FAMILY SAFE WHICH, LIKE ALL BIZARRO SAFES, HAS NO LOCK, HIS MISERLY FATHER APPEARS...

URK!!...MY BABY! HIM THROW AWAY MY MISER'S HOARD!

SERVES YOU RIGHT FOR BEING A MISER!

INTO THE KITCHEN FLASHES THE CHILD'S ANGRY FATHER, AND HE RETURNS...

ME *PUNISH* YOU BY MAKING YOU EAT UP ALL THIS *ICE CREAM!*

DADDY, PLEASE DON'T MAKE ME EAT THAT AWFUL STUFF! ME PROMISE NOT TO BE BAD NO MORE! *WAH-HHH!*

PRESENTLY...

AS BIG REWARD FOR SOLVING CASE, ME GIVE YOU THIS WORN-OUT TIRE! AND FOR *TIP*... A BROKEN BOTTLE!

¡GASP!--YOU VERY GENEROUS! THANKS!

PRESENTLY, AS *BIZARRO NO. 1* RETURNS HOME...

A USED TIRE!!... OH-HHH, HOW SWEET! JUST WHAT ME NEED FOR MY CAR... BECAUSE *BIZARRO-LOISES* CAN'T FLY LIKE MEN BIZARROS! YOU *DARLING!!*

¡CHUCKLE! NOTHING AM TOO GOOD FOR *YOU!*

SOON AFTERWARD, AT THE *BIZARRO WORLD'S* TWISTED VERSION OF *METROPOLIS' DAILY PLANET* BUILDING...

EXTRA, EXTRA!

DAILY ᴴTRAE
DETECTIV BIZARRO NO. 1 SOLVES BAFELING KRIME

NEXT DAY, AS AN EMERGENCY LOUDSPEAKER BLARES...

CALLING ALL POLICE! CRIME AT PUBLIC SQUARE!

UH-OH! MAYBE THIS AM JOB FOR *ME!*

A FEW SECONDS LATER, AT THE SPOT WHERE THE *PALACE OF JUNK* HAD BEEN STANDING...

OH, NO! BEAUTIFUL PALACE AM G-GONE! IN ITS PLACE AM... *HORRIBLE UGLY MUSEUM OF "ART"...!*

ME AM THE MAYOR! COME INSIDE!

ART MUSEUM

⑥

30

SHORTLY, INSIDE...

;CHOKE; --REVOLTING! ...NOT ONLY DOES BUILDING LOOK AWFUL, BUT IT AM NOW FILLED WITH...;URP!! UGLY JUNK!

;SOB!!

CURATOR

APOLLO

ME HEREBY HIRE YOU TO SOLVE THIS TERRIBLE CRIME WHICH VIOLATES BIZARRO CODE BECAUSE YOU ARE DUMBER THAN WHOLE BIZARRO POLICE FORCE PUT TOGETHER!

ME PROMISE TO CATCH GUILTY BIZARRO WHO USED HIS SUPER-STRENGTH TO COMMIT THIS...;UGH!!...GHASTLY CRIME! HIM GOT TWISTED BRAIN!...AH!! AM GETTING IDEA!

BIZARRO NO. 1

PRESENTLY...

ME AM BIZARRO DETECTIVE ON TRAIL OF IMPORTANT CASE! ARE YOU DOCTOR, OR INMATE?

AM DOCTOR! STEP IN, BIZARRO NO. 1!

BIZARRO LUNATIC ASYLUM

INMATES OF THE BIZARRO INSANE ASYLUM ARE FREAK BIZARROS WHO, BECAUSE THE IMITATOR MACHINE DIDN'T AFFECT THEIR MINDS, CAN THINK AND SPEAK NORMALLY, THOUGH THEY STILL HAVE SUPER-POWERS...

POOR CHAPS! THEM BUILD THINGS PERFECTLY BECAUSE THEM ARE MENTALLY SICK!

TELL ME, DOCTOR, IS THERE ANY BIZARRO "TREATMENT" CAN BE USED TO CURE THEM?

BIZARRO NO. 1

7

HEY, INTERNE! SHOW *BIZARRO NO 1* CLEVER WAY US CURE PATIENTS!

SURE, DOC!

THIS AM HOW US *KNOCK SENSE* INTO THEM HEADS!

HIT ME SOME MORE! I'M BEGINNING TO FEEL *MUCH BETTER!* AHHH!

POW

BAM

SOK!!

PRESENTLY...

THE DOCTOR TOLD ME NO PATIENTS HAVE ESCAPED LATELY. IF A LUNATIC DIDN'T COMMIT CRIME, THEN SOMEBODY ELSE DID! SOMEONE WITH CLEVER MOTIVE, MAYBE! *WAIT...!!*

BIZARRO NO. 1

¡GASP!! WHY ME NOT THINK OF THIS BEFORE? CRIMINAL IN MYSTERY STORIES AM ALWAYS *LEAST SUSPECTED PERSON!* WHO AM LEAST PERSON ME WOULD SUSPECT? OUR RESPECTED *MAYOR*, THAT WHO! ..WHY? 'CAUSE HIM GOT NO *MOTIVE!!!*

SOON, AT THE MAYOR'S HOME...

GRR-RR! – YOU ARE CRIMINAL WHO RUINED *PALACE OF JUNK!*

BUT ME GOT *NO MOTIVE...* AND DON'T FORGET... *ME* HIRED YOU TO SOLVE CASE!

⑧

RIGHT! NO MOTIVE, AM GOOD *MOTIVE!* FACT YOU HIRED ME AM *PROOF* YOU ARE VILLAIN! DON'T RESIST! ME GOING TO TAKE AWAY YOUR POWERS BY FIRING *NON-SUPER RAY-GUN* AT YOU!

DON'T SHOOT HIM... YET!

TURNING, *BIZARRO NO.1* SIGHTS THE MAYOR'S *BIZARRO-LOIS* WIFE...

LET MY HUSBAND FINISH HIS PAINTING FIRST! PAINTING AM HIS HOBBY!

UH...*YOU* DID...*THAT?!!*

YES!

YOU PAINTED THIS...THIS *MASTERPIECE?* YOU DID THIS?...*YOU?...YOU??!!*

ME DID IT! -- WHY YOU ASK??

IMPOSSIBLE FOR *ANYONE* WHO COULD PAINT *THIS MARVELOUS* PICTURE BUILD THAT HORRIBLE ART MUSEUM! ...YOU *INNOCENT!!*

FIND REAL CULPRIT *SOON,* OR ME FIRE YOU... *GET OUT!!*

LATER, IN THE HOME OF THE NO.1 *BIZARRO* FAMILY...

¡MOAN! -- ME NO CLOSER TO CATCHING VILLAIN THAN WHEN ME START CASE!

DON'T GIVE UP, DARLING! I LOVE YOU! YOU HAND- SOMEST BIZARRO ON THIS WORLD!

SUDDENLY, ASTOUNDINGLY...

HI, FOLKS! ME *BIZARRO- KLTPZYXM!*

PUFF!

YIPE! HIM AM *BIZARRO* DOUBLE OF *MR. MXYZPTLK,* IMP FROM 5TH DIMENSION WHO PESTERS *SUPERMAN!* ONLY WAY *SUPERMAN* CAN GET RID OF *MXYZPTLK* AM...

...TO TRICK HIM INTO SAYING HIS NAME *BACKWARDS!* THEN IMP RETURNS TO HIS OWN DIMENSION FOR AT LEAST 30 DAYS!

B-BUT HOW COULD THERE BE A *BIZARRO* OF *MXYZPTLK??...* HOW?...*HOW???*

9

"AWP! ME KNOW WHAT HAPPENED! WHEN *BIZARRO, JUNIOR* WAS FOOLING AROUND WITH *DUPLICATOR RAY MACHINE*, RAY SHOT UP THROUGH FORTRESS' CEILING OPENING..."

 "...AND FOCUSED ON *MR. MXYZPTLK* WHO WAS FLYING PAST *BIZARRO WORLD* WHILE HIM WAS VISITING THIS DIMENSION! IMPERFECT RAY CREATED IMPERFECT *MXYZPTLK* DUPLICATE... *BIZARRO-KLTPZYXM!!!*"

CEILING OPENER LEVER

STRANGE RAY CREATE *ME!*

YES, THAT HAPPENED! --UNLIKE *MXYZPTLK*, ME HATE MISCHIEF...BECAUSE ME AM *OPPOSITE* OF HIM! ME USE MY MAGIC POWERS ONLY FOR *GOOD!* FOR INSTANCE, SEE WHAT ME NOW DO TO YOUR CRUMMY HOUSE!...*ALAKAZOOKUS!!*

BIZARRO NO. 1

A SPLIT INSTANT AFTERWARD...

BEHOLD! SLOPPY HOUSE AM NOW...*GORGEOUS!*

OH, MY! HIM MAKE OUR LOVELY HOME L-LOOK *AWFUL!*

¡GASP!¡ --ME SEE IT ALL NOW! YOU AM VILLAIN WHO RUINED *PALACE OF JUNK!* ADMIT IT!

CORRECTION! ME *IMPROVED* IT! I LIKE TO DO GOOD THINGS!

GET RID OF HIM, HONEY, BEFORE *KLTPZYXM* MESSES UP *EVERYTHING!*

HM-MM... *SUPERMAN* GETS RID OF *MXYZPTLK* BY MAKING HIM SAY HIS NAME BACKWARDS!...UH...SINCE *KLTPZYXM* AM OPPOSITE OF *MXYZPTLK*, ME MUST TRICK THIS *BIZARRO* PEST INTO SAYING HIS NAME FORWARDS!

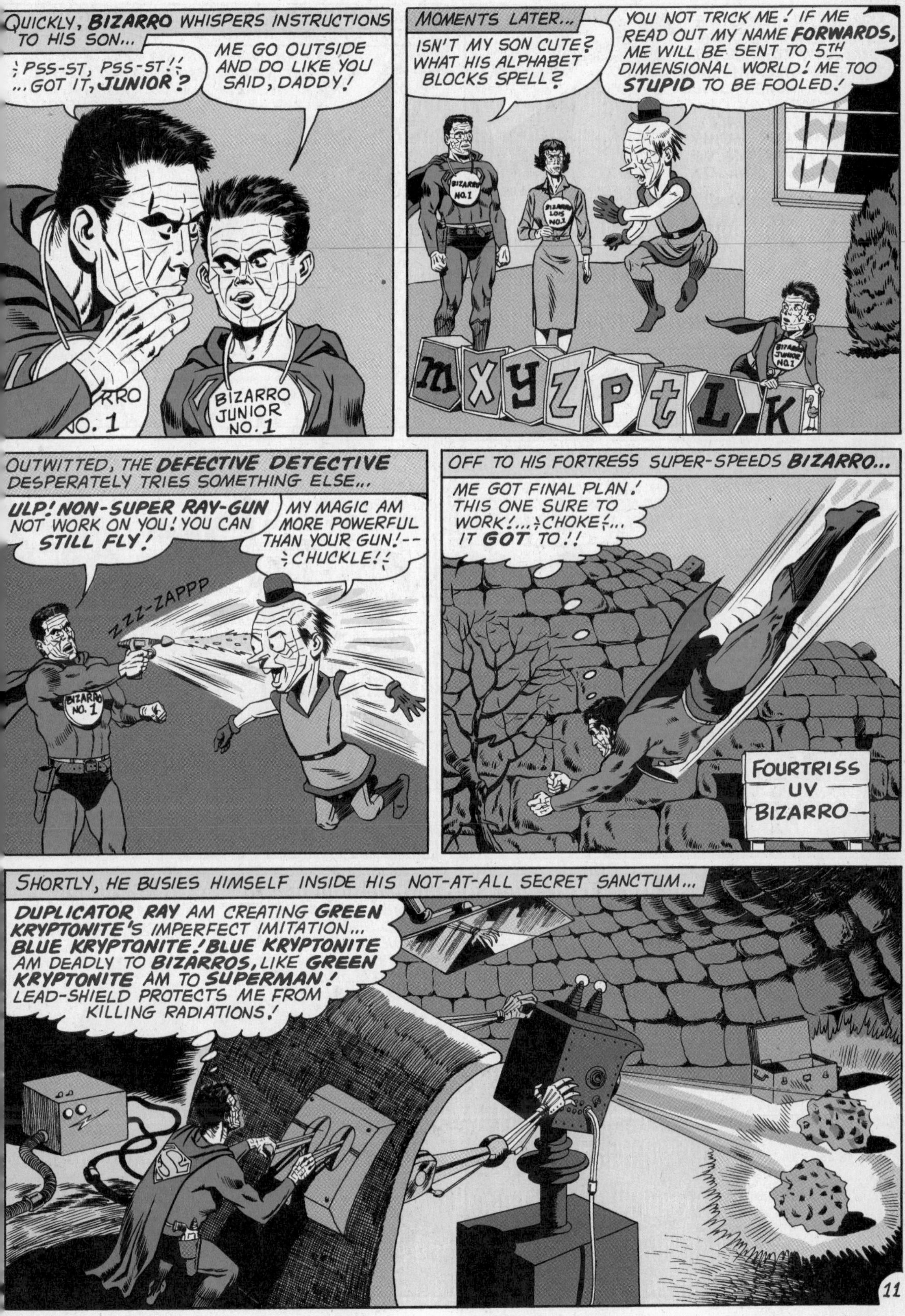
QUICKLY, BIZARRO WHISPERS INSTRUCTIONS TO HIS SON...
PSS-ST, PSS-ST! ...GOT IT, JUNIOR?
ME GO OUTSIDE AND DO LIKE YOU SAID, DADDY!
BIZARRO JUNIOR NO. 1
MOMENTS LATER...
ISN'T MY SON CUTE? WHAT HIS ALPHABET BLOCKS SPELL?
YOU NOT TRICK ME! IF ME READ OUT MY NAME FORWARDS, ME WILL BE SENT TO 5TH DIMENSIONAL WORLD! ME TOO STUPID TO BE FOOLED!
BIZARRO NO. 1
MXYZPTLK
OUTWITTED, THE DEFECTIVE DETECTIVE DESPERATELY TRIES SOMETHING ELSE...
ULP! NON-SUPER RAY-GUN NOT WORK ON YOU! YOU CAN STILL FLY!
MY MAGIC AM MORE POWERFUL THAN YOUR GUN!-- CHUCKLE!
ZZZ-ZAPPP
BIZARRO NO. 1
OFF TO HIS FORTRESS SUPER-SPEEDS BIZARRO...
ME GOT FINAL PLAN! THIS ONE SURE TO WORK!... CHOKE!... IT GOT TO!!
FOURTRISS UV BIZARRO
SHORTLY, HE BUSIES HIMSELF INSIDE HIS NOT-AT-ALL SECRET SANCTUM...
DUPLICATOR RAY AM CREATING GREEN KRYPTONITE'S IMPERFECT IMITATION... BLUE KRYPTONITE! BLUE KRYPTONITE AM DEADLY TO BIZARROS, LIKE GREEN KRYPTONITE AM TO SUPERMAN! LEAD-SHIELD PROTECTS ME FROM KILLING RADIATIONS!
11

NOW METAL CLAWS ME OPERATE AM PUTTING **BLUE KRYPTONITE** INTO LEAD BOX WHICH ME CAN CARRY UNHARMED, SINCE DEADLY RADIATION CAN'T PASS THROUGH LEAD!... CEILING MIRROR SHOWS ME WHAT AM HAPPENING BEHIND LEAD-SHIELD!

SUPER-SWIFTLY, THE PATHETICALLY DIM-WITTED SLEUTH FLIES HOMEWARD...

AH, THERE AM **KLTPZYXM** BELOW! WHEN **BLUE KRYPTONITE** WEAKENS AND PAINS HIM, HIM GLADLY GO TO 5TH DIMENSION!

BUT...

OH, NO! RADIATIONS OF **BLUE KRYPTONITE** DON'T HARM YOU, EITHER!

¡SOB!

YOU UNDERESTIMATE MY MAGICAL POWERS AGAIN! HA, HA! INSTEAD OF HURTING ME, RADIATIONS FEEL... **PLEASANT!**

NOW YOU NEVER BE ABLE TO ARREST **KLTPZYXM**, AND... AND PUT HIM IN JAIL...¡SOB!¡

AS DETECTIVE, ME AM MISERABLE FLOP--¡SOB!¡

WAH-HHH!

BIZARRO LOIS NO. 1

BIZARRO NO. 1

BIZARRO JUNIOR NO. 1

UNEXPECTEDLY...

ARREST? YOU WANT ARREST ME? WHY YOU NOT SAY SO IN FIRST PLACE ??... **ME SURRENDER!** JAIL ME!! ME WON'T RESIST!

HUH ???... ME DON'T UNDERSTAND! WHY YOU SURRENDER?

DON'T YOU SEE, DARLING? THE REAL **MR. MXYZPTLK** WOULD USE TRICKS TO AVOID ARREST, BUT **KLTPZYXM**... HIS DIRECT **OPPOSITE**... AM TOO **GOOD** TO RESIST **LAW!**

THREE CHEERS FOR LAW!... HOORAY, HOORAY, HOORAY!

BIZARRO NO. 1

12

YIPPEE! ME SOLVED CASE! ME ARRESTED VILLAIN!

OH, WHAT DANDY DETECTIVE YOU AM!

HIM GREAT!

STOP GLOATING! TAKE ME TO JAIL, ALREADY... *WHAMMO!!* BIZARRO-HOUSE CHANGE BACK TO WAY YOU WERE BEFORE!

SHORTLY, IN THE *BIZARRO* JAIL...

WINDOW AM IN FLOOR! THAT AM BACKWARD FROM EARTH!...ME WON'T BE HERE LONG! SINCE ME AM GUILTY, *BIZARRO* LAWS GAVE ME *SHORT SENTENCE!*

THAT EVENING, AS THE UNIVERSE'S STUPIDEST DETECTIVE RELAXES AT HOME BY READING A MYSTERY, HE READS THE ENDING *FIRST*...

SO BUTLER DID IT, EH?

13

GEE, THIS MUST BE GREAT MYSTERY STORY! ME CAN HARDLY WAIT UNTIL ME READ THROUGH *WHOLE BOOK BACKWARDS,* TO *BEGINNING*...SO ME CAN LEARN HOW IT *STARTS!*...WHAT *SUSPENSE!!*

THE END

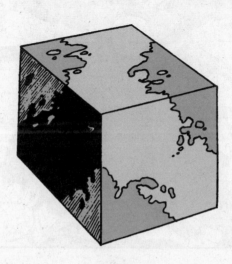

TALES of the BIZARRO WORLD

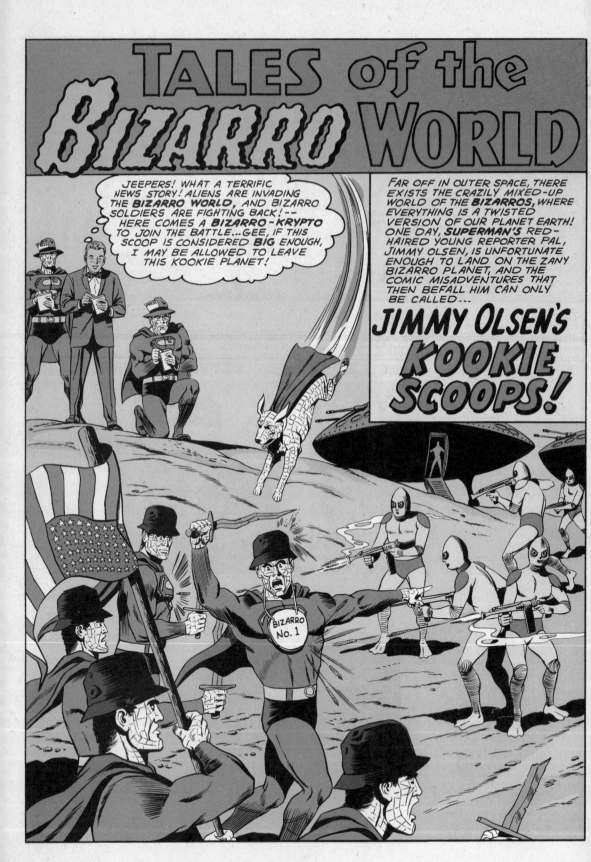

JEEPERS! WHAT A TERRIFIC NEWS STORY! ALIENS ARE INVADING THE *BIZARRO WORLD*, AND BIZARRO SOLDIERS ARE FIGHTING BACK!-- HERE COMES A *BIZARRO-KRYPTO* TO JOIN THE BATTLE...GEE, IF THIS SCOOP IS CONSIDERED *BIG* ENOUGH, I MAY BE ALLOWED TO LEAVE THIS KOOKIE PLANET!

FAR OFF IN OUTER SPACE, THERE EXISTS THE CRAZILY MIXED-UP WORLD OF THE *BIZARROS*, WHERE EVERYTHING IS A TWISTED VERSION OF OUR PLANET EARTH! ONE DAY, *SUPERMAN'S* RED-HAIRED YOUNG REPORTER PAL, JIMMY OLSEN, IS UNFORTUNATE ENOUGH TO LAND ON THE ZANY BIZARRO PLANET, AND THE COMIC MISADVENTURES THAT THEN BEFALL HIM CAN ONLY BE CALLED...

JIMMY OLSEN'S KOOKIE SCOOPS!

BIZARRO No. 1

ONE DAY, AT THE **DAILY PLANET**, AS EDITOR PERRY WHITE BAWLS OUT IMPETUOUS YOUNG NEWSHAWK JIMMY OLSEN...

"CITY'S WATER COMMISSIONER TAKES OCEAN CRUISE"... YOU CALL **THAT A BIG STORY?**

BUT...

LISTEN CLOSELY, OLSEN...WHEN A MAN BITES A DOG, **THAT'S NEWS!** OR... IF THE MOON RISES IN THE MORNING, INSTEAD OF THE SUN, **THAT'S NEWS, TOO. GET IT?**

I...GOT IT, CHIEF!

THEN DON'T TURN IN IDIOTIC, UNIMPORTANT DRIVEL! GIVE ME SCOOPS THAT ARE EXCITING, DIFFERENT, AND **IMPORTANT!** NOW GET OUT! AND DON'T CALL ME CHIEF!

YES... ...CHIEF! Whew!

NEXT MORNING, ON HIS DAY OFF, AS JIMMY DRIVES ALONG THE FOG-SHROUDED COUNTRYSIDE...

WOW!– A SPACE SHIP!... I'LL INVESTIGATE!

MINUTES LATER...

HEY! THERE GOES MY PAL **SUPERMAN** INTO THE SHIP, CARRYING SOME MACHINERY, AND THERE'S SOMEONE WITH HIM... MY BOSS, PERRY WHITE! WAIT FOR **ME!!**

AN INSTANT AFTER JIMMY RACES IN, THE VESSEL'S DOOR SLAMS SHUT AND THE SHIP BLASTS SKYWARD...

YIPES!... LEMME OUTA HERE!!

VRROOOMMM

INSIDE THE ROCKET SHIP HURTLING INTO OUTER SPACE, THE YOUTHFUL REPORTER MAKES A SHOCKING DISCOVERY...

I WAS MISTAKEN! YOU'RE *BIZARRO,* THE DISTORTED DUPLICATE OF *SUPERMAN*... AND THIS IS -- ¡*GULP!*¡-- A *B-BIZARRO-PERRY WHITE!*

BIZARRO NO. 1

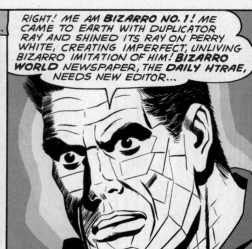

RIGHT! ME AM *BIZARRO NO. 1!* ME CAME TO EARTH WITH DUPLICATOR RAY AND SHINED ITS RAY ON PERRY WHITE, CREATING IMPERFECT, UNLIVING BIZARRO IMITATION OF HIM! *BIZARRO WORLD* NEWSPAPER, THE *DAILY HTRAE,* NEEDS NEW EDITOR...

...BECAUSE OLD EDITOR RETIRED *BIZARRO-WHITE* MAKE GREAT EDITOR! REASON ME USE SPACE SHIP IS WHITE NOT SUPER, LIKE ME, AND NO CAN FLY IN SPACE!

ME HIRE YOU TO WORK ON *DAILY HTRAE,* JIMMY!

NO! TAKE ME BACK TO EARTH!!

BIZARRO NO. 1

GR-RR! ME THROW YOU OUT OF SPACE SHIP IF YOU WON'T WORK ON *BIZARRO* NEWSPAPER!

¡*GROAN!*¡ MY *SUPERMAN* SIGNAL-WATCH DOESN'T WORK ACROSS OUTER SPACE! I CAN'T SIGNAL MY PAL FOR HELP!

X-IT DORE

I'M TRAPPED! WAIT! I ACCEPT THE JOB!!

GOOD!

SPLENDID! BUT REMEMBER, BOY... ME WANT GREAT STORIES FROM YOU! TERRIFIC SCOOPS!

BIZARRO NO. 1

PRESENTLY...

¡*GASP!*-- I *CAN'T* BE SEEING STRAIGHT! TH-THAT PLANET IS *SQUARE-SHAPED!!*

THAT AM *BIZARRO WORLD!* IT AM YOUR NEW HOME FROM NOW ON, YOU LUCKY, RED-HEADED NEWSHAWK!

3

AFTER THEY LAND, JIMMY TAKES A SIGHT-SEEING STROLL ON THE MAD WORLD...

BUILDINGS LEAN AT ALL ANGLES! *EVERYTHING'S* A MIXED-UP VERSION OF THINGS ON EARTH, LIKE THIS PECULIAR IMITATION OF THE *DAILY PLANET* BUILDING...

THAT CLOCK HAS ITS NUMERALS SCRAMBLED IN SUCH A MANNER THAT IT'S UTTERLY USELESS! AND THAT BIZARRO WORLD FLAG NEXT TO IT LOOKS LIKE IT ESCAPED FROM A NIGHTMARE!!

SUDDENLY, A STARTLING SURPRISE...

GOSH! THEY'VE EVEN GOT A *BIZARRO-KRYPTO* HERE! HE'S AS POWERFUL AS *SUPERMAN'S* SUPERDOG PET!

NEXT, JIMMY SEES...

ME FROM BIZARRO *INCOME TAX BUREAU!* IS TIME FOR GOVERNMENT TO PAY PEOPLE ANNUAL TAX! HERE AM SOME MONEY! TAKE IT, OR BE *PUNISHED!*

≀GASP!≀--IT'S THE *REVERSE* OF EARTH! AND HERE, THEY USE *COAL* FOR MONEY!!

AFTERWARD, IN THE NEWSROOM OF THE *DAILY HTRAE*...

SO THAT'S THE *KOOKIE CODE* THEY LIVE BY!--OW!

BIZARRO CODE
US DO *OPPOSITE* OF ALL EARTHLY THINGS! US *HATE* BEAUTY! US *LOVE* UGLINESS! IS *BIG CRIME* TO MAKE ANYTHING *PERFECT* ON *BIZARRO WORLD!*

AND TO THINK I'M STUCK HERE UNTIL *SUPERMAN* RESCUES ME...IF EVER!-- ≀GROAN≀--I'VE LEARNED THAT EVERYONE HERE LOOKS LIKE THE ORIGINAL *BIZARRO NO. 1* AND HIS WIFE *BIZARRO-LOIS NO. 1*, BECAUSE THE OTHERS ARE DUPLICATES MANUFACTURED BY AN *IMITATION MACHINE!*

OFFICE

4

OBSERVING JIMMY'S DEPRESSED EXPRESSION, A **BIZARRO-LOIS** STAFF-MEMBER CONSOLES HIM...

ME GLAD YOU SAD, BECAUSE THAT MEAN YOU AM **HAPPY!**

WHAT CRAZILY TWISTED LOGIC!

EDITOR

YOU NOT HANDSOME LIKE **BIZARRO** MEN, BUT ME LIKE YOU ANYWAY, EVEN IF YOU **DON'T** LOOK SO GOOD!

THANKS A HEAP!

JEEPERS! WITH A CHEERY FRIEND LIKE THIS, WHO NEEDS ENEMIES??

AS JIMMY IS SUMMONED INTO THE EDITOR'S OFFICE...

HOLY CATS! THE **PERRY WHITE-BIZARRO'S** TWISTED MEMORY DIMLY RECALLS THE REAL MR. WHITE'S FONDNESS FOR CIGARS! ONLY THIS **BIZARRO** DUPLICATE OF PERRY PREFERS **EXPLODING CIGARS!**

BANNG!

JIMMY, ME GOT GOOD NEWS FOR YOU! WRITE THREE GREAT SCOOPS AND YOU GET **WONDERFUL PRIZE!**

SWELL!

HE MUST MEAN THEY'LL REWARD ME BY RETURNING ME TO EARTH!

EAGERLY, JIMMY SCOURS THE MAD CITY IN SEARCH OF A SCOOP, UNTIL...

}GASP!{ -- THOSE BIZARROS ARE DELIBERATELY SETTING FIRE TO THAT MOVIE THEATRE WITH THEIR HEAT VISION!

MOVIE THEATUR

FIRE ALARUM BOX

WHAT A STORY! I'LL TURN IN A FIRE ALARM SO FIREMEN WILL SPEED HERE AND EXTINGUISH THE FIRE BEFORE IT GETS COMPLETELY OUT OF CONTROL!

FIRE ALARM BOX

⑤

BUT WHEN THE BIZARRO FIREMEN ARRIVE...

HUH? ARE THEY *CRAZY*? INSTEAD OF *FIGHTING* THE FIRE, THE FIREMEN ARE THROWING *FUEL* ON IT, SO THE BLAZE WILL *SPREAD*!

THAT WHAT *BIZARRO* FIREMEN *ALWAYS* DO! WE *NEVER* PUT OUT A FIRE!

GASOLEAN

BUT...GREAT SCOTT! IF THE FIRES AREN'T PUT OUT, WHY DOESN'T THE WHOLE PLANET BURN?

IT RAIN EVERY FOUR HOURS ON *BIZARRO* WORLD...

...SEE?!!

I SEE! YE GODS, THAT MOVIE HOUSE IS NOW NOTHING BUT CHARRED WRECKAGE... INCLUDING THE CANDY-COUNTER...

MAN, WHAT A GREAT SCOOP!

THEATER

KANDY KOWNTER

PRESENTLY, AT THE *DAILY HTRAE*...

YOU CALL *THIS* BIG STORY?... "MOVIE THEATER BURNS DOWN"! SO WHAT? WHO CARES? THIS AM DULL... BORING!

GEE, I THOUGHT IT WAS TERRIFIC! ...S-SORRY!

BANG!

SHORTLY AFTERWARD...

IDIOT! LOOK AT GREAT STORY IN RIVAL PAPER!

OW! TO THE BIZARROS, THE THEATER BURNING *WASN'T* NEWS! BUT THE TOASTING OF A MARSHMALLOW BAR *WAS*! WHAT A WEIRD HEADLINE THIS IS!

The Daily Noose

MARSHMALLOWS GET TOASTID IN THEATUR FIRE; THEM SURE TASTE GOOD!

KANDY KOWNTER

JIMMY, HOW YOU EXPECT GET BIG PRIZE IF YOU MUFF *IMPORTANT* STORIES? WHY YOU NOT SMART LIKE *ME*? AND... *CALL ME CHIEF!!!*

OKAY, CHIEF!

AWP! OH, MY ACHING HEAD! THIS *BIZARRO* WHACKINESS IS GETTING ME!

6

OH, NO! HERE COMES THAT PESTY *BIZARRO-LOIS* AGAIN!

POOR JIMMY! IT AM AWFUL SHAME THE WAY *BIZARRO-WHITE* HIM PICK ON YOU! ME SURE YOU GET THAT BIG PRIZE, YET! ... TAKE ME TO LUNCH!

PRESENTLY, IN A NEARBY RESTAURANT...

GEE WHIZ! ARE YOU ACTUALLY GOING TO EAT *ALL THAT?!!*

OF COURSE! ME AM ON DIET! MUST EAT *ALL* THIS SO ME BE *SURE* TO LOSE WEIGHT!

AFTERWARD, STILL SEEKING A COLOSSAL SCOOP, JIMMY TOURS THE CITY...

GOSH! LOOK WHO'S IN THAT *BIZARRO* PRISON RECREATION-ROOM! A *BIZARRO-MXYZPTLK!* NOW I'VE SEEN EVERYTHING!

A MOMENT LATER...

QUICK, PALS! SMOOTH OUT MOUND OF DIRT ME FORM WHILE BURROWING, SO NOBODY KNOW ME AM BREAKING *INTO* JAIL!

ON EARTH, THEY BUST *OUT* OF PRISON! HERE, IT'S THE *OPPOSITE!!*

SUPER-SPEEDILY, THE WOULD-BE CONVICT'S FRIENDS OBLIGE...

COAST AM CLEAR! BROOM AM MAKING GROUND PERFECTLY *NEAT* AGAIN SO NOBODY GET WISE TO OUR FRIEND'S SNEAKY TRICK!

GOOD! NOW US FLY AWAY! ... :SNICKER!:

BACK TO THE NEWSPAPER OFFICE SCURRIES JIMMY...

"BIZARRO BREAKS INTO JAIL"! ... BIG SCOOP! THAT HAPPEN *ALL* THE TIME! WHEN YOU GOING RECOGNIZE *GOOD* STORY WHEN YOU SEE IT?

:CHOKE!: ... I ... I'LL TRY *HARDER,* CHIEF ...

EDITOR

BANNG!

44

SHORTLY... IDIOT! YOU GOOFED AGAIN! LOOK AT HEADLINE IN **RIVAL PAPER!**

AGAIN?!!

WHAT'S SO NEWSWORTHY ABOUT **THAT??!**

Daily Noose

TWO BIZARROS ARRESTID FOR SWEEPING DIRT!

STUPID! THEM WAS BREAKING **BIZARRO CODE!** AM AGAINST LAW TO MAKE ANYTHING PERFECT ON THIS PLANET! THEM SWEPT GROUND **PERFECTLY NEAT!**

≶MOAN≷--IF I DON'T GET OFF THIS PLANET SOON, I'LL GO NUTS, TOO!!

DON'T BE DISCOURAGED, JIMMY! ME AM SURE YOU WILL GET BIG PRIZE, NO MATTER **HOW** DUMB YOU BE!

MOST OF ALL, I'VE GOT TO GET AWAY FROM **HER!** SHE GIVES ME THE CREEPS!

LATER, AS ALIEN SPACE SHIPS ATTACK THE **BIZARRO WORLD**, AND A SQUAD OF **BIZARRO SOLDIERS** STREAK AT THE INVADERS, JIMMY COVERS THE EVENT WITH BIZARRO REPORTERS...

WOW! THE ALIENS' MIGHTY POWER-RAYS AREN'T HARMING THE **BIZARRO** WARRIORS ONE BIT!

8

AND AS THE ENEMY SHIPS ALIGHT...

NOW THE ALIENS ARE FIRING DIAMOND-TIPPED PROJECTILES, BUT EVEN THE SUPER-HARD DIAMONDS CAN'T HARM THE INVULNERABLE BIZARROS!...UH-OH! HERE COMES BIZARRO-KRYPTO!

BLAM!

BLAM!

BUT THEN, TO THE ALIENS' CONFUSION...

??...THE FOE NO LONGER RESISTS! SCOUT LZ-489! GO FIND OUT WHY!

GASP!--THE DOPEY BIZARROS HAVE TEMPORARILY LOST INTEREST IN THE INVASION AND ARE PLAYING WITH BIZARRO-KRYPTO!

AS THE ALIEN SCOUT INVESTIGATES...

A SNEAKY ALIEN, HAH? YOWRP-PP! ME GO GET 'IM!

THE BIZARROS QUIT FIGHTING THE INVADERS TO PLAY WITH THE POOCH! WHAT STUNNING NEWS!

MOMENTS LATER, THE PUZZLED INVADERS ARE TREATED TO SOME TYPICALLY TWISTED BIZARRO REASONING...

BIZARRO WORLD SURRENDER BECAUSE IF US LOSE, THAT MEAN US WIN!

HE DOESN'T MAKE SENSE, BUT THAT DOESN'T MATTER!...OUR FORCES ARE VICTORIOUS!

AS WORD OF THE SURRENDER SWIFTLY SPREADS, THE BIZARROS DIG A GIANT STOREHOUSE WITHIN THE PLANET'S INTERIOR, WHERE THEY HIDE THEIR "VALUABLES," WHICH ARE IN REALITY...JUNK!

OUR TREASURES AM SAFE HERE!

THEM ALIENS WON'T GET OUR GARBAGE! US WILL PROTECT IT TO THE LAST SCRAP!

SINCE ALL INVADERS DEMAND TRIBUTE, US WILL GIVE THEM WORTHLESS STUFF LIKE JEWELS, GOLD, AND FRESH FOOD!

9

WHEN THE BIZARROS DEFIANTLY OFFER THE TRIBUTE TO THEIR CONQUERORS...

ALL THESE TREASURES FOR... US? THIS IS TOO GOOD TO BE TRUE! THERE **MUST** BE A CATCH!

I AGREE WITH YOU IT IS A **TRAP** OF SOME SORT! OTHERWISE, WHY SHOULD THEY BE SO GENEROUS?

FEARFULLY, THE INVADERS FLEE OFF INTO THE COSMOS...

WE HAD NO CHOICE! THEY HAD SOME TRICK IN MIND, OFFERING US ALL THOSE VALUABLE GIFTS!

IF WE STAYED, WE'D HAVE BEEN DOOMED ...I THINK!

EAGERLY, JIMMY TURNS IN HIS STORY, BUT...

DID YOU LIKE IT?

"ALIENS CAPTURE BIZARRO WORLD, THEN FLEE"!... SAP! YOU HOPELESS! ME SHOW YOU **IMPORTANT** STORY IN RIVAL PAPER!

GET IT?!-- IF MAN BITES DOG, THAT **NOT** NEWS, RIGHT? BUT IF **DOG BITE MAN** THAT **AM** NEWS!

ERP!--THAT'S JUST THE OPPOSITE OF WHAT EARTH EDITORS CONSIDER IMPORTANT!

The Daily Noose
DOG BITES MAN

ME DISAPPOINTED! HOW YOU EVER GONNA WIN **BIG PRIZE**??

¡CHOKE!:...I GUESS I N-NEVER WILL! TRY AS I MAY, I CAN'T THINK BACKWARDS, SIDEWAYS AND UPSIDE DOWN, LIKE THESE PATHETICALLY TWISTED DUPLICATES OF **SUPERMAN!**

SHORTLY...

YOU LUCKY KID, YOU! BIZARRO-LOIS HERE PUT IN GOOD WORD FOR YOU WITH HER DADDY WHO PUBLISH **DAILY HTRAE!** YOU GET BIG PRIZE, EVEN IF YOU **NOT** GET SCOOPS!

HOORAY!

10

THANKS, BIZARRO-LOIS! IF NOT FOR YOU, I WOULDN'T GET THE PRIZE I SO BADLY WANT: BEING SENT BACK TO EARTH!

NO, NO! THE BIG PRIZE IS... YOU WILL BE MARRIED TO HER... TOMORROW!

WHAT?!... WAIT A MINUTE! I DON'T WANT TO MARRY HER! I...!

US AM BIZARRO-LOIS' BROTHERS! IF YOU NOT MARRY OUR SISTER, US INSULTED!

WHEN US INSULTED, US GET SUPER-ANGRY! SOCK WHOEVER US MAD AT, WITH SUPER-POWERFUL FISTS!... YOU GOING MARRY OUR SISTER... HAH???

BUT OF COURSE!!! PHYSICALLY, I'M NO MATCH FOR THEM! ...I'LL USE MY WITS!!

THAT NIGHT, IN HIS BIZARRO WORLD APARTMENT, JIMMY RACKS HIS BRAINS, UNTIL...

HA, HA, HA! I GOT IT!... LET'S FACE IT! I'M TEE-RIFIC!

NEXT DAY, AT THE BIZARRO WEDDING CEREMONY...

BEFORE ME PRONOUNCE JIMMY OLSEN AND BIZARRO-LOIS MAN AND WIFE, IF ANYONE OBJECT LET HIM SPEAK NOW, OR FOREVER SHUT UP!

ME OBJECT!!!

UP RACES A BIZARRO-JIMMY...!

:PANT, PANT!:... ME WANT MARRY BIZARRO-LOIS MYSELF!

:CHUCKLE!:... LAST NIGHT I SLIPPED INTO A LAB AND CREATED THIS IMPERFECT, UNLIVING DUPLICATE OF MYSELF, WITH A DUPLICATOR RAY MACHINE!

11

I FIGURED THAT MY DUPLICATE, WITH HIS TWISTED BIZARRO MIND, WOULD LOVE BIZARRO-LOIS, BECAUSE I DON'T!

PLEASE MARRY ME!

BECAUSE YOU MUCH HAND-SOMER, ME WILL MARRY YOU INSTEAD OF HIM!

AND SO BIZARRO-LOIS WEDS BIZARRO-JIMMY...

FOR LOSING SUCH A GREAT CATCH, YOU BE PUNISHED! ME SEND YOU BACK TO EARTH IN SPACE SHIP!

YIPEE!

LATER...

POOR JIMMY! ME FEEL SORRY FOR HIM! OH, WELL, ME GUESS US CAN'T ALL BE LUCKY!

WHEEE! EARTH, HERE I COME!

AFTER THE SHIP REACHES OUR WORLD, AND JIMMY RETURNS TO THE DAILY PLANET...

I WANT SCOOPS, UNDERSTAND?!

WHAT A RELIEF TO BE HOME, AGAIN! GOSH, I EVEN ENJOY BEING BAWLED OUT BY THE REAL PERRY WHITE!

12

THE End.

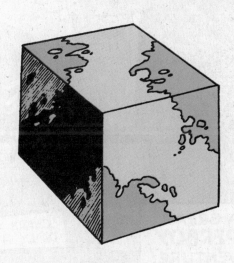

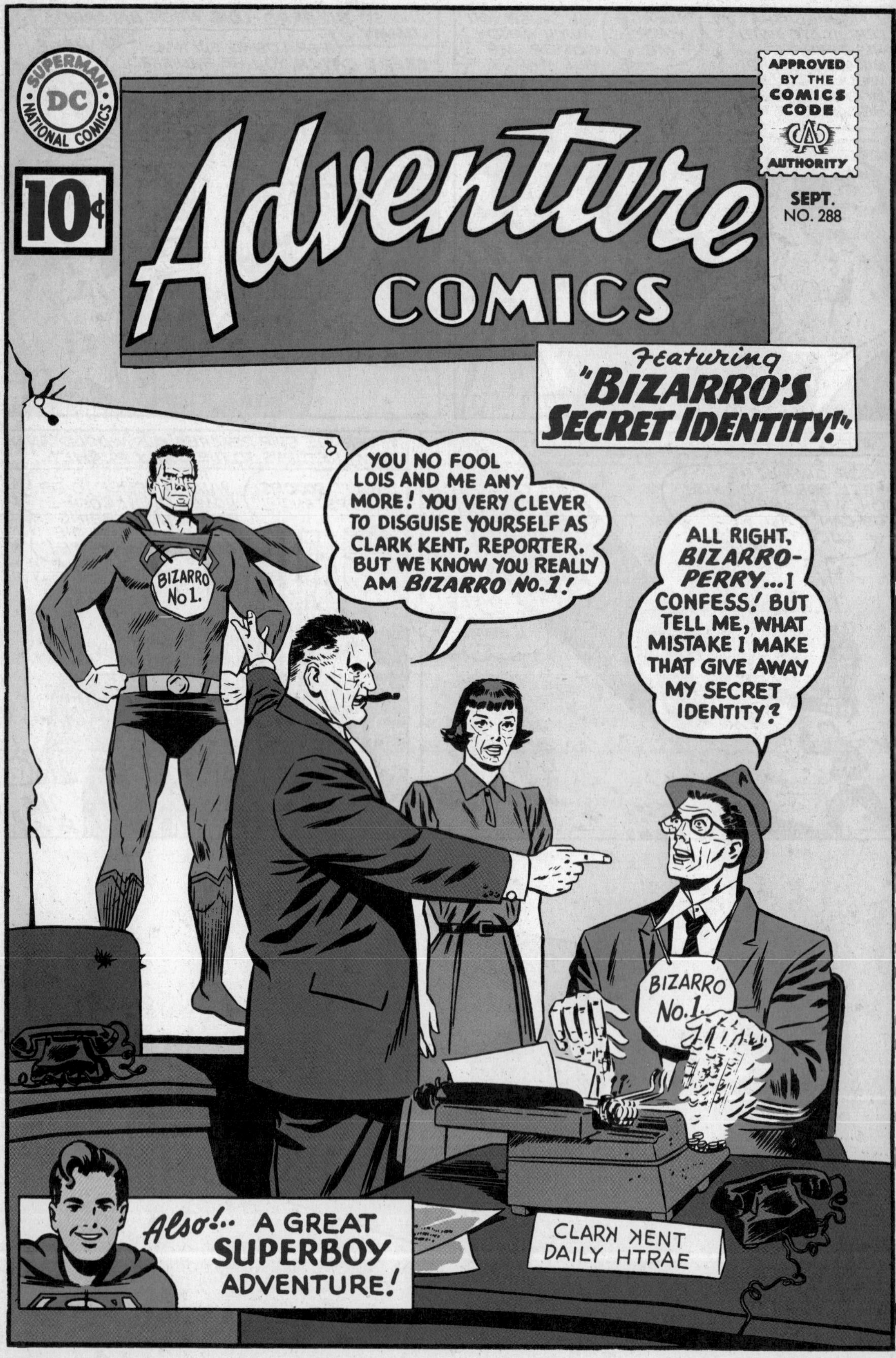
SUPERMAN DC NATIONAL COMICS
10¢
Adventure COMICS
APPROVED BY THE COMICS CODE AUTHORITY
SEPT. NO. 288
Featuring "BIZARRO'S SECRET IDENTITY!"
BIZARRO No1.
YOU NO FOOL LOIS AND ME ANY MORE! YOU VERY CLEVER TO DISGUISE YOURSELF AS CLARK KENT, REPORTER. BUT WE KNOW YOU REALLY AM BIZARRO NO.1!
ALL RIGHT, BIZARRO-PERRY...I CONFESS! BUT TELL ME, WHAT MISTAKE I MAKE THAT GIVE AWAY MY SECRET IDENTITY?
BIZARRO No.1
Also!.. A GREAT SUPERBOY ADVENTURE!
CLARK KENT DAILY HTRAE

TALES of the BIZARRO WORLD

EVERYTHING ON THE COCKEYED, MIXED-UP **BIZARRO WORLD** IS A CRAZY VERSION OF THINGS AS THEY ARE HERE ON EARTH! HOWEVER, ONE SET OF CIRCUMSTANCES REMAINS THE **SAME!** JUST AS **SUPERMAN** HAS SUPER-POWERS, THE IMPERFECT **BIZARRO** VERSIONS OF THE **MAN OF STEEL** ALSO POSSESS SUPER-POWERS! AND JUST AS THE LOIS LANE OF EARTH IS NON-SUPER, SO ARE THE BIZARRO-LOISES NON-SUPER!-- HOWEVER... SHOCKINGLY... THIS ALL CHANGES ONE AMAZING DAY WHEN THE **BIZARRO WORLD** BECOMES SUDDENLY AWARE OF A MYSTERIOUS STUPOR-WOMAN IN THE ADVENTURE OF...

BIZARRO'S SECRET IDENTITY!

IT AM...STUPOR-WOMAN!...HM-MM- ME WONDER WHO AM HER **SECRET** IDENTITY??

:CHUCKLE!:...WOULD BIZARRO NO. 1 BE SHOCKED TO LEARN THAT STUPOR-WOMAN AM NONE OTHER THAN ME, HIS LOVING WIFE, BIZARRO-LOIS NO. 1!!

BIZARRO NO. 1

WHO AM STUPOR-WOMAN?

NOBODY KNOW HER IDENTITY!

FAR OUT IN THE UNIVERSE EXISTS THE STRANGEST, WHACKIEST PLANET IN THE ENTIRE COSMOS...IT IS THE **SQUARE BIZARRO WORLD,** INHABITED BY STRANGE CREATURES WHO ARE IMPERFECT DUPLICATES OF **SUPERMAN,** LOIS LANE, PERRY WHITE AND OTHER METROPOLIS CHARACTERS...

EVERYTHING'S UTTERLY ZANY ON THIS WORLD, THE EXACT OPPOSITE OF EARTH, AND TO PROVE IT, LET'S LOOK IN ON THE **NO.1 BIZARRO FAMILY** EARLY ONE MORNING...

BE SURE TO BRUSH YOUR TEETH, SON!

BATHROOM

BIZARRO LOIS NO. 1

ME AM BRUSHING MY TEETH WITH **SHOE-POLISH** RIGHT **NOW,** MAMA!

GOOD BOY!

SHOE POLISH

BIZARRO JUNIOR NO.1

AND NOW ME AM POLISHING MY SHOES WITH **TOOTHPASTE!** IS YOU **PROUD** OF ME, MAMA?

ME SURE AM! **BIZARRO JUNIOR NO.1,** YOU AM WITHOUT A DOUBT THE **MESSIEST** SIGHT A MOTHER EVER SAW!... ME PROUD OF YOU!

NOW ME AM MUSSING UP MY HAIR... SO ME WILL LOOK **EVEN SLOPPIER!** THAT WAY, ME MAKE **BIG HIT** WITH GIRLS AT SCHOOL! NO BIZARRO GIRL LIKE KID WHO LOOKS... UGH!... NEAT!

SHORTLY...

HURRY UP AND EAT **DINNER*** OR YOU BE LATE FOR SCHOOL, SON!

OKAY, DAD! CHICKEN MY FAVORITE FOOD IN THE MORNING!

BIZARRO JUNIOR NO.1

*NOTE: ON THE BIZARRO WORLD, ALL INHABITANTS EAT A HEAVY DINNER UPON AWAKENING...A LIGHT BREAKFAST IS THEIR EVENING MEAL!!

2

PRESENTLY...

HO-BOY! THIS SURE TASTE **GREAT!** YOU AM MARVELOUS COOK, LOIS!

THANK YOU, DEAR! MY RECIPE IS TO THROW AWAY THE POTATOES, AND COOK ONLY THE **PEELINGS!**

AFTER *JUNIOR* LEAVES FOR SCHOOL...

WHAT AM BOTHER YOU, DEAR? YOU LOOK MORE VACANT-EYED THAN USUAL...

ME AM BORED STIFF! ME SICK OF BEING TIED DOWN TO HOUSE...

AS WE WARNED YOU, THINGS ARE **DIFFERENT** ON THE BIZARRO WORLD!

ALL MALE BIZARROS OF **SUPERMAN** HAVE SUPER-POWERS, CAN FLY WHERE THEY PLEASE! BIZARRO-LOIS LANES **NOT** HAVE SUPER-POWERS! ME GOING GET JOB BEFORE THIS BOREDOM DRIVE ME SANE...!

DON'T CRY! ME UNDER-STAND, BABY...!

ME BORED, TOO, WITH NOTHING TO DO BUT BE BIGGEST SHOT ON WHOLE DARN PLANET! HMM... ME GOT IDEA!!... WE BOTH BECOME REPORTERS! *BIZARRO-PERRY WHITE*, EDITOR OF *DAILY HTRAE*, MY FRIEND! HE HIRE US!

OH, DARLING! WE BOTH BE REPORTERS NOW-- JUST LIKE ORIGINAL CLARK KENT AND LOIS LANE!

AND SO, NEXT DAY, AT THE *DAILY HTRAE*, BIZARRO NO.1 AND HIS WIFE BECOME NEWSHOUNDS...

WELCOME TO STAFF!

THANK YOU TOO MUCH, *BIZARRO-JIMMY OLSEN!*

HERE COME BOSS-MAN *BIZARRO-WHITE!*

LOIS, ME GOT GREAT ASSIGNMENT FOR YOU! GO TO *BIZARRO JAIL* AND SEE IF YOU CAN FIND STORY DULL ENOUGH TO MAKE FRONT PAGE!

ME GO RIGHT AWAY, PERRY!

EN ROUTE, SHE STOPS TO MAKE SOME PURCHASES, AND SOON, AT THE JAIL...

FROM ME, TO YOU!

AIN'T SHE SWEET? BIZARRO-LOIS NO. 1 AM BRINGING GIFTS FOR PRISON GUARDS! SHE GOT BIG HEART!

AMONG THE BIZARRO CONVICTS VASTLY IMPRESSED BY HER KINDNESS IS BIZARRO-KLTPZYXM, WHO WAS CREATED BY BIZARRO JUNIOR NO. 1, WHILE THE YOUNGSTER WAS MEDDLING WITH HIS FATHER'S DUPLICATOR RAY MACHINE...

HOW NICE! SHE DESERVES TO BE REWARDED!

UNLIKE MISCHIEVOUS MR. MXYZPTLK, KLTPZYXM IS VERY GOOD AND WOULDN'T DREAM OF USING HIS MAGICAL POWERS TO FREE HIMSELF FROM PRISON...

PS-SST, LADY! BECAUSE YOU SO SWELL, ME WILL USE MY MAGIC TO GIVE YOU SUPER-POWERS!

YOU... WHAT??!!

BIZARRO LOIS NO. 1

THE NEXT MOMENT...

HEY... CAREFUL!... YOU AM BENDING JAIL BARS WITH YOUR SUPER-STRENGTH! KEEP THIS SECRET! IF OTHER BIZARRO WOMEN LEARN THAT WIFE OF PLANET'S LEADER GOT SUPER-POWERS, THEY WILL DEMAND THOSE POWERS, TOO! NOW STRAIGHTEN BARS!

GOSH!... THANKS!!

BIZARRO LOIS NO. 1

LATER, ALONE AT HOME, BIZARRO-LOIS NO. 1 CREATES A SUPER-COSTUME FOR HERSELF FROM ONE OF HER HUSBAND'S SPARE UNIFORMS...

THERE! NOW ME ABLE FLY AT SUPER-SPEED WITHOUT CLOTHES BURNING OFF!

BIZARRO LOIS NO. 1

AND SO IS CREATED...STUPOR-WOMAN, THE ONLY FEMALE WITH SUPER-POWERS ON THE BIZARRO WORLD!!

ME WILL USE MY POWERS TO HELP ALL BIZARRO WOMEN! ...LADY BIZARROS HAVE NO FEAR... STUPOR-WOMAN, SHE AM HERE!!!

INTO ACTION HURTLES THE BONEHEAD OF STEEL...!

UP...DOWN...AND... AND...AWA-AAAY??

THERE GO BIZARRO-KRYPTO! HIM SURE LOOK PUZZLED! ...¡CHUCKLE!¿

WHO THAT?

VERY SOON...

BAW-WWWWWWW!

HM-MM! THAT BIZARRO-LOIS...IN DISTRESS! THIS AM A JOB FOR STUPOR-WOMAN! GOODIE!

¡GASP!¿ A...A... BIZARRO WOMAN WHO CAN FLY! WHO ARE YOU?

ME AM STUPOR-WOMAN, CHAMPION OF ALL WEAK LOIS LANES! NOW...TELL ME YOUR PROBLEM!

THOSE UGLY FLOWERS AM RUINING MY PRETTY WEED-GARDEN, THAT WHAT MY PROBLEM AM!

HAVE NO FEAR... STUPOR-WOMAN, SHE AM HERE!!

SWIFTLY FLYING ALONG, STUPOR-WOMAN PLUCKS AWAY THE PRETTY FLOWERS SO THAT THE WEEDS ALONE REMAIN...

THESE SPACE WEEDS AM STRONG LIKE WIRE, NOT WEAK LIKE EARTH WEEDS!

5

AFTERWARD...

OH, THANK YOU, **STUPOR-WOMAN!** WHENEVER ME SMELL THESE WEEDS, ME THINK OF **YOU!**

¡CHOKE!¡...ME AM TOUCHED BY THAT **GREAT COMPLIMENT!!**

LATER, **STUPOR-WOMAN** FINDS ANOTHER BIZARRO-LOIS IN NEED OF AID...

WHAT YOUR PROBLEM, DEARIE?

MY HUSBAND BUILD THIS HOUSE, BUT HE FORGOT TO BUILD A ROAD TO HIGHWAY!

SUPER-SOON...

¡GASP!¡...**STUPOR-WOMAN** AM SUPER-SWIFTLY BUILDING A GLASS ROAD AT SUPER-SPEED, USING HER HEAT VISION TO MELT SAND INTO GLASS! HOW **SUPER!**

MOMENTS LATER...

THANK YOU, **STUPOR-WOMAN!** HOW **BRILLIANT** OF YOU TO HAVE BUILT THIS **SHORT-CUT** ROAD FOR ME TO HIGHWAY!

ME ALWAYS GLAD TO PERFORM SUPER-FEATS FOR BEAUTIFUL BIZARRO WOMEN!

SOME SHORT-CUT! ACTUALLY, **STUPOR-WOMAN** HAS BUILT A **LONG,** ZIG-ZAG ROAD!

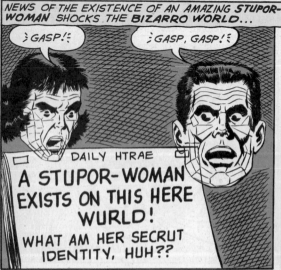

NEWS OF THE EXISTENCE OF AN AMAZING **STUPOR-WOMAN** SHOCKS THE **BIZARRO WORLD...**

¡GASP!¡

¡GASP, GASP!¡

DAILY HTRAE

A STUPOR-WOMAN EXISTS ON THIS HERE WURLD!

WHAT AM HER SECRUT IDENTITY, HUH??

THAT EVENING, AT **BREAKFAST,** IN THE NUMBER ONE BIZARRO FAMILY HOME...

WHO CAN **STUPOR-WOMAN** BE?

SEARCH ME!

ME HOPE HIM **NOT** SEARCH ME, OR MAYBE HIM FIND **CLUE!**

BIZARRO LOIS NO. 1

NEXT DAY, ON A BIZARRO GOLF COURSE...

GOLF BORES ME, BUT ME GOT TO PLAY IT, LIKE PRESIDENTS EISENHOWER AND KENNEDY, ON EARTH! SINCE ME AM LEADER OF BIZARRO WORLD, ME GOT TO KEEP UP THIS TRADITION!

OKAY! START PLAYING BIZARRO GOLF... NOW!!

ME BEGIN BY BURROWING INTO GROUND UNDER COURSE'S FIRST HOLE!

BANG!

A MOMENT LATER, WITHIN A SMALL, SCOOPED-OUT CAVERN BENEATH THE HOLE...

FIVE!!!

MY "X-RAY" VISION AM GUIDING MY SHOT!

UP OUT OF THE GROUND SUPER-SWIFTLY FLIES BIZARRO NO. 1...

AH-HHHH... GOLF-BALL ME HIT AM FLYING UP OUT OF HOLE...

SECONDS LATER...

HURRAY! ME GOT A TEE IN ONE!!

GOOD SHOT, BUDDY-PAL! YOU PLAY GOOD, LIKE A GOLFER SHOULD!

HA, HA! ON EARTH, STUPID GOLFERS HIT BALL FROM TEE INTO HOLE!

MEANWHILE, BIZARRO-LOIS NO. 1, IN HER DISGUISE OF STUPOR-WOMAN, IS FLYING ON PATROL...

UH-OH! ME AM PASSING UPRIGHT TOWER OF PISA WHICH HAVE BIZARRO WORLD NATIONAL SYMBOL OF VULTURE ON IT, SO ME MUST SHOW PROPER RESPECT, BY SALUTING!

7

As she streaks over the golf-course, her super-hearing picks up a conversation below...

EVERYBODY WONDERING WHAT IS *STUPOR-WOMAN'S* SECRET IDENTITY! SINCE YOU AM OUR LEADER, AND YOUR WIFE AM TOP WOMAN OF OUR WORLD, MAYBE *SHE* AM STUPOR-WOMAN... YES?

HM...MMM... ME GETTING IDEA...

AWP! MY HUSBAND ACTING *SUSPICIOUS!* ME BETTER HURRY HOME AND GET BUSY! HIM *SURE* TO ASK WHAT ME DID ALL DAY, SINCE HIM KNOW ME DIDN'T GO TO DAILY HTRAE OFFICE TODAY!

Arriving home, *STUPOR-WOMAN* swiftly bakes 1,000 pies...

HIM MAY COME HOME ANY SECOND! ME GOT TO WORK *FAST* SO HIM WON'T SUSPECT ME GOT *SUPER-POWERS!!!*

A few moments after she removes her action costume, her mate arrives...

--998 --999 --1,000 PIES! --ONLY FEMALE WITH SUPER-POWERS COULD BAKE THIS MANY PIES! THIS *PROVES* YOU AM STUPOR-WOMAN!

URK! M-ME STUPIDLY GAVE MYSELF AWAY!

WAIT... *MY WIFE SUPER??*-- NO! IT *COULDN'T* BE! YOU PROBABLY BOUGHT THEM PIES IN BAKERY!-- YEAH! THAT AM IT, HA, HA.!

WHAT A RELIEF! HIM TALKED HIM-SELF OUT OF THE TRUTH WHICH AM RIGHT UNDER HIS BIZARRO NOSE!

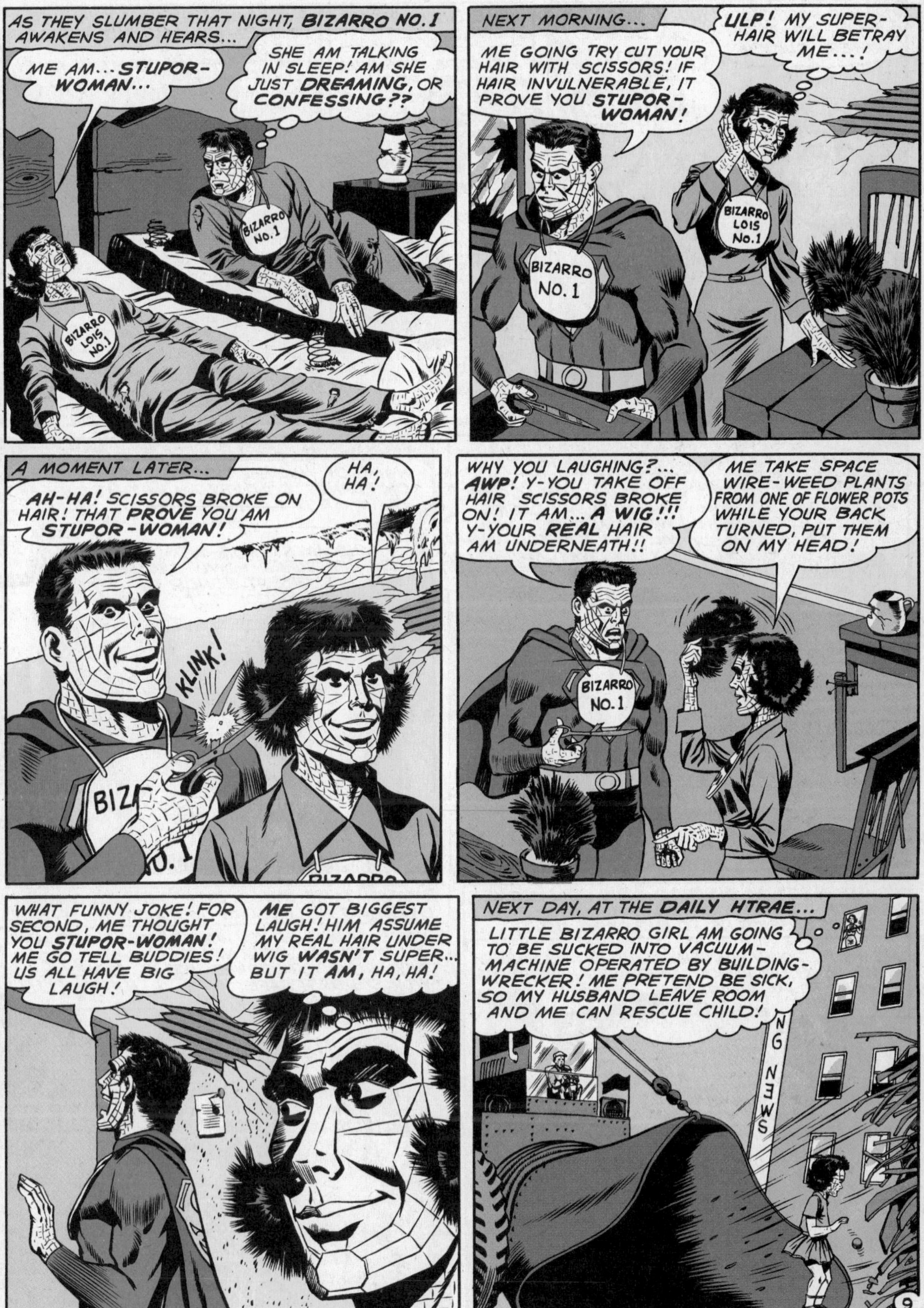
AS THEY SLUMBER THAT NIGHT, BIZARRO NO.1 AWAKENS AND HEARS...
ME AM... STUPOR-WOMAN...
SHE AM TALKING IN SLEEP! AM SHE JUST DREAMING, OR CONFESSING??
BIZARRO NO.1
BIZARRO LOIS NO.1
NEXT MORNING...
ME GOING TRY CUT YOUR HAIR WITH SCISSORS! IF HAIR INVULNERABLE, IT PROVE YOU STUPOR-WOMAN!
ULP! MY SUPER-HAIR WILL BETRAY ME...!
BIZARRO NO.1
BIZARRO LOIS NO.1
A MOMENT LATER...
AH-HA! SCISSORS BROKE ON HAIR! THAT PROVE YOU AM STUPOR-WOMAN!
HA, HA!
KLINK!
WHY YOU LAUGHING?... AWP! Y-YOU TAKE OFF HAIR SCISSORS BROKE ON! IT AM... A WIG!!! Y-YOUR REAL HAIR AM UNDERNEATH!!
ME TAKE SPACE WIRE-WEED PLANTS FROM ONE OF FLOWER POTS WHILE YOUR BACK TURNED, PUT THEM ON MY HEAD!
BIZARRO NO.1
WHAT FUNNY JOKE! FOR SECOND, ME THOUGHT YOU STUPOR-WOMAN! ME GO TELL BUDDIES! US ALL HAVE BIG LAUGH!
ME GOT BIGGEST LAUGH! HIM ASSUME MY REAL HAIR UNDER WIG WASN'T SUPER... BUT IT AM, HA, HA!
NEXT DAY, AT THE DAILY HTRAE...
LITTLE BIZARRO GIRL AM GOING TO BE SUCKED INTO VACUUM-MACHINE OPERATED BY BUILDING-WRECKER! ME PRETEND BE SICK, SO MY HUSBAND LEAVE ROOM AND ME CAN RESCUE CHILD!
NG NEWS
9

OH--ME FEEL DIZZY! YOU GO TAKE DRINK OF WATER, QUICK!

YES, DEAR!

WHILE *BIZARRO NO.1* DRINKS...

ME HOPE THIS WILL MAKE *HER* FEEL BETTER!

ICE WATER

BIZARRO-LOIS NO.1 CHANGES TO *STUPOR-WOMAN* AND PERFORMS THE RESCUE...

JUST IN TIME!

BACK TO THE NEWSPAPER OFFICE SHE FLIES, CHANGING IDENTITIES JUST BEFORE HER HUSBAND RETURNS...

BETTER, NOW?

UH-HUH!

HM-MM. ME LOOKED THROUGH MY OFFICE WINDOW AND THOUGHT ME SAW *STUPOR-WOMAN* FLY THIS WAY! MAYBE LOIS AM HER! ME SET TRAP!!

ZZZZZ

BIZARRO LOIS NO.1

SHORTLY, IN PERRY'S OFFICE...

NAME OF WINNER OF "*UGLIEST WOMAN ON PLANET*" CONTEST AM IN THAT SAFE-- IT AM *BEST* SAFE ON WORLD!

IF LOIS AM *STUPOR-WOMAN*, SHE'LL USE HER SUPER-POWERS TO SEE IF *SHE* HAS *GREAT HONOR* OF WINNING CONTEST!

AS PERRY LEAVES *BIZARRO-LOIS NO.1* ALONE IN HIS OFFICE TO PROOF-READ AN ARTICLE, HE TELLS HIS SUSPICIONS TO *BIZARRO NO.1*...

ME WRITE DOWN WINNER'S NAME MY X-RAY VISION REVEAL TO ME AM IN SAFE!

AH-HA! MY SUPER-SENSES HAVE EXPOSED HER!

REVEALING HIS DISCOVERY TO *BIZARRO-WHITE*, *BIZARRO NO.1* LOOKS ON A MOMENT LATER, AS...

NAME OF WINNER YOU WROTE ON PAPER AM...*YOUR NAME!* THIS PROVE YOU LOOKED INTO WORLD'S BEST SAFE, WITH X-RAY VISION!-- YOU AM *STUPOR-WOMAN!*

THEY GOT ME!-- WAIT!....NO!... THEY HAVEN'T!!!

BIZARRO LOIS NO.1

10

Panel 1: SECONDS LATER, IN PERRY'S OFFICE...

YES, ME COULDN'T RESIST PEEKING INTO SAFE! BUT ME DID IT BY JUST WALKING *BEHIND* SAFE! BIZARRO SAFES GOT NO BACK TO THEM!

LITTLE NAPOLEON'S GHOST! ME FORGOT THAT-- ME HUMBLY APOLOGIZE, LOIS!

Panel 2: BUT LATER, AT THE *NUMBER ONE BIZARRO FAMILY HOME*...

LOIS, MY SUPER-SENSES CAUGHT YOU IN ACT OF USING SUPER-POWERS IN PERRY'S OFFICE! HOW YOU GET POWERS THAT MADE YOU *STUPOR-WOMAN??*

KLTPZYXM GAVE THEM TO ME... ;SOB!;

Panel 3: OH, NO! ACCORDING TO *BIZARRO LAW*, IT AM AWFUL CRIME TO ACCEPT GIFT FROM CONVICT! US COULD BOTH BE EXILED FROM *BIZARRO WORLD* FOR THAT! HOW COULD YOU...?!!

BOO-HOO! ME S-SORRY! ME WISH ME *NEVER HAD* THEM SUPER-POWERS AT ALL...! ;SOB!!;

Panel 4: MEANWHILE, FLYING THROUGH OUTER-SPACE, THE REAL *MR. MXYZPTLK* HAS WITNESSED EVERYTHING...

;CHUCKLE!; NOW TO CREATE SOME MISCHIEF OF MY OWN! I HEREBY MAGICALLY COMMAND *EVERYONE* ON THE *BIZARRO WORLD* TO FORGET *STUPOR-WOMAN* EVER EXISTED!

Panel 5: AND BIZARRO-LOIS NO.1, I ORDER YOU TO NO LONGER HAVE SUPER-POWERS!... BIZARRO NO.1, I COMMAND YOU TO WANT TO BECOME *STUPOR-MAN*!... HA, HA! SOMEDAY I'LL HAVE A REAL SHOWDOWN WITH THAT GOODY-GOODY *BIZARRO* DUPLICATE OF ME!... BYE-BYE, *BIZARRO WORLD!*

Panel 6: AS MXYZPTLK'S COMMAND INSTANTLY WORKS...

;PUFF!; ...HELP ME REARRANGE THIS HEAVY FURNITURE, INSTEAD OF PLAYING WITH THAT FAKE RUBBER-NOSE!

ME WILL CRUSADE AS *STUPOR-MAN* AND HAVE *BIZARRO KENT* SECRET IDENTITY! WHEN I WEAR THIS RUBBER-NOSE NOBODY BE ABLE GUESS WHO *STUPOR-MAN* REALLY AM!... ;CHUCKLE!;

Panel 7: AND SO, IN THE DAYS THAT FOLLOW, A *STUPOR-MAN* IS BORN...

HOORAY! STUPOR-MAN SPLASHED MUD ON MY DRESS. NOW IT SO DIRTY MAYBE ME WIN PRIZE AT FASHION SHOW!

WHO AM HIS *SECRET IDENTITY??*

11

DIMLY RECALLING **SUPERMAN'S** DUAL-PERSONALITY SET-UP ON EARTH, **BIZARRO NO.1** SECURES A JOB ON THE **DAILY HTRAE** IN HIS SECRET IDENTITY OF **BIZARRO-KENT.** THEN, ONE AFTERNOON...

CONFESS, CLARK KENT! WE KNOW YOU AM REALLY BIZARRO NO.1!

¡GASP!¡... HOW YOU GUESS MY SECRET IDENTITY? WHAT MISTAKE I MADE??

YOU AM TYPING AT SUPER-SPEED AND ABSENT-MINDEDLY WEARING BIZARRO NO.1 MEDALLION IN PLAIN VIEW!

SINCE **YOU** AM SECRETLY **BIZARRO NO.1,** WHO AM SECRETLY **BIZARRO KENT,** THAT DEFINITELY PROVE **YOU** AM ALSO **STUPOR-MAN!!**

ME ADMIT IT! ME DROP SUPER-IDENTITIES!

¡CHUCKLE!¡... BUT YOU MUST ADMIT ME AM PRETTY DARNED GOOD! ON EARTH THEY HAVEN'T GUESSED, FOR YEARS, THAT CLARK KENT AM SECRET IDENTITY OF **SUPERMAN!**... BUT, ME!...**HA!!**... ME AM SO **TERRIFIC,** MY SECRET IDENTITY WAS FOUND OUT ON **MY FIRST CASE!!!**

Thl End.

12

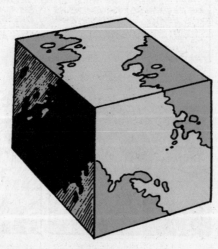

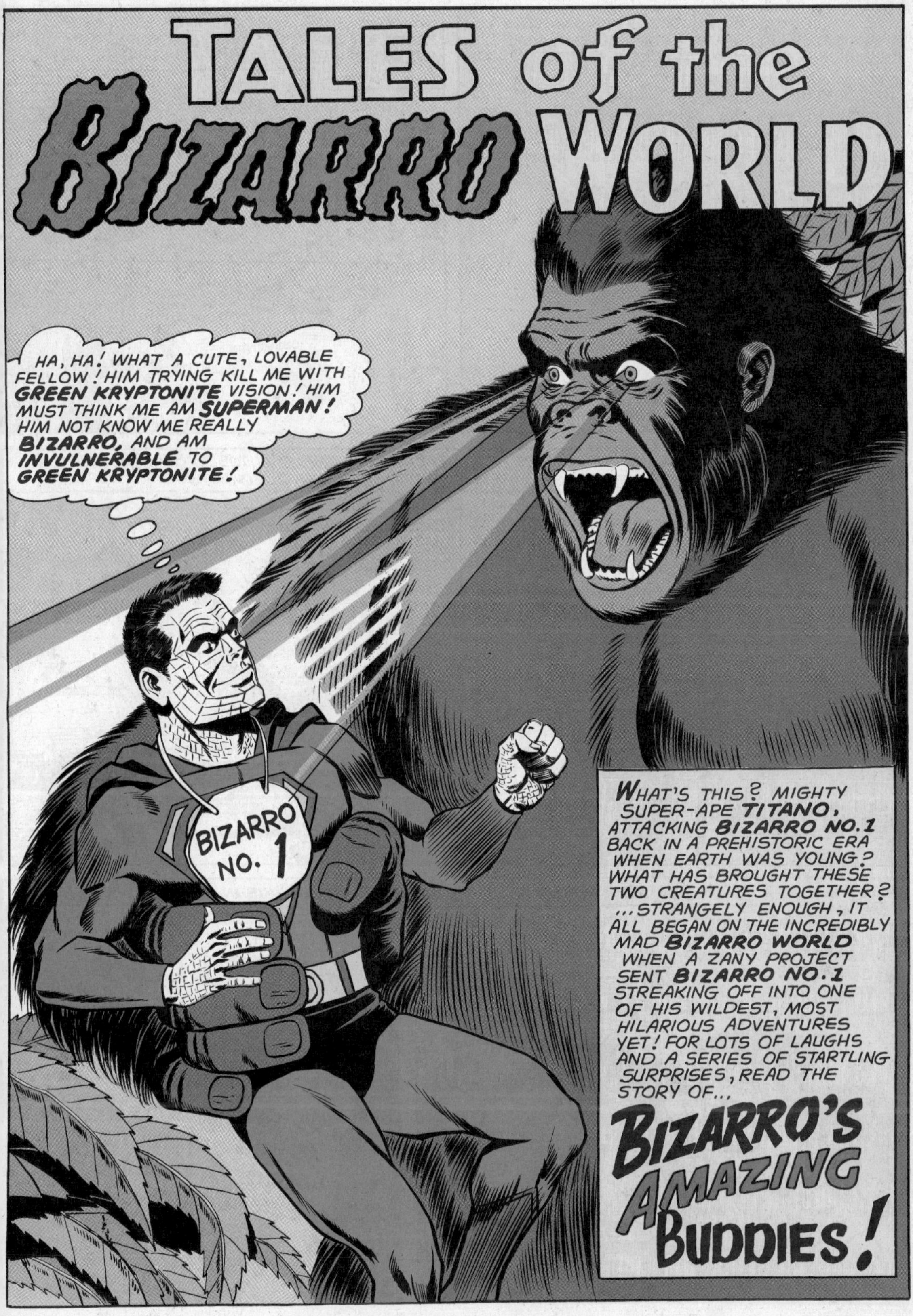
TALES of the BIZARRO WORLD
HA, HA! WHAT A CUTE, LOVABLE FELLOW! HIM TRYING KILL ME WITH GREEN KRYPTONITE VISION! HIM MUST THINK ME AM SUPERMAN! HIM NOT KNOW ME REALLY BIZARRO, AND AM INVULNERABLE TO GREEN KRYPTONITE!
BIZARRO NO. 1
WHAT'S THIS? MIGHTY SUPER-APE TITANO, ATTACKING BIZARRO NO.1 BACK IN A PREHISTORIC ERA WHEN EARTH WAS YOUNG? WHAT HAS BROUGHT THESE TWO CREATURES TOGETHER? ...STRANGELY ENOUGH, IT ALL BEGAN ON THE INCREDIBLY MAD BIZARRO WORLD WHEN A ZANY PROJECT SENT BIZARRO NO.1 STREAKING OFF INTO ONE OF HIS WILDEST, MOST HILARIOUS ADVENTURES YET! FOR LOTS OF LAUGHS AND A SERIES OF STARTLING SURPRISES, READ THE STORY OF...
BIZARRO'S AMAZING BUDDIES!

FAR OFF IN OUTER SPACE EXISTS THE STRANGEST, WHACKIEST PLANET IN THE ENTIRE WORLD... THE **SQUARE BIZARRO WORLD!**

EVERYTHING ON THIS CRAZY PLANET IS UTTERLY ZANY! FOR EXAMPLE, THIS IS HOW A HAPPY **BIZARRO**-LOIS WIFE DEMONSTRATES HER AFFECTION...

FACT YOU AM THROWING DISHES **PROVE** YOU LOVE ME, DARLING! HOW **LUCKY** ME AM!!

ON THIS MADCAP WORLD, EVERYONE ENTERS THROUGH **EXITS**, AND LEAVES THROUGH **ENTRANCES**...!

MOMMY, WHY EARTH PEOPLE ENTER THROUGH ENTRANCES, AND EXIT THROUGH EXITS?

BECAUSE THEM AM **STUPID, THAT'S WHY!**

INTRANCE

EGGSIT

BIZARRO WORLD AUTOS **STOP** FOR **GREEN** TRAFFIC LIGHTS, AND **GO** WHEN THE TRAFFIC LIGHTS TURN **RED**...

YOU DROVE THROUGH **GREEN LIGHT!** THAT AM AGAINST LAW!

AND WHEN AN AUTO ON THIS MAD WORLD GETS A "CAR WASH"...

HOW **BEAUTIFULLY** YOUR EMPLOYEES AM MESSING UP CAR WITH MUDDY WATER HOSE!

IF YOU FIND ONE CLEAN SPOT LEFT ON CAR, LADY, YOU GET REFUND!

CAR WASH INC.

BEHIND ALL THIS INCREDIBLE WHACKINESS IS THE **BIZARRO CODE**...

BIZARRO CODE

US DO OPPOSITE OF ALL EARTHLY THINGS! US HATE **BEAUTY**! US LOVE **UGLINESS**! IS BIG CRIME TO MAKE ANYTHING PERFECT ON **BIZARRO WORLD!**

AND NOW LET US LOOK IN ON SOME TYPICAL **BIZARRO** CHILDREN WATCHING AN EARTH TV SHOW, ON A TV SET EQUIPPED WITH A SUPER-ANTENNA...

BAW-WWW! DANIEL BOONE AM ESCAPING FROM THAT **NICE** INDIAN!

≀SHUDDER≀-- HOW **DREADFUL** THOSE --UGH!--TV EARTH HEROES AM!

MEANWHILE, A FURIOUS DEBATE RAGES AT THE **BIZARRO** WORLD'S CAPITOL, THE **UPRIGHT TOWER OF PISA**...

DOWN WITH EARTH HERO TV SHOWS.!!

THEM AM REVOLTING.!!

INSIDE THE TOWER, A LEADING **BIZARRO** SICKOLOGIST VIGOROUSLY PROTESTS...

BIZARRO COUNCIL, THEM TV EARTH HEROES AM GIVING **BIZARRO** YOUTHS DAY-MARES! THEM AM RUINING OUR BRATS' MENTAL HEALTH!

ZZZZZ!

THIS MUST STOP! IF NECESSARY, ME WILL SMASH EVERY TV SET ON THIS HERE PLANET!

CALM YOURSELF!

THE PLANET'S RULER, **BIZARRO NO. 1**, ANNOUNCES...

FRANKENSTINE

ABOMIMABLE SNOWMANN

ME WILL CREATE NEW **BIZARRO** WORLD TV SERIES! IT WILL BE ABOUT "**GREAT HEROES OF PAST**"! REAL-LIFE **WORTH-WHILE** HEROES WHO **DESERVE** TO BE **ADMIRED**, LIKE THESE...

③

ME WILL TRAVEL THROUGH TIME-BARRIER INTO EARTH'S PAST! THEN ME WILL WRITE TV STORIES ABOUT WHAT ME LEARN ABOUT THEM HEROES!

GOOD! ESPECIALLY SINCE THEY WILL BE **REAL** HEROES, NOT MADE-UP FICTION CHARACTERS!

FRANK

65

SHORTLY AFTERWARD, THE *BIZARRO WORLD'S* RULER BIDS HIS FAMILY FAREWELL...

GOODBYE, *BIZARRO-LOIS NO. 1!* GOODBYE *BIZARRO JUNIOR NO. 1!* AND MOST OF ALL, GOODBYE *BIZARRO-KRYPTO!*

GOODBYE! DON'T HURRY BACK!

ACROSS SPACE TO THE PLANET EARTH HURTLES THE ORIGINAL IMPERFECT *SUPERMAN* DUPLICATE...

LUCKY FOR *SUPERMAN,* ME AM TOO BUSY TO FIGHT WITH HIM RIGHT NOW!

INTO THE TIME-BARRIER SUPER-SPEEDS *BIZARRO...*

ME WILL TRAVEL JUST FEW YEARS INTO PAST, TO TIME WHEN FIRST *ABOMINABLE SNOWMAN* WAS SEEN ON EARTH!

EMERGING OUT OF THE TIME-BARRIER, *BIZARRO* SOARS ABOVE THE HIMALAYAN MOUNTAINS, SEARCHING FOR SOME SIGN OF THE FABULOUS MAN-BEAST...

WHERE AM YOU, *ABOMINABLE?*

MEANWHILE, IN THE VICINITY, A PARTY OF EXPLORERS TOIL UPWARD, STRAINING THEIR EYES FOR THE SAME OBJECTIVE...

DO YOU THINK THE ASTOUNDING SNOW-CREATURE THE NATIVES CALL *YEHTI REALLY* EXISTS, ASQUITH?

WE MAY SOON KNOW, MACDUFF!

GLIMPSING A MOVING SHADOW, *BIZARRO* STREAKS DOWN ONTO A SNOWY MOUNTAIN-LEDGE, BUT...

AWW-WWP! YOU NOT *ABOMINABLE SNOWGUY!* YOU JUST MOUNTAIN-BEAR! HEY! STOP HUGGING ME!!

4

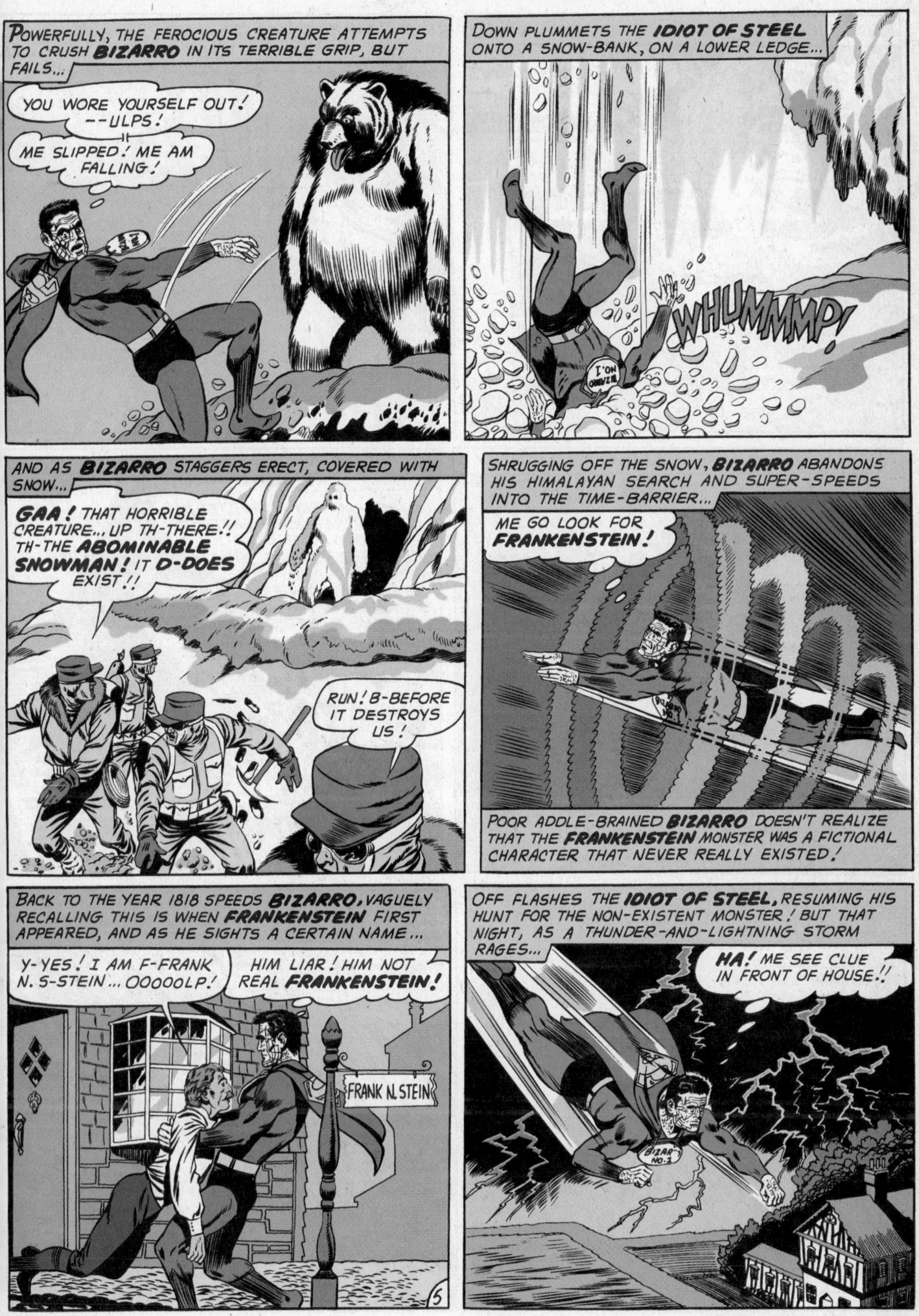
POWERFULLY, THE FEROCIOUS CREATURE ATTEMPTS TO CRUSH BIZARRO IN ITS TERRIBLE GRIP, BUT FAILS...
YOU WORE YOURSELF OUT! --ULPS!
ME SLIPPED! ME AM FALLING!
DOWN PLUMMETS THE IDIOT OF STEEL ONTO A SNOW-BANK, ON A LOWER LEDGE...
WHUMMMP!
AND AS BIZARRO STAGGERS ERECT, COVERED WITH SNOW...
GAA! THAT HORRIBLE CREATURE... UP TH-THERE!! TH-THE ABOMINABLE SNOWMAN! IT D-DOES EXIST!!
RUN! B-BEFORE IT DESTROYS US!
SHRUGGING OFF THE SNOW, BIZARRO ABANDONS HIS HIMALAYAN SEARCH AND SUPER-SPEEDS INTO THE TIME-BARRIER...
ME GO LOOK FOR FRANKENSTEIN!
POOR ADDLE-BRAINED BIZARRO DOESN'T REALIZE THAT THE FRANKENSTEIN MONSTER WAS A FICTIONAL CHARACTER THAT NEVER REALLY EXISTED!
BACK TO THE YEAR 1818 SPEEDS BIZARRO, VAGUELY RECALLING THIS IS WHEN FRANKENSTEIN FIRST APPEARED, AND AS HE SIGHTS A CERTAIN NAME...
Y-YES! I AM F-FRANK N. S-STEIN... OOOOOLP!
HIM LIAR! HIM NOT REAL FRANKENSTEIN!
FRANK N. STEIN
5
OFF FLASHES THE IDIOT OF STEEL, RESUMING HIS HUNT FOR THE NON-EXISTENT MONSTER! BUT THAT NIGHT, AS A THUNDER-AND-LIGHTNING STORM RAGES...
HA! ME SEE CLUE IN FRONT OF HOUSE!!

WHILE LIGHTNING FLASHES, AND THUNDER CRASHES...

A SPIKE! DID IT FALL OUT OF FRANKENSTEIN'S HEAD...??

BA-RROOM

BIZARRO NO. 1

INSIDE THE HOUSE, AS BOOMING THUNDERBOLTS AWAKEN A WOMAN, SHE LOOKS OUT OF HER BED-ROOM WINDOW IN TIME TO SEE...

A MONSTER!...OH! TH-THAT GH-GHASTLY FACE...!

LIGHTNING STRIKE SPIKE!—ME ONLY FEEL TICKLE!

BIZARRO NO. 1

TOSSING AWAY THE SPIKE, BIZARRO STREAKS AWAY...

CLUE NO GOOD! ME FLY INTO TIME-BARRIER AND LOOK FOR EVEN GREATER HERO THAN FRANKENSTEIN!

BIZA NO.

TO THE WOMAN, IT SEEMS THAT BIZARRO SIMPLY VANISHED...!

TH-THAT GHASTLY, FRIGHTENING FIGURE! THAT UNFORGETTABLY MONSTROUS FACE! DID I IMAGINE IT?...WAIT! THAT APPARITION AND THAT NAME HE UTTERED-- FRANKENSTEIN-- HAS GIVEN ME A WEIRD INSPIRATION!

IMMEDIATELY, SHE SITS DOWN TO WRITE A FANTASTIC, TERRIFYING NOVEL, FATED TO THRILL MANY MILLIONS OF READERS FOR MANY GENERATIONS...

Frankenstein by Mary W. Shelley

OUT OF THE TIME-BARRIER AND INTO THE YEAR 1301 A.D., IN THE MIDDLE AGES, SPEEDS THE IDIOT OF STEEL...

THEM SAY THE DEVIL WAS FIRST SEEN HERE! ME FIND HIM!!

6

SOON...

CLEFT IN GROUND AM GOOD PLACE FOR DEVIL TO HIDE! ME LOOK FOR HIM HERE!

DOWN INTO A PHOSPHORESCENTLY GLOWING SUBTERRANEAN CAVE CRASHES *BIZARRO*...

YOO-HOO!--HEY! YOU AROUND HERE SOMEWHERE, DEVIL? ME WANT MAKE BIG TV HERO OF YOU!

HIM NOT ANSWER! HIM EITHER BASHFUL, OR NOT **HERE**!

BACK UP TO THE GROUND'S SURFACE SPEEDS A DISAPPOINTED *BIZARRO*, THEN...

HM-MMM! AM THEM **GHOSTS** DANCING ON MOUNTAIN PEAK? MAYBE SATAN HAVING MEETING WITH SOME BUDDY-PALS!

BUT AS HE FLIES TO INVESTIGATE...

TOO BAD! "GHOSTS" AM ONLY FOG-WISPS!...HOW CAN ME CONTACT SATAN? **WAIT**! ME GETTING DEVILISH IDEA! HA, HA!

LAUGHING WILDLY, *BIZARRO* CRASHES DOWN INTO THE GROUND...

HAW, HAW! SINCE SATAN AM A SLIPPERY FELLOW TO CATCH, ME START OFF BY DIGGING FOR **OIL**! X-RAY VISION REVEAL OIL DEPOSIT BELOW!

THEN, AS HE CRASHES BACK TO THE SURFACE, HAVING CREATED AN OIL POOL...

NOW ME AM READY TO GET "HORNS FOR THE DEVIL," HA, HA, HA!

7

OFF STREAKS **BIZARRO,** SEARCHING UNTIL HE FINDS THE SKELETON OF A LONG DEAD STEER...

ME NEED THEM HORNS MORE THAN YOU DO, OLD SPORT! ME BORROW THEM!

AFTERWARD, **BIZARRO** MAKES A "TAIL" OUT OF ROPE, THEN HE ATTACHES THE HORNS AND "TAIL" TO HIMSELF.

NOW THAT ME AM CHEAP IMITATION OF SATAN, ME FLY BACK TO OIL POOL!

RETURNING TO THE POOL, THE **IDIOT OF STEEL** IGNITES THE OIL WITH HIS HEAT VISION...

SATAN WON'T LIKE IT IF ME GIVE BAD IMITATION OF HIM!

NEXT, **BIZARRO** DRINKS A GREAT DRAUGHT OF THE BURNING OIL...

WHEN HE COME TO COMPLAIN, ME GRAB HIM, TELL HIM ABOUT MY IDEA TO MAKE HIM LOVABLE TV HERO OF **BIZARRO WORLD** BRATS!

AS **BIZARRO** SPURTS THE FLAMING OIL FROM HIS MOUTH...

ME WILL OFFER HIM TERRIFIC DEAL! STAR BILLING! FAT CUT OF ALL PROFITS!--UH-OH! TH-THAT SHADOW... FROM BEHIND...MUST BE **HIM!**

SWIFTLY TURNING, THE **IDIOT OF STEEL** SEES, INSTEAD OF SATAN, A TERRIFIED BEGGAR FROM A NEARBY VILLAGE...

SPARE ME, SPARE ME...!

TOO BAD! ME THOUGHT HIM WAS DEVIL!

8

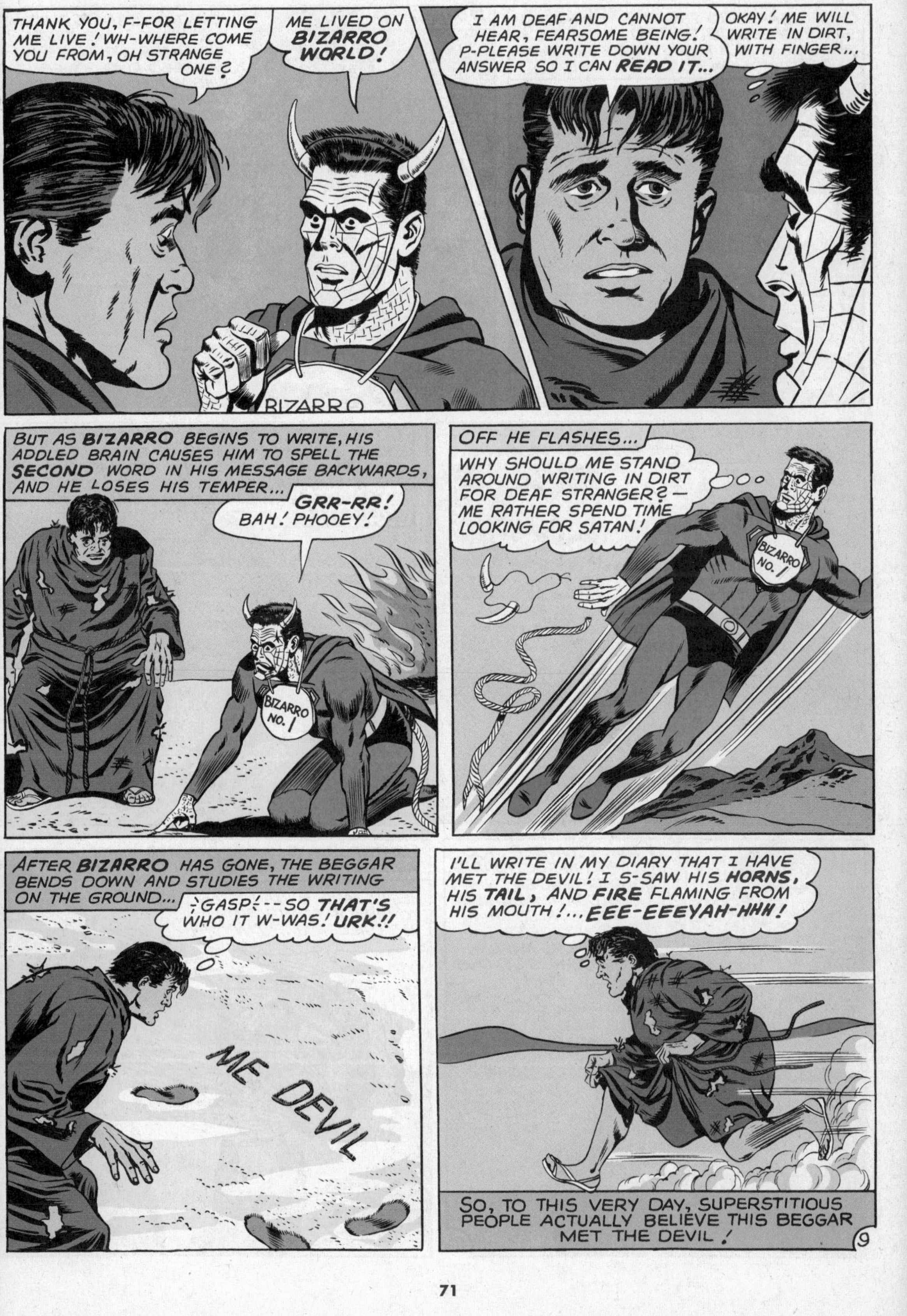
THANK YOU, F-FOR LETTING ME LIVE! WH-WHERE COME YOU FROM, OH STRANGE ONE?
ME LIVED ON BIZARRO WORLD!
BIZARRO
I AM DEAF AND CANNOT HEAR, FEARSOME BEING! P-PLEASE WRITE DOWN YOUR ANSWER SO I CAN READ IT...
OKAY! ME WILL WRITE IN DIRT, WITH FINGER...
BUT AS BIZARRO BEGINS TO WRITE, HIS ADDLED BRAIN CAUSES HIM TO SPELL THE SECOND WORD IN HIS MESSAGE BACKWARDS, AND HE LOSES HIS TEMPER...
GRR-RR! BAH! PHOOEY!
BIZARRO NO. 1
OFF HE FLASHES...
WHY SHOULD ME STAND AROUND WRITING IN DIRT FOR DEAF STRANGER? — ME RATHER SPEND TIME LOOKING FOR SATAN!
BIZARRO NO. 1
AFTER BIZARRO HAS GONE, THE BEGGAR BENDS DOWN AND STUDIES THE WRITING ON THE GROUND...
¡GASP!--SO THAT'S WHO IT W-WAS! URK!!
ME DEVIL
I'LL WRITE IN MY DIARY THAT I HAVE MET THE DEVIL! I S-SAW HIS HORNS, HIS TAIL, AND FIRE FLAMING FROM HIS MOUTH!... EEE-EEEYAH-HHH!
SO, TO THIS VERY DAY, SUPERSTITIOUS PEOPLE ACTUALLY BELIEVE THIS BEGGAR MET THE DEVIL!
9

ONCE AGAIN INTO THE TIME-BARRIER SUPER-SPEEDS *BIZARRO*, THEN BACK THROUGH IT TO A PREHISTORIC ERA THAT EXISTED MILLIONS OF YEARS AGO...

MAYBE HERE, ME FIND SOMEONE WORTH FEATURING ON *BIZARRO WORLD* TV!

PRESENTLY...

GIANT DINOSAURS FIGHTING SO WHAT? WHO CARES? AUDIENCES WOULD YAWN!-- ME NEED FIND SOMEONE WHO WOULD MAKE THEM LAUGH--NOT SOME SCARY MONSTER LIKE ROBIN HOOD OR DANIEL BOONE!

SUDDENLY, A GIANT, HAIRY PAW CLUTCHES THE SUPER-TALENT SCOUT FROM THE *BIZARRO WORLD*...

HOORAY! GOOD LUCK, AT LAST!

LITTLE DOES *BIZARRO* KNOW IT, BUT HE IS BEING ATTACKED BY NONE OTHER THAN *TITANO*, THE SUPER-APE *SUPERMAN* HAD CAST THROUGH THE TIME-BARRIER INTO THE PAST...AND *TITANO* HAS MISTAKEN *BIZARRO* FOR *SUPERMAN!*

ROARRR

HOORAY! I FIND MY STAR!

HIM *LOVABLE*, TOO! CUTE, AFFECTIONATE, AND TENDER! HIM COULD PLAY *ROMANTIC* ROLES, ALSO! HIM WOULD BE SENSATIONAL AS MARILYN MONROE'S LEADING MAN!

GRATEFULLY, *BIZARRO* TEARS HIMSELF FREE AND REWARDS *TITANO*...

HERE, TAKE BANANAS AS TOKEN OF ADMIRATION! ME CALL YOU..."*TINY*"!

???

10

INTO THE TIME-BARRIER, THEN OUT OF IT AND BACK TOWARD HIS OWN WORLD FLIES *BIZARRO*...

ME AM COMING, *BIZARRO WORLD!* AND HAVE ME GOT WONDERFUL NEWS!...WOW!!

PRESENTLY, AT A *BIZARRO* TELEVISION STATION...

BIZARRO BOYS AND GIRLS, ME HAVE MADE SKETCH OF STAR OF NEW *TV* SERIES! HE AM *TINY*, REAL-LIFE HERO ME MET IN EARTH'S PAST!

TINY

INSTANTLY, *BIZARRO* YOUTHS FLY INTO THE STATION LIKE A HORDE OF BEES... I...I...I...

BIZARRO NO.1, YOU AM LIAR!

THERE NO SUCH ANIMAL AS "TINY"!

"TINY" AM *STEAL* OF EARTH MOVIE HERO *KING KONG! SEE!!!* THEM LOOK *ALIKE!*

WBIZ TV

KING KONG

SWIFTLY, WORD FLASHES AROUND THE *BIZARRO* WORLD...

BIZARRO NO.1 HOAXED EVERYBODY!

HE TRICKED US!

HE PULL OUR INVULNERABLE LEGS!

OUT OF THE TV STATION SLINKS *BIZARRO NO.1*...

EVERYONE STARING AT M-ME! THEM THINK ME HAVE B-BETRAYED THEM!--;CHOKE;

STATION

WBIZ TV

11

SHORTLY, IN THE *BIZARRO NO. 1* HOME...

:SOB:- ME AM *DISGRACED!*

:SOB:- IF YOU DISGRACED, ME DISGRACED, TOO!

:SOB: -US, TOO!.

COME OUT, BIZARRO NO. 1!! RIGHT NOW!!!

:SOB!:

AS *BIZARRO NO. 1* OBEYS THE SHOUT, HE DISCOVERS..

Y-YOU PEOPLE **DON'T** H-HATE ME ??

NO! *US LOVE YOU* FOR HOAXING US. AS MAYOR, ME GIVE YOU MEDAL FOR PULLING SNEAKY, CHEATING TRICK ON US. HOW CLEVER YOU BE TO FOOL US THAT *TINY* WAS YOUR IDEA, WHEN YOU REALLY STEAL IT FROM *KING KONG!*

THEM LOVE ME, *BIZARRO-LOIS NO. 1,* DARLING! THEM STUPID IDIOTS *LOVE* ME!

YOU ADORABLE CHEAT, YOU!

12

AND SO, AS OUR TALE ENDS, *BIZARRO NO. 1* IS LAVISHLY HONORED FOR A FEAT HE HADN'T EVEN PERFORMED! DOES THIS SEEM KOOKIE TO YOU?— WELL, WHAT *ELSE* DID YOU EXPECT ON THE MAD *BIZARRO WORLD?* HMM-MMMMMMM ???

THE END

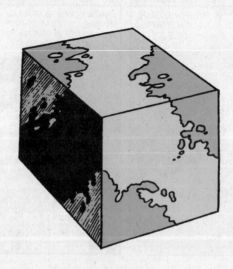

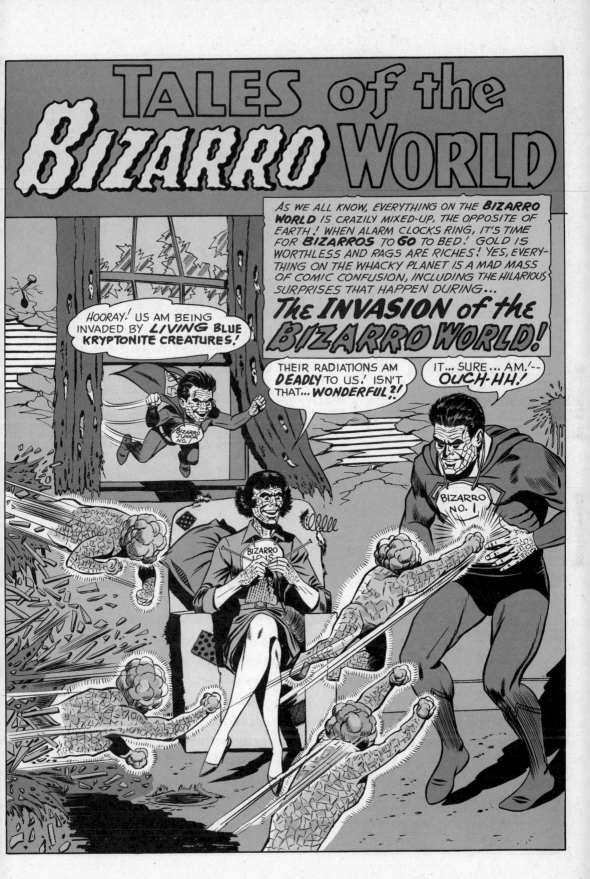

TALES of the BIZARRO WORLD

As we all know, everything on the **BIZARRO WORLD** is crazily mixed-up, the opposite of EARTH! When alarm clocks ring, it's time for **BIZARROS** to **GO** to bed! Gold is worthless and rags are riches! Yes, everything on the whacky planet is a mad mass of comic confusion, including the hilarious surprises that happen during...

The INVASION of the BIZARRO WORLD!

HOORAY! US AM BEING INVADED BY *LIVING* BLUE KRYPTONITE CREATURES!

THEIR RADIATIONS AM **DEADLY** TO US! ISN'T THAT... **WONDERFUL?!**

IT... SURE... AM.'-- OUCH-HH!

BIZARRO JUNIOR NO. 1

BIZARRO LOIS

BIZARRO NO. 1

FAR OUT IN SPACE THERE EXISTS THE GOOFIEST PLANET IN THE ENTIRE UNIVERSE... THE SQUARE **BIZARRO WORLD!** IT IS THE HOME PLANET OF THE PATHETIC, STUPID **BIZARRO** CREATURES WHO ARE IMPERFECT DUPLICATES OF **SUPERMAN** AND HIS FRIENDS...

EVERYTHING THERE IS A MAD, REVERSED VERSION OF EARTHLY CUSTOMS...FOR INSTANCE, **BIZARROS** SLEEP WITH THEIR **FEET**, INSTEAD OF THEIR **HEADS**, ON PILLOWS...!

ON THE **BIZARRO WORLD**, **PEDESTRIANS** HONK HORNS WHEN THEY WANT **AUTOMOBILES** TO GET OUT OF THE WAY...

THEM CRAZY WOMEN PEDESTRIANS DON'T KNOW HOW TO **WALK!**

HONNK HONNKK!

AT **BIZARRO** RACE TRACKS, THE MECHANICAL RABBITS DO THE **CHASING**...

HA, HA! THEM DUMB BUNNIES NEVER CATCH UP, BECAUSE **ME, BIZARRO-KRYPTO**, GOT **SUPER-SPEED!**... HYUK! HYUK!

AND THE **BIZARRO** DICTIONARY... WELL, IT'S AS CRAZILY SCRAMBLED AS THE WITS OF THE **BIZARROS**...

BIZARRO DIKSHUNERY

ZERO --HI-EST MARKE ENY STEWDENT KAN GET!

YESTURDAY --THE DAE AFTUR TUMORROW...MAYBEE.

WOULD -- TREES AR MADE UV WOULD.

WOLFF -- A NICE PET.

WALNUT -- IDIOT WHUT STARES ATT WALLS.

VEGETABLE --SUM KINDA TABLE.

TREE -- WUN, TWOO, TREE

TAX -- NAILS.

SUPPER -- SUPERMAN HAS SUPPER-POWURS

STRAWBURRIES --PUNK BURRIES WICH TASTE LIKE STRAW.

SIDEWALK --PECULYUR WAY UV WALKIN.

SHOEMAKER -- GUY WHO MAKES HATS.

SELFISH -- SELL FISH, UV COARSE.

SCHOOLROOM --TORTURE CHAMBUR.

SAWDUST -- WHAT GUY WHO FELL IN DURT SAW.

NOON --MIDNITE.

KINGDUMB --SMART COUNTREE.

DANDELION -- NICE KING UV BEASTS.

CHESTNUT -- GUY ALWAYZ SHOWIN' OFF HIS CHEST.

BELONG --BE NOT SHORT.

(2)

NOW LET US LOOK IN ON THE **NUMBER ONE BIZARRO FAMILY** AT AN ESPECIALLY SUPER-CRUCIAL MOMENT...!

¡GASP! ¡--CHOKE! ¡URK!!!

WHAT AM WRONG, DARLING?

BIZARRO NO. 1

BIZARRO LOIS NO. 1

BIZARRO JUNIOR

MY SUPER-HEARING DETECT **RUMBLING NOISES** UNDERGROUND! --THIS C-CAN MEAN ONLY ONE THING!... **BIZARRO WORLD** AM GOING BLOW UP LIKE PLANET **KRYPTON** DID!

OH, HOW AWFUL!

DIMLY, **BIZARRO NO. 1** RECALLS HOW **SUPERMAN'S** FATHER, JOR-EL, HAD VAINLY ATTEMPTED TO ESCAPE **KRYPTON'S** DOOM...

I'LL BUILD SPACE SHIPS, LARA, AND SAFELY FLY ALL OF US TO ANOTHER WORLD BEFORE **KRYPTON** EXPLODES!

ME DO THAT, TOO!!!

BUT WHEN THE LEADER OF THE **BIZARRO** PLANET TRIES TO WARN THE OTHER **BIZARROS**...

OUR WORLD GOING BLOW UP! US **MUST** ESCAPE!

SO WHAT?!

¡YAWN!

BIZARRO NO. 1

LATER...

NOBODY INTERESTED! ME BUILD SPACE SHIP, SAVE OWN FAMILY, LIKE JOR-EL DID!

STUPIDLY, **BIZARRO** FAILS TO REALIZE HE DOESN'T **NEED** A SPACE SHIP, BUT COULD FLY HIS FAMILY TO ANOTHER WORLD UNDER HIS OWN POWER!

SHORTLY...

WHAT WRONG **NOW**?

ONE THING! ME DON'T KNOW **HOW** TO BUILD SPACE SHIP!

YOU BETTER DO SOMETHING SOON, DADDY, BEFORE OUR WHOLE WORLD BLOW UP! RUMBLING NOISES UNDER GROUND GETTING **LOUDER**!

BIZARRO LOIS

BIZARRO NO. 1

BIZARRO JUNIOR NO. 1

③

77

MEANWHILE, IN A COUNTRYSIDE FIELD, THE REAL REASON FOR THE UNDERGROUND NOISES BECOMES APPARENT...

MONSTERS MADE OF LIVING *BLUE KRYPTONITE* ARE BURROWING TO SURFACE FROM INSIDE PLANET!

LOOK! CREATURES' RADIATIONS AM WEAKENING AND *KILLING BIZARROS* JUST LIKE *GREEN KRYPTONITE* CAN HARM *SUPERMAN!*

IRRESISTIBLY, THE FANTASTIC INVADERS MARCH ACROSS THE SQUARE WORLD, RUTHLESSLY SMASHING EVERYTHING IN THEIR PATH, THE *BLUE KRYPTONITE* RADIATIONS STOPPING ALL *BIZARROS* WHO GET IN THEIR WAY...

DO THE *BIZARROS* INSTANTLY FORM BATTLE SQUADRONS TO GALLANTLY FIGHT THIS HORRIFIC MENACE?...ER...NO...

US AM BEING INVADED! HOW *LOVELY!*

HA, HA! TOMORROW AM *CHRISTMAS* ON *BIZARRO WORLD!* US CELEBRATE INVASION AND HOLIDAY AT SAME TIME, ON *JULY 4!*

THAT NIGHT, ON *CHRISTMAS EVE, BIZARRO No.1* DISGUISES HIMSELF...

ME STUFFED PILLOWS IN SANTA COSTUME, AND PUT ON FAKE BEARD! HOW ME LOOK, NOW?

HA, HA! YOU MAKE DELIGHTFUL *BIZARRO-CLAUS!*

MOMENTS LATER, *BIZARRO-CLAUS* SPEEDS THROUGH THE NIGHT SKY IN A SLED DRAWN BY HIS PET, *BIZARRO-KRYPTO*...

♪ JINGLE-BELLS, JINGLE-BELLS, JUNK GETS IN MY WAY...♪

④

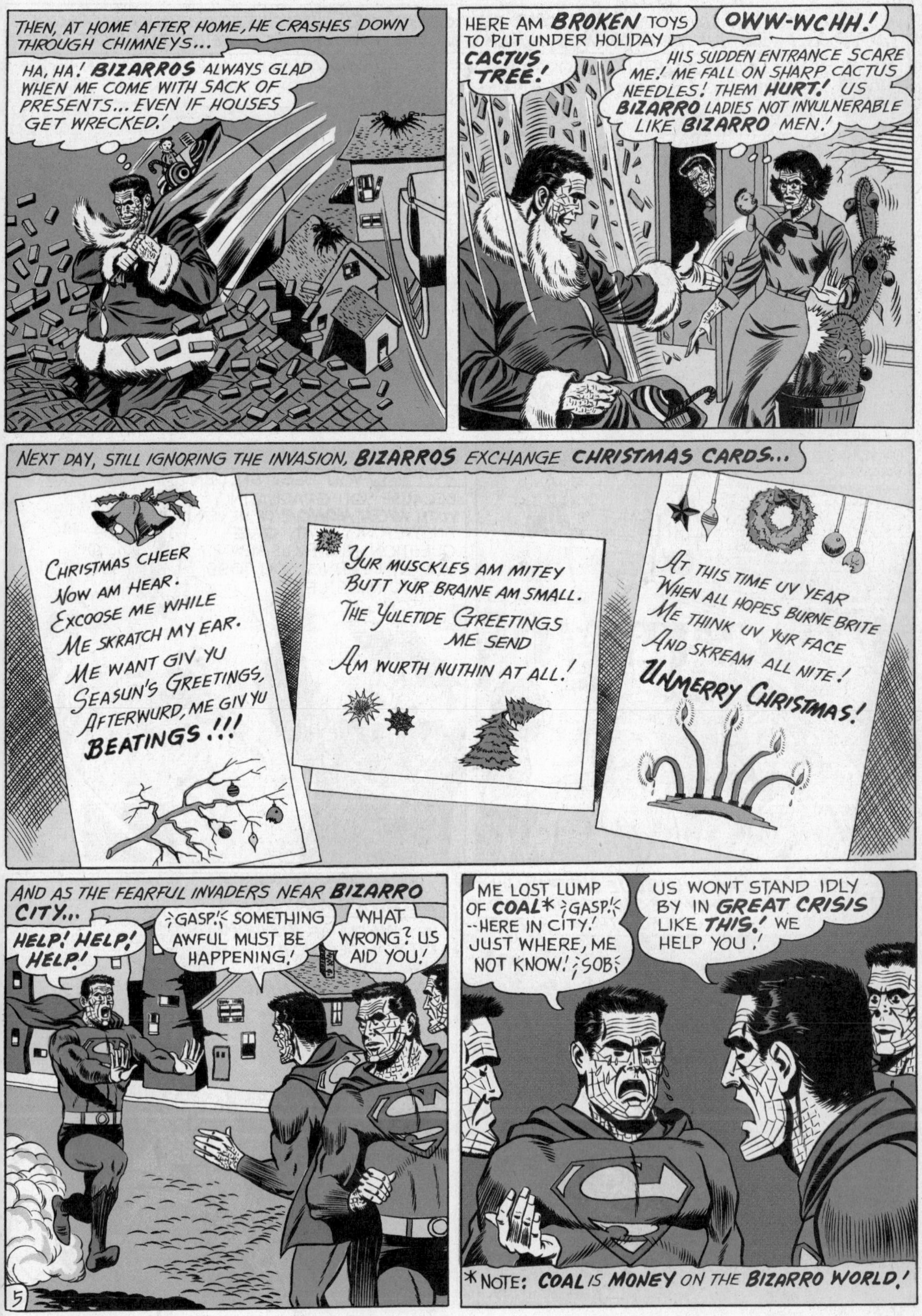

THEN, AT HOME AFTER HOME, HE CRASHES DOWN THROUGH CHIMNEYS...
HA, HA! BIZARROS ALWAYS GLAD WHEN ME COME WITH SACK OF PRESENTS... EVEN IF HOUSES GET WRECKED!
HERE AM BROKEN TOYS TO PUT UNDER HOLIDAY CACTUS TREE!
OWW-WCHH!
HIS SUDDEN ENTRANCE SCARE ME! ME FALL ON SHARP CACTUS NEEDLES! THEM HURT! US BIZARRO LADIES NOT INVULNERABLE LIKE BIZARRO MEN!
NEXT DAY, STILL IGNORING THE INVASION, BIZARROS EXCHANGE CHRISTMAS CARDS...
CHRISTMAS CHEER NOW AM HEAR. EXCOOSE ME WHILE ME SKRATCH MY EAR. ME WANT GIV YU SEASUN'S GREETINGS, AFTERWURD, ME GIV YU BEATINGS!!!
YUR MUSCKLES AM MITEY BUTT YUR BRAINE AM SMALL. THE YULETIDE GREETINGS ME SEND AM WURTH NUTHIN AT ALL!
AT THIS TIME UV YEAR WHEN ALL HOPES BURNE BRITE ME THINK UV YUR FACE AND SKREAM ALL NITE!
UNMERRY CHRISTMAS!
AND AS THE FEARFUL INVADERS NEAR BIZARRO CITY...
HELP! HELP! HELP!
GASP! SOMETHING AWFUL MUST BE HAPPENING!
WHAT WRONG? US AID YOU!
5
ME LOST LUMP OF COAL* GASP! --HERE IN CITY! JUST WHERE, ME NOT KNOW! SOB
US WON'T STAND IDLY BY IN GREAT CRISIS LIKE THIS! WE HELP YOU!
*NOTE: COAL IS MONEY ON THE BIZARRO WORLD!

INTO THE CITY GRIMLY STALK THE **BLUE KRYPTONITE CREATURES**, INTENDING TO DESTROY THE CRAZILY SHAPED BUILDINGS...BUT THE **BIZARROS**, WILDLY SEARCHING FOR THE LOST PIECE OF COAL, BEAT THEM TO IT...

NOT UNDER **THIS** BUILDING!

OR THIS ONE, EITHER!

HOORAY! ME FOUND IT! US CAN STOP WRECKING CITY NOW!

ON TOWARD THE **BIZARRO COLLEGE** CHARGE THE INVADERS, PREPARING TO SMASH IT TO SMITHEREENS...

BUT... SECONDS BEFORE THE INVADERS CAN TEAR IT DOWN... YOU BEST STUDENT BECAUSE YOU GRADUATING WITH **HIGH HONOR** OF NEVER ANSWERING EVEN **ONE** QUESTION RIGHT! US REWARD YOU BY LETTING YOU TOSS ATOMIC MISSILE AT SCHOOL!

OH, GOODY!

BIZARRO COLLEGE

THUS, BEFORE THE MONSTROUS **BLUE KRYPTONITE CREATURES** CAN DESTROY THE COLLEGE, THE SCHOOL'S TOP STUDENT DOES THE JOB FOR THEM...

BWAAMMMM

TOO LATE, A SUDDEN THOUGHT DAWNS ON THE **BIZARRO MAYOR...**

HEY, **WAIT!** IF **BIZARRO CITY** AM DESTROYED BY INVADERS, ME WILL BE MAYOR OF... **NOTHING!** STOP THEM!

OKAY, ONLY SHUT UP!

TROUBLE-MAKER!

TO THE ATTACK SPEEDS A FLYING SQUADRON OF **BIZARRO** VOLUNTEERS...

SPECTATORS CHEER US BECAUSE THEY SURE WE GOING TO STOP INVASION.' SORRY, BUT ORDERS AM ORDERS.'

HOORAY! HOORAY!

HOWEVER, DEADLY **BLUE KRYPTONITE** RADIATIONS WIPE OUT THE FIRST WAVE...

LOOK! INVADERS DESTROY OUR DEFENDERS.'

LET'S SHOW US AM GOOD SPORTS!

AND SO THE **BIZARROS** CHEER ON THEIR FOES...

RACKETY-ZACKETY LET'S GIVE A CHEER! NICE-NICE INVADERS US **GLAD** YOU AM HERE! YAA-AAA, MONSTERS !!!

HOORAY, HOORAY US NOW! THEM AM DESTROYING US YIPPETY-ZIPPETY-DIPPITY WOW.!! YAAA-AAA, MONSTERS .!!

HOWEVER, THE **BIZARRO MAYOR** PERSISTS...

¡SOB.!¡--IF ME LOSE SOFT JOB AS MAYOR, ME WILL HAVE TO **WORK** FOR LIVING! **GET RID OF INVADERS.'** ¡SOB.!¡

ALL RIGHT, ALL RIGHT, ALL RIGHT! JUST STOP COMPLAINING!

BIZARRO NO. 1

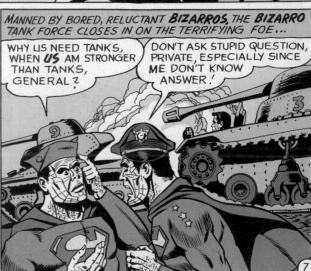

MANNED BY BORED, RELUCTANT **BIZARROS**, THE **BIZARRO** TANK FORCE CLOSES IN ON THE TERRIFYING FOE...

WHY US NEED TANKS, WHEN **US** AM STRONGER THAN TANKS, GENERAL?

DON'T ASK STUPID QUESTION, PRIVATE, ESPECIALLY SINCE ME DON'T KNOW ANSWER.'

7

THE **BIZARROS** IN THE TANKS PERISH, JUST AS THE FIRST WAVE HAD...

AARGH!

HA, HA! **BLUE KRYPTONITE** RADIATIONS AM DESTROYING OUR SOLDIERS, AGAIN!

LET'S **CELEBRATE!**

WHAT A WORLD.!!... SOON, WHILE UNDER ATTACK, **BIZARRO CITY** IS THE SCENE OF A FRANTIC JAMBOREE...

MUSIC AM GOING BE PLAYED BY "**BIZARRO COOL CAT COMBO**" LED BY **BIZARRO-HIPSTER NO. 1**"!

THAT AM **ME**, FOLKS! HA, HA, HAA-AAAA!

BIZARRO NO. 1

"**WEEP-AND-WAIL BIZARRO LOIS**" AM GOING BE SING! SAY SOMETHING TO FANS, "**WEEP-AND-WAIL**"!

DON'T LET THOSE DARLING INVADERS THINK US DON'T APPRECIATE INVASION! **EVERYBODY DANCE!**

AND SO, AS THE "**BIZARRO COOL CAT COMBO**" FRACTURES A HASTILY IMPROVISED **BIZARRO** ROCK-AND-ROLL TUNE...

B COOL CAT COMBO

..."**WEEP-AND-WAIL BIZARRO-LOIS**" MANGLES A MELODY, AS ONLY **SHE** CAN --!

OH, THEM BLUE, BLUE-EE-OO MONSTERS WRIGGLED TO THE ATTACK! THEIR CRAZY, COOL, COOL RADIATION **KNOCKED US FLAT!** BUT US LOVES IT... YEAH, YEAH, YEAH US **LOVES** IT... YEAH, YEAH, YEAH!

♪ THEM AM AWFUL TO SEE ♫ BUT JIMMINY GOLLY-GEE THEM AM REAL GOOD-LOOKIN' NEXT TO -}UGH{- YOU'N ME!

8

MOMENTARILY, THE GHASTLY INVADERS HALT, AND THE **BIZARROS** DANCE EVEN **MORE** WILDLY...

SO WELCOME, *BLUE MONSTERS*, WE AM **GLAD** YOU CAME! DESTROY, DESTROY, US LOVES YOU JUST THE SAME! OOBAHDEYOOBAY-- URF...URF...OOLEEAHKOOLEEAH-- URP, URP!

♪ UP WENT THE MONSTER! ♪ **DOWN** WENT *BIZARRO!* WHO GIVES A HANG OR A RING-DING-DANG? YEOOWWWW!!

♪ JUST GO-GO --GO!! ♪ BLUE, BLUE--TRUE BLUE ♪ MAH-UN-STERS! SQUEEDLEEYAH...VOOM!!

AS THE FRENZIED JAMBOREE ENDS, *BIZARRO NO.1* AND HIS BUDDIES DISCOVER, TO THEIR HORROR...

AWP! --THEM INVADERS BUILT ROCKET-RAY WHICH AM...÷ GASP!÷-- CH-CHANGING OUR **SQUARE** WORLD INTO A...÷ SHUDDER÷... ROUND WORLD! THEM AM **FIENDISH FIENDS!**

FINALLY ANGERED, THE **BIZARROS** RETALIATE...

BIZARRO-LOISES CAN'T BE HARMED BY *BLUE KRYPTONITE* RADIATIONS, SINCE THEM AM IMPERFECT DUPLICATES OF EARTH GIRL LOIS LANE! WE THROW GIRLS UP IN AIR!

9

AS THEIR PARACHUTES OPEN AND GENTLY LOWER THEM TOWARD THE FOE, THE *BIZARRO-LOISES* FIRE RAY-GUN BOLTS AT THE INVADERS, BUT...

ENEMY UNHARMED BY RAY-GUNS.!

BIZARRO No. 1 WILL THINK OF SOMETHING ELSE.!

SWIFTLY, THE *BIZARRO* LEADER GETS ANOTHER INSPIRATION...

ME LOVE IDEA! *GREEN KRYPTONITE* CAN'T GO THROUGH LEAD AND HARM *SUPERMAN!* SO US WILL BUILD LEAD ARMOR, AT SUPER-SPEED! IT'LL PROTECT *ALL BIZARROS* FROM *BLUE KRYPTONITE* RADIATIONS.!

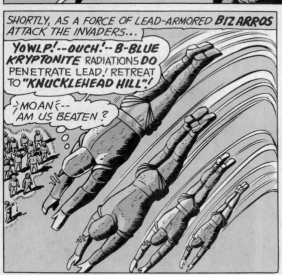

SHORTLY, AS A FORCE OF LEAD-ARMORED *BIZARROS* ATTACK THE INVADERS...

YOWLP.!--OUCH.!--B-BLUE KRYPTONITE RADIATIONS *DO* PENETRATE LEAD! RETREAT TO *"KNUCKLEHEAD HILL"!*

MOAN!-- AM US BEATEN?

MINUTES AFTERWARD...

LOOK, *BIZARRO NO. 1* OUR SONS AM STREAKING TO ATTACK ENEMY IN LEAD ARMOR US MADE TO PROTECT EVERYBODY! THEM WILL BE D-DESTROYED...!

NO! GO BACK, *BIZARRO BRATS.!*...GO BACK! LEAD ARMOR WON'T PROTECT YOU.!!

BUT, TO THE ASTONISHMENT OF THE ADULT *BIZARRO* SOLDIERS...

GREAT FRANKENSTEIN! OUR KIDS AM NOT HARMED BY RADIATIONS! *BIZARRO* BRATS AM WHIPPING FOES! INVADERS AM FLEEING UNDERGROUND AGAIN.!!

SOON...

WHAT YOU KNOW! *BOY BIZARROS* WON WAR.!

HOW'D YOU KIDS DO IT, *BIZARRO JUNIOR No. 1*?

ME TOO DUMB TO REMEMBER! *YOU* EXPLAIN, *BIZARRO-OLSEN.!*

10

THE **BIZARRO** REPORTER, WHO IS AN IMPERFECT DUPLICATE OF JIMMY OLSEN OF EARTH, OBLIGES...

WHEN ME SAW OUR ARMY GET BEATEN, ME MADE SUGGESTION TO **BIZARRO** KIDS...

" IN RESPONSE, KIDS FLEW ME TO YOUR **FOURTRISS UV BIZARRO**. THERE, I ORDERED THEM TO COME OUT OF THEIR LEAD ARMOR, THEN ME SHONE **DUPLICATOR-RAY** ON THEIR ARMOR..."

RAY AM MAKING **IMPERFECT** LEAD-ARMOR! SINCE **BLUE KRYPTONITE** AM IMPERFECT **GREEN KRYPTONITE**, BLUE KRYPTONITE RAYS WON'T PENETRATE **IMPERFECT LEAD**!

AS **BIZARRO-OLSEN'S** BOSS, EDITOR **BIZARRO-WHITE**, APPEARS...

YOUR PLAN WORKED!

GREAT JOB, JIMMY! ME REWARD YOU BY **LOWERING** YOUR SALARY!

THANKS, CHIEF! ¡CHOKE! ME DON'T DESERVE SUCH **GENEROSITY**!

⑪

AFTER THE **BIZARROS** SUPER-SWIFTLY REPAIR ALL DAMAGE TO THEIR CITY AND MAKE THE **BIZARRO WORLD** SQUARE ONCE MORE...

PHOOIE! THINGS AM **DULL** NOW!

CHEER UP! IF US **LUCKY**, SOME OTHER AWFUL CREATURES WILL INVADE US SOON!

⑭ END

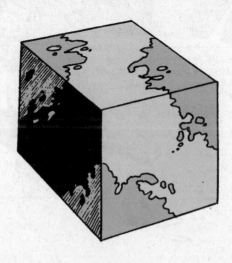

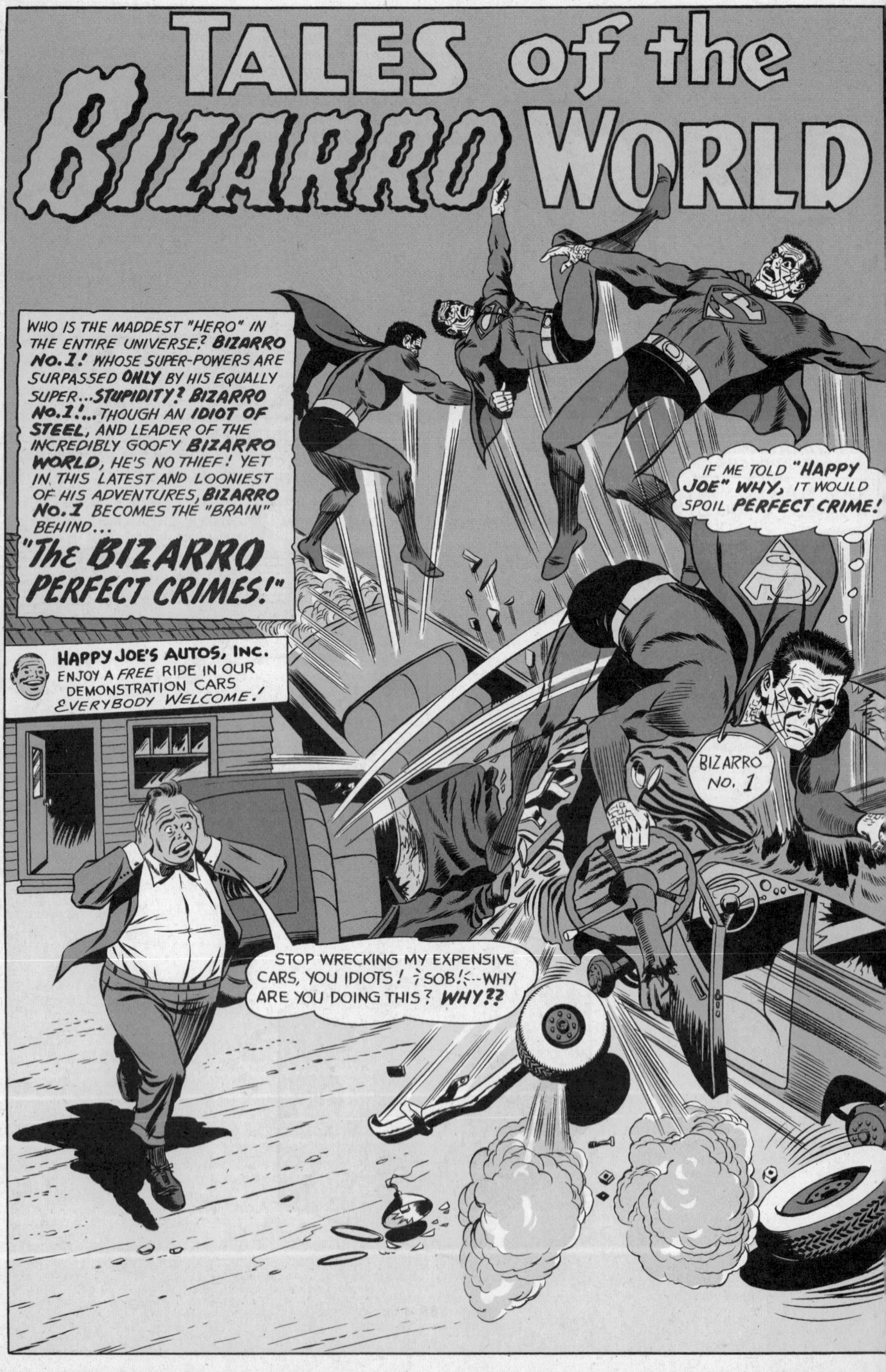
TALES of the BIZARRO WORLD
WHO IS THE MADDEST "HERO" IN THE ENTIRE UNIVERSE? BIZARRO NO. 1! WHOSE SUPER-POWERS ARE SURPASSED ONLY BY HIS EQUALLY SUPER...STUPIDITY? BIZARRO NO. 1!...THOUGH AN IDIOT OF STEEL, AND LEADER OF THE INCREDIBLY GOOFY BIZARRO WORLD, HE'S NO THIEF! YET IN THIS LATEST AND LOONIEST OF HIS ADVENTURES, BIZARRO NO. 1 BECOMES THE "BRAIN" BEHIND...
"The BIZARRO PERFECT CRIMES!"
IF ME TOLD "HAPPY JOE" WHY, IT WOULD SPOIL PERFECT CRIME!
HAPPY JOE'S AUTOS, INC.
ENJOY A FREE RIDE IN OUR DEMONSTRATION CARS
EVERYBODY WELCOME!
BIZARRO NO. 1
STOP WRECKING MY EXPENSIVE CARS, YOU IDIOTS! ¡SOB!¡--WHY ARE YOU DOING THIS? WHY??

WAY, WAY, **WAY** OUT IN THE UNIVERSE EXISTS THE CRAZIEST PLANET IN THE ENTIRE COSMOS... IT IS THE SQUARE **BIZARRO WORLD!**

EVERYTHING... BUT **EVERYTHING** ON THIS WHACKY WORLD IS ZANILY MIXED-UP! FOR INSTANCE...

YIPE!

ARF!

ARF!

THAT'S RIGHT! ON THIS PLANET, POSTMEN BARK AT DOGS, INSTEAD OF VICE VERSA!

SHEER LUNACY REIGNS EVERYWHERE, EVEN IN KITCHENS OF **BIZARRO** HOMES...

GO TAKE LONG WALK! ME MAKING **INSTANT COFFEE!**

GROAN --THAT TAKE **ONE HOUR** TO MAKE!

BIZARRO LOIS NO. 1

INSTUNT COUGHEE

BIZARRO NO. 1

ON THIS CUBE-SHAPED WORLD, **PARENTS** GET REPORT CARDS, AND THEIR **KIDS** SIGN THE CARDS...

BECAUSE YOUR REPORT-CARD GRADES AM SO MISERABLY **ROTTEN,** ME FORBID YOU TO SPANK ME FOR ENTIRE MONTH!

CHOKE --US SORRY!

IN **BIZARRO** COURTROOMS, LAWYERS ARGUE **AGAINST** THEIR OWN CLIENTS...

ME GOT SNEAKING HUNCH MY CLIENT AM GUILTY AS SIN! GIVE HIM LONG SENTENCE, YOUR DISHONOR!

MY LAWYER AM DOING PEACHY-DANDY JOB OF **FRAMING** ME! HA, HA!

AND IN THE **BIZARRO** MADCAP VERSION OF EARTH'S WALL STREET...

HOORAY! MY **BIZARRO GAS AND FUEL COMPANY** STOCK WENT **DOWN** SIX POINTS! MY WIFE WILL BE **SO** HAPPY!! GOODY-GOODY!!

2

COAL IS USED FOR MONEY ON THE **BIZARRO WORLD!** HERE, WE SEE THREE **BIZARRO** MAIDENS TOSSING THREE LUMPS OF COAL IN A FOUNTAIN AND MAKING WISHES...

ME **DON'T** WISH TO EVER BE RICH!

ME **DON'T** WISH ME WAS FAMOUS!

ME **DON'T** WISH TO MEET MY DREAM-MAN!

AND NOW, LET US LOOK IN ON **BIZARRO NO. 1** AND **BIZARRO-LOIS NO. 1** AS THEY WATCH A **BIZARRO** HISTORY PAGEANT...

THE BRITISH **AREN'T** COMING!

PROGRAM SAY HIM AM PAUL REVERE!

NEXT, ANOTHER HISTORICAL EVENT, **BIZARRO**-STYLE, IS PORTRAYED--**LINCOLN** HAVING HIS BEARD SHAVED OFF...!

IMPOSSIBLE! **BIZARRO** MEN'S HAIR AM INVULNERABLE, AND **CAN'T** BE CUT!... OH, ME SEE! ACTOR AM JUST WEARING **MAKE-UP!**

THEN BABE RUTH IS INCORRECTLY DEPICTED AS BEING THE BASEBALL PLAYER WHO SCORED THE MOST **BUNTS,** INSTEAD OF THE MOST HOME-RUN **HITS...**

NOW HIM GOING **STEAL ALL THE BASES** AND **SELL** THEM AT **PAWN-SHOP!**

AFTERWARD, ANOTHER EVENT OF HISTORY IS MANGLED...

OUTLAW WYATT EARP, ME GET YOU AS SURE AS MY NAME AM **SHERIFF JESSE JAMES!!**

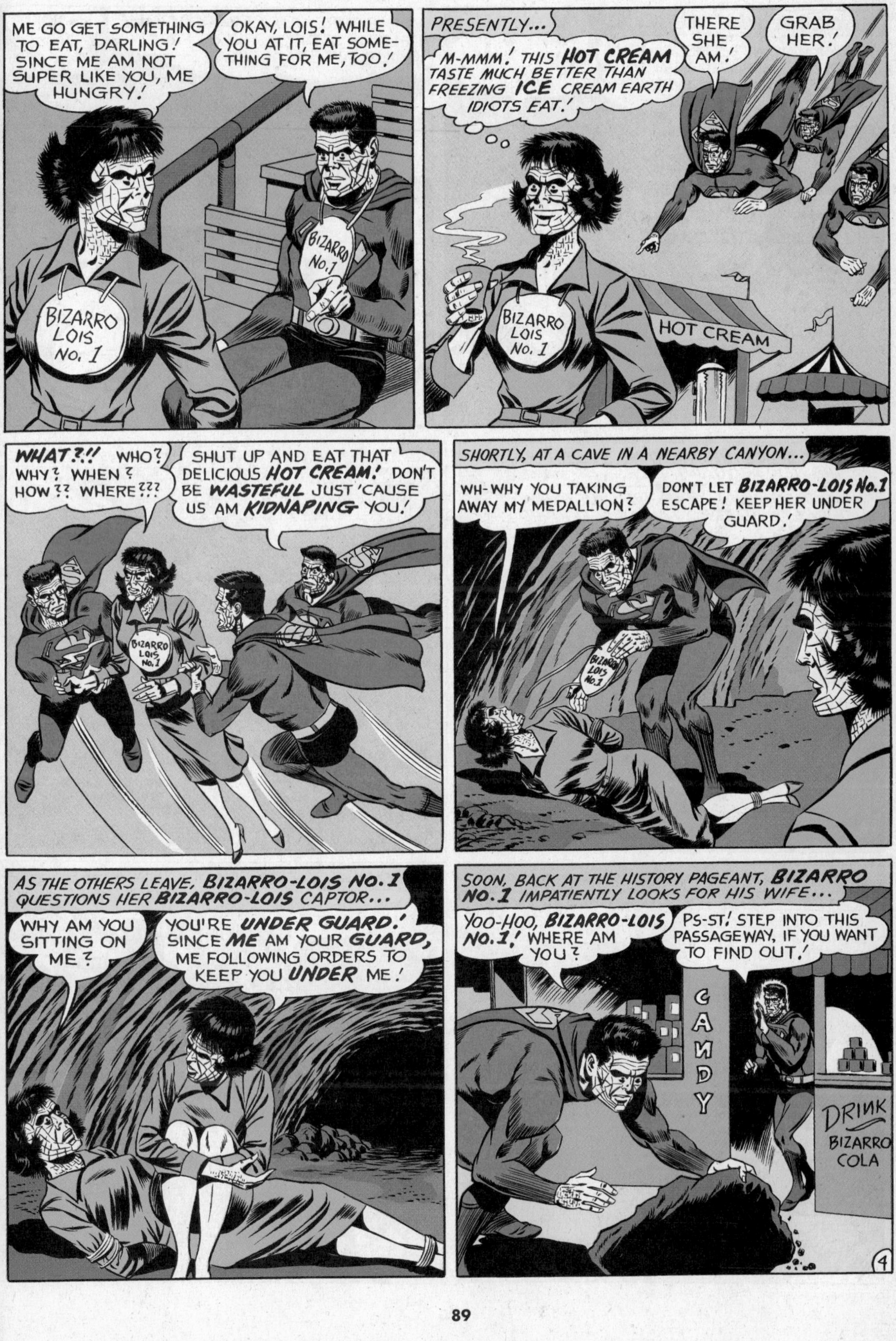

ME GO GET SOMETHING TO EAT, DARLING! SINCE ME AM NOT SUPER LIKE YOU, ME HUNGRY!
OKAY, LOIS! WHILE YOU AT IT, EAT SOMETHING FOR ME, TOO!
BIZARRO No. 1
BIZARRO LOIS No. 1
PRESENTLY...
M-MMM! THIS HOT CREAM TASTE MUCH BETTER THAN FREEZING ICE CREAM EARTH IDIOTS EAT!
THERE SHE AM!
GRAB HER!
BIZARRO LOIS No. 1
HOT CREAM
WHAT?!! WHO? WHY? WHEN? HOW?? WHERE???
SHUT UP AND EAT THAT DELICIOUS HOT CREAM! DON'T BE WASTEFUL JUST 'CAUSE US AM KIDNAPING YOU!
BIZARRO LOIS No. 1
SHORTLY, AT A CAVE IN A NEARBY CANYON...
WH-WHY YOU TAKING AWAY MY MEDALLION?
DON'T LET BIZARRO-LOIS No. 1 ESCAPE! KEEP HER UNDER GUARD!
AS THE OTHERS LEAVE, BIZARRO-LOIS NO. 1 QUESTIONS HER BIZARRO-LOIS CAPTOR...
WHY AM YOU SITTING ON ME?
YOU'RE UNDER GUARD! SINCE ME AM YOUR GUARD, ME FOLLOWING ORDERS TO KEEP YOU UNDER ME!
SOON, BACK AT THE HISTORY PAGEANT, BIZARRO NO. 1 IMPATIENTLY LOOKS FOR HIS WIFE...
YOO-HOO, BIZARRO-LOIS NO. 1! WHERE AM YOU?
PS-ST! STEP INTO THIS PASSAGEWAY, IF YOU WANT TO FIND OUT!
CANDY
DRINK BIZARRO COLA
4

AS *BIZARRO No.1* OBEYS...

THIS AM YOUR WIFE'S MEDALLION! IS PROOF US KIDNAPED HER! DO LIKE US SAY, OR YOU NEVER SEE *BIZARRO-LOIS No.1* AGAIN!

BIZARRO LOIS No. 1

≥CHOKE≥-- WHAT YOU W-WANT ME SHOULD DO?

YOU FIGURE OUT *PERFECT CRIME*, HELP US GET RICH, AND US FREE YOUR WIFE! IS CLEAR?

≥CHOKE≥ YES...

OFF INTO SPACE *BIZARRO No.1* FLIES, TRAILED BY HIS NEW ACQUAINTANCES...

ME GOT DO WHAT THEY SAY, OR *BIZARRO-LOIS No. 1* DOOMED!

HIM MUST HAVE ALREADY FIGURED OUT *PERFECT CRIME!* WHAT MARVELOUSLY TWISTED BRAIN!

THROUGH THE UNIVERSE FLASH THE BIZARRE FOUR, UNTIL...

AH-HA! HIM LEADING US TO PLANET EARTH!

AS THEY SPEED DOWN TOWARD A GARBAGE DUMP, NEAR *METROPOLIS*...

SOME TRUCKS BELOW AM HEADING TOWARD DUMP! FOLLOW ME, AND BE QUIET.'

DON'T TRY TRICK US, OR YOU BE SORRY!

BIZARRO No. 1

PRESENTLY...

WHY US HIDING HERE?

YOU SOON SEE! ...SHH-HHH!

BIZARRO No. 1

A FEW MINUTES LATER... THIS IS A GOOD SPOT TO DUMP THE RUBBISH! LET 'ER GO, BOYS!

AND AS THE JUNK RAINS DOWN ON THE CROUCHING *BIZARROS*...

¡GASP!--WORN-OUT SHOES! BROKEN BOTTLES!

CIGAR BUTTS! RUSTY NAILS! BENT OLD TIN CANS! WHAT A FORTUNE!

QUIET! IF THEM HEAR US, CRIME WON'T BE *PERFECT!*

AFTER THE TRUCKS LEAVE, AND THE RUBBISH IS GATHERED...

ME DID MY PART, LEADING YOU TO THIS VALUABLE LOOT! NOW TELL ME WHERE YOU HIDE MY KIDNAPED WIFE!

NOT UNTIL YOU PULL *ONE MORE PERFECT CRIME!*

YOU RATS! YOU PROMISED...!

DO LIKE US SAY OR YOU NEVER HEAR NAGGING VOICE OF YOUR WIFE AGAIN!

AND YOU NEVER AGAIN TASTE HER AWFUL COOKING!

¡CHOKE!-- YOU WIN! BUT THIS'LL BE LAST PERFECT CRIME! FOLLOW ME!

HA, HA! *BIZARRO NO.1* DON'T DARE DEFY US!

US GOT HIM WHERE US WANT HIM! HA! HA!

MINUTES LATER...

HAPPY JOE'S AUTOS, INC. ENJOY A *FREE* RIDE IN OUR DEMONSTRATION CARS *EVERYBODY WELCOME!*

ME GOT IDEA FOR ANOTHER *PERFECT CRIME!* LISTEN CLOSELY...!

IF US LISTEN WHILE STANDING ANY *CLOSER* TOGETHER, US GET SQUASHED FLAT!

6

MOMENTS AFTER *BIZARRO NO. 1* ISSUES INSTRUCTIONS, *"HAPPY JOE"* UNHAPPILY SEES...

URK! WH-WHAT ARE YOU MONSTERS DOING IN MY CARS? GET OUT! *HELP!!*

US TAKING FREE RIDE, LIKE SIGN SAY!

AS *BIZARRO NO. 1* HAD PLANNED, TWO CARS SPEED AHEAD OF THE OTHER TWO CARS, REVERSE DIRECTION, THEN...

YOU'LL CRASH!

THAT AM THE IDEA, *"HAPPY JOE"*!

NEXT INSTANT...

GAA! MY EXPENSIVE DEMONSTRATION CARS ARE SMASHING, BUT THOSE CRAZY MONSTERS DON'T APPEAR HURT AT ALL!

KA-POWW

BWWUMMMPP

AFTERWARD...

BECAUSE AUTO TIRES AM *NOW* RIPPED, THEM AM *VALUABLE* TREASURES!

WHAT A PERFECTLY *PERFECT* CRIME!

OOLP!

LET MY WIFE GO NOW!

UH--NOT *YET!* YOU GOT PULL STILL *ONE MORE* PERFECT STEAL!

BIZARRO NO. 1

7

GR-RR! YOU BREAK PROMISE! ME OUGHT TO...!

GET TOUGH, AND YOU NEVER SEE WIFE AGAIN!

THINK OF ANOTHER **PERFECT CRIME,** FAST!

SOON, **BIZARRO NO. 1** LEADS THE OTHERS TO AN EMPTY LUMBER-CAMP, UP NORTH, WHERE...

GRAB SAWS, AND HELP ME CUT DOWN FOREST!

WHO WANTS **TREES?** THEM AIN'T **VALUABLE!**

DON'T ARGUE! OBEY MASTERMIND!

IN THE TWINKLING OF AN EYE, THE IMPERFECT IMITATIONS OF **SUPERMAN** LEVEL THE ENTIRE FOREST WITH THEIR SAWS...

HM-MM! WHAT HAS **BIZARRO NO. 1** GOT IN MIND?

NEXT, **BIZARRO NO. 1** GATHERS TOGETHER...

TREES WORTHLESS, BUT **SAWDUST** WORTH FORTUNE, RIGHT?

RIGHT! ⌇DROOL⌇--WHAT MARVELOUS **LOOT!**

AS THE LUMBER-CAMP FOREMAN RETURNS FROM TOWN WITH HIS CREW...

IMPOSSIBLE! ALL THE TREES ARE CUT DOWN! BUT ACCORDING TO OUR CONTRACT'S TERMS, WE'LL STILL GET PAID! ... WOW! I'LL PHONE THE NEWSPAPERS!

8

SHORTLY... STOP GLOATING OVER LOOT, ALREADY, AND TELL ME WHERE YOU'VE HIDDEN MY KIDNAPED WIFE ON *BIZARRO WORLD!*

US TELL YOU *AFTER* YOU GET VALUABLE LOOT FOR US *ONE MORE TIME!*

WAIT HERE! ME FLY TO OTHER SIDE MOUNTAIN! ME WANT BE ALONE, AND THINK THIS THROUGH TO ILLOGICAL CONCLUSION!

TAKE ALL TIME YOU WANT, BUT BE BACK IN *ONE MINUTE!*

PRESENTLY, ALONE AND MISERABLE, *BIZARRO NO. 1* PONDERS... ⸗SOB⸗ --THEM VILLAINOUS *BIZARROS* WILL *NEVER* LET *BIZARRO-LOIS NO. 1* GO! IF ONLY ME COULD THINK OF WAY OUT OF THIS *TRAP...!*

BEFORE THE MINUTE IS UP... HERE COMES *BIZARRO NO. 1* AROUND MOUNTAIN! HIM MADE UP MIND!

UNLESS HIM MADE RIGHT DECISION, HIM BE MIGHTY SORRY!

ME GOT SENSATIONAL IDEA! FOLLOW ME INTO OUTER SPACE, THEN DO LIKE ME DO!

FIRST US BUILD SPACE-GLOBE TO CARRY OUR LOOT IN!

THROUGH SPACE TO ANOTHER SOLAR SYSTEM THE FOUR FORMS SUPER-SPEED, INTO A YOUNG FLAMING PLANET'S ATMOSPHERE... *BIZARRO NO. 1* BLOWING SUPER-BREATH AT FIERY PLANET! US DO SAME!

⑨

94

MIGHTILY, THE SUPER-FOUR EXTINGUISH THE FLAMES...

≥GASP!≤--THIS YOUNG PLANET AM IN COAL-ERA STAGE OF ITS FORMATION!

NOW THAT US BLEW OUT FLAMES, PLANET AM GIGANTIC HUNK OF COAL!

YOW! NOTHING MORE VALUABLE THAN COAL! HOW SMART OF BIZARRO NO. 1 TO FIGURE HOW US COULD CHANGE FLAMING PLANET INTO ...≥DROOL≤... THIS!!

SECONDS LATER, ON THE PLANET'S SURFACE...

HA, HA, HA! COAL! COAL!

YOU NOW RICHEST BIZARROS IN UNIVERSE! NOW TELL ME--WHERE YOU HIDE MY WIFE?

SHE IS IN CAVE IN BIRCH CANYON ON BIZARRO WORLD! NOW GO AWAY! DON'T BOTHER US!

SECONDS LATER, BEHIND A CERTAIN MOUNTAIN ON EARTH...

HUH? HOW CAN YOU BE ME, WHEN ME AM ME?!

THE ANSWER OBVIOUSLY IS...

...THAT I'M NOT YOU! THERE! I'VE REMOVED MY PLASTIC MASK!

≥GASP!≤--YOU AM... SUPERMAN! B-BUT HOW--WHY...??

BIZARRO No. 1

"HEARING A RADIO NEWS FLASH ABOUT THAT LEVELLED FOREST, I FLEW THERE TO INVESTIGATE, IN TIME TO OVERHEAR THOSE VILLAINOUS BIZARROS THREATEN YOU..."

SO THAT'S WHAT'S BEHIND THE MYSTERY! --I'LL HELP BIZARRO NO. 1!

BIZARRO No. 1

10

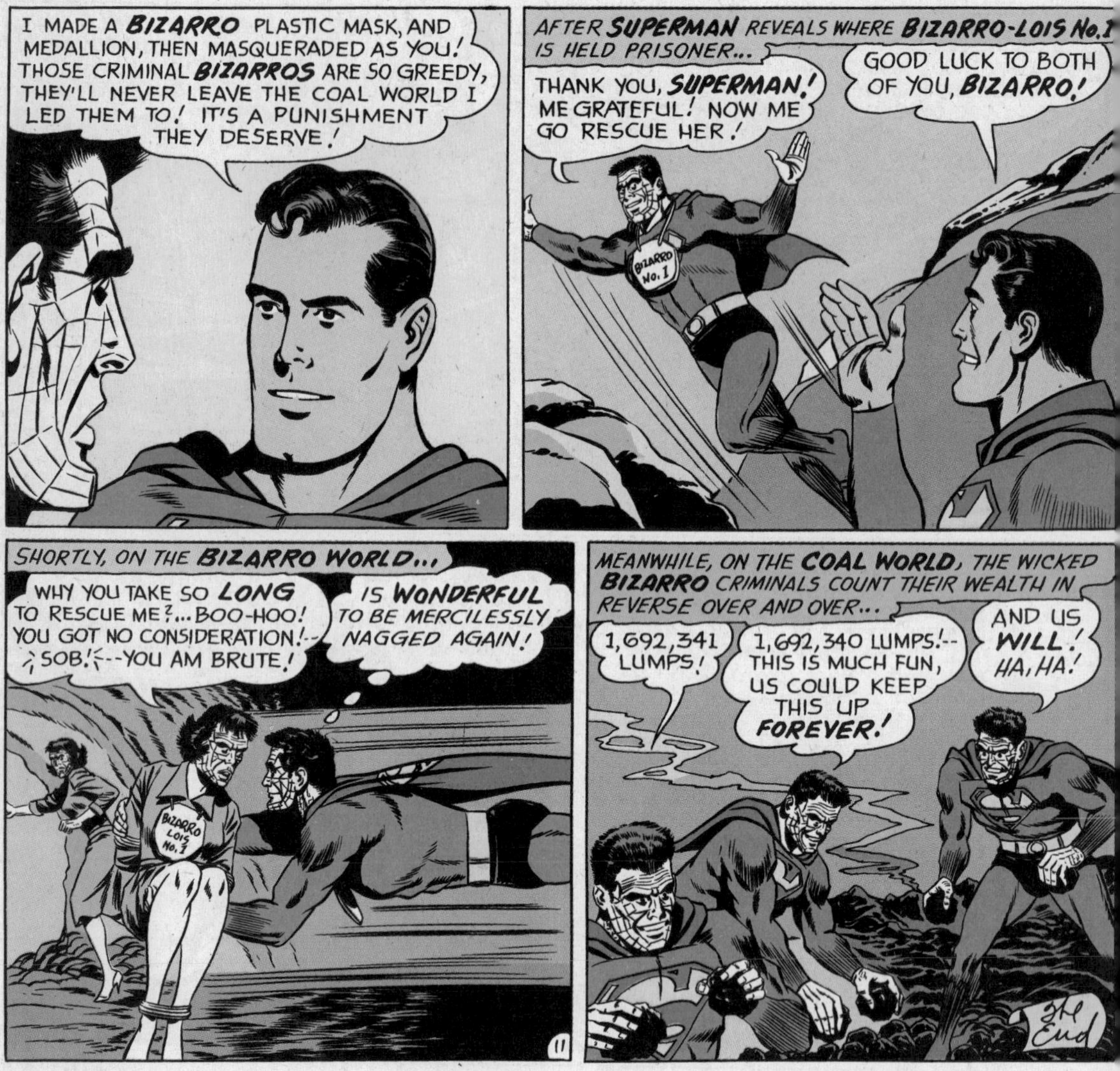
I MADE A BIZARRO PLASTIC MASK, AND MEDALLION, THEN MASQUERADED AS YOU! THOSE CRIMINAL BIZARROS ARE SO GREEDY, THEY'LL NEVER LEAVE THE COAL WORLD I LED THEM TO! IT'S A PUNISHMENT THEY DESERVE!
AFTER SUPERMAN REVEALS WHERE BIZARRO-LOIS No.1 IS HELD PRISONER...
THANK YOU, SUPERMAN! ME GRATEFUL! NOW ME GO RESCUE HER!
GOOD LUCK TO BOTH OF YOU, BIZARRO!
BIZARRO No. 1
SHORTLY, ON THE BIZARRO WORLD...
WHY YOU TAKE SO LONG TO RESCUE ME?...BOO-HOO! YOU GOT NO CONSIDERATION!--SOB!--YOU AM BRUTE!
IS WONDERFUL TO BE MERCILESSLY NAGGED AGAIN!
BIZARRO LOIS No. 1
11
MEANWHILE, ON THE COAL WORLD, THE WICKED BIZARRO CRIMINALS COUNT THEIR WEALTH IN REVERSE OVER AND OVER...
1,692,341 LUMPS!
1,692,340 LUMPS!-- THIS IS MUCH FUN, US COULD KEEP THIS UP FOREVER!
AND US WILL! HA, HA!
The End

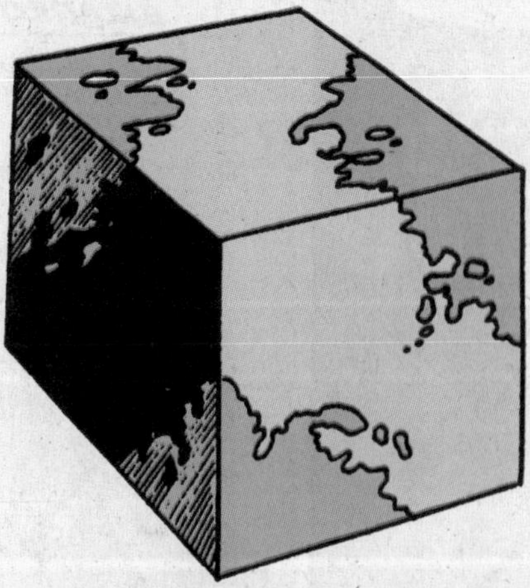

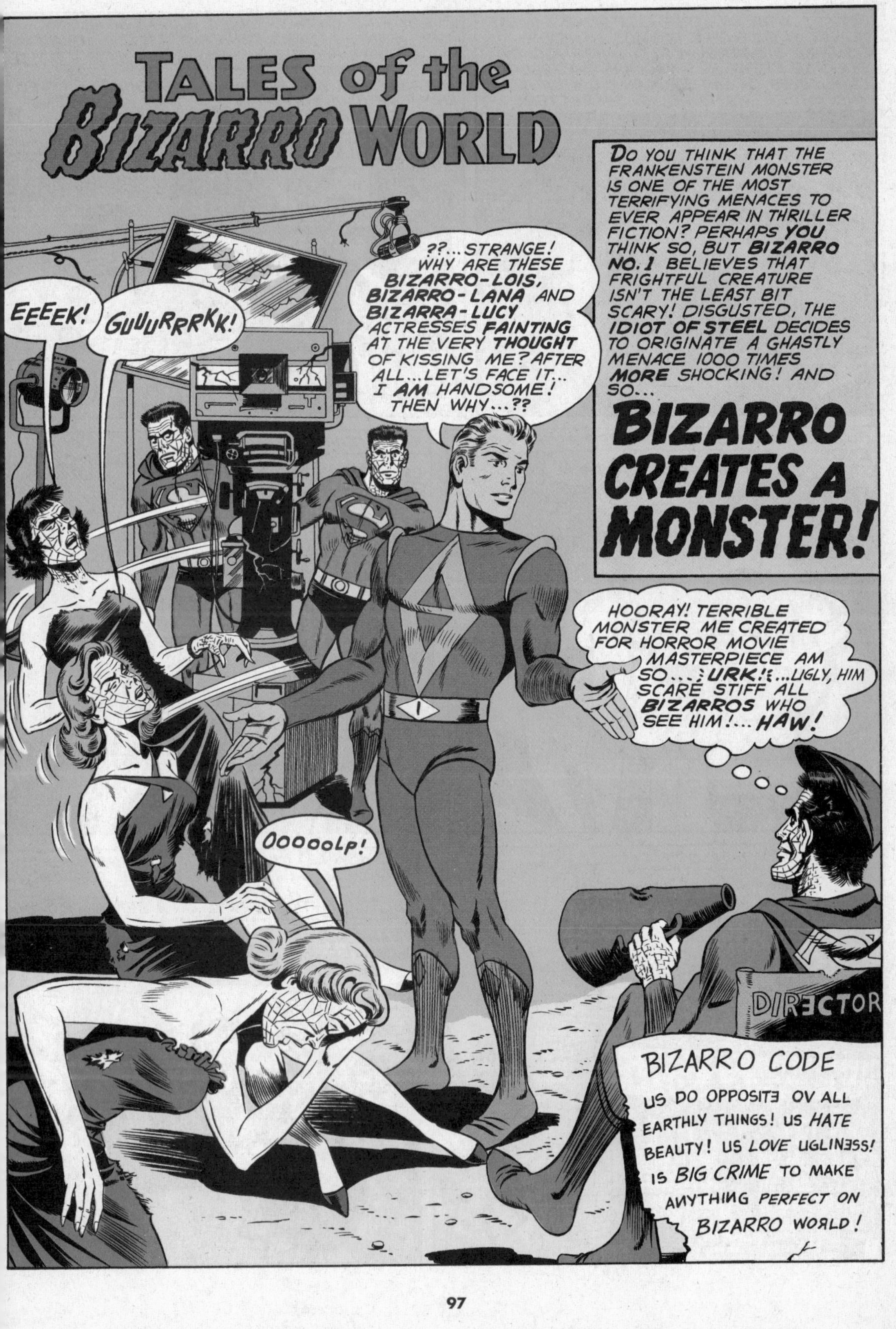
TALES of the BIZARRO WORLD
DO YOU THINK THAT THE FRANKENSTEIN MONSTER IS ONE OF THE MOST TERRIFYING MENACES TO EVER APPEAR IN THRILLER FICTION? PERHAPS YOU THINK SO, BUT BIZARRO NO. 1 BELIEVES THAT FRIGHTFUL CREATURE ISN'T THE LEAST BIT SCARY! DISGUSTED, THE IDIOT OF STEEL DECIDES TO ORIGINATE A GHASTLY MENACE 1000 TIMES MORE SHOCKING! AND SO...
BIZARRO CREATES A MONSTER!
EEEEK!
GUUURRRKK!
??...STRANGE! WHY ARE THESE BIZARRO-LOIS, BIZARRO-LANA AND BIZARRA-LUCY ACTRESSES FAINTING AT THE VERY THOUGHT OF KISSING ME? AFTER ALL...LET'S FACE IT... I AM HANDSOME! THEN WHY...??
HOORAY! TERRIBLE MONSTER ME CREATED FOR HORROR MOVIE MASTERPIECE AM SO...URK!...UGLY, HIM SCARE STIFF ALL BIZARROS WHO SEE HIM!...HAW!
OOOOOLP!
DIRƎCTOR
BIZARRO CODE
US DO OPPOSITƎ OV ALL EARTHLY THINGS! US HATE BEAUTY! US LOVE UGLINƎSS! IS BIG CRIME TO MAKE ANYTHING PERFECT ON BIZARRO WORLD!

FAR OUT IN THE UNIVERSE EXISTS THE ZANIEST PLANET IN THE ENTIRE COSMOS... IT IS THE **SQUARE BIZARRO WORLD**, INHABITED BY STRANGE CREATURES WHO ARE IMPERFECT DUPLICATES OF **SUPERMAN**, LOIS LANE, AND OTHER METROPOLIS CHARACTERS...

EVERYTHING ON THIS PLANET IS UTTERLY WHACKY, AND ITS DIM-WITTED DENIZENS THINK IN **REVERSE** FROM EARTH PEOPLE. FOR INSTANCE...

BECAUSE THIS AM "**MOTHERS'** DAY," ME GIVE **YOU** GIFT, DADDY!

I GET NOTHING! OH, WELL! THAT AM WAY THE EGG ROLLS!

FILTER CIGARETTES ARE SMOKED AT THE **WRONG** ENDS...!

IT'S WHAT'S UP **BACK** THAT COUNTS!

IN A BIZARRO BALL-PARK...

EVERYBODY GO HOME! GAME CALLED ON ACCOUNT OF **GOOD** WEATHER!

BAH! WHY WE NOT HAVE CLOUD-BURST?!!

SKY AM DISAPPOINTINGLY **CLEAR**!

AT A BIZARRO SALOON...

THE DRINKS AM **ON THE HOUSE**!

LIVEWOOD GULCH SAJOEN

AND NOW LET US LOOK IN ON THE **NO.1 BIZARRO FAMILY** AS THEIR **ULTRA-POWERFUL** TELEVISION SET PICKS UP A **FRANKENSTEIN** MOVIE TELECAST FROM EARTH ON A **SHOCK TV SHOW**...

FRANKENSTEIN MONSTER AM NICE!

BIZARRO No.1

2

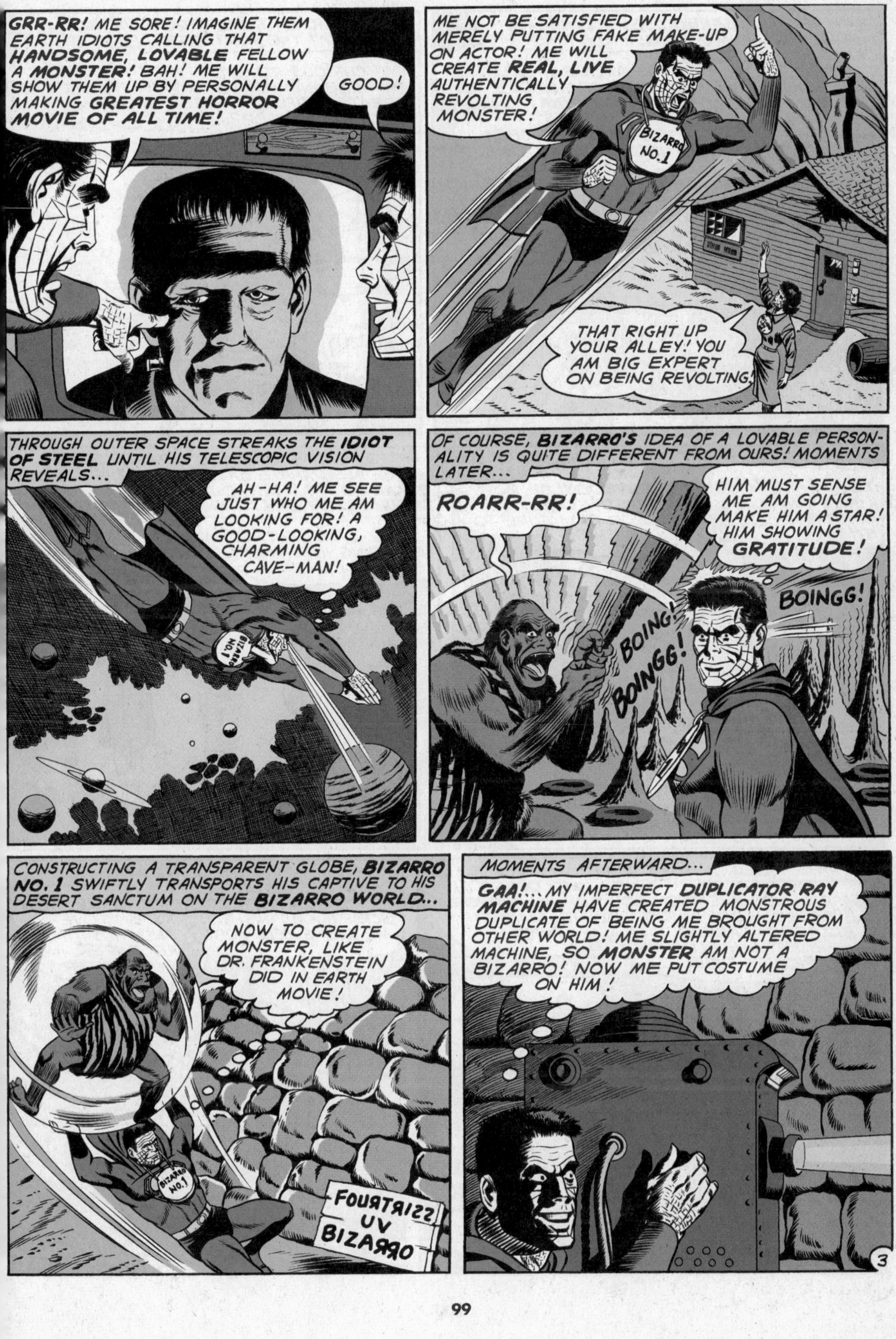
GRR-RR! ME SORE! IMAGINE THEM EARTH IDIOTS CALLING THAT HANDSOME, LOVABLE FELLOW A MONSTER! BAH! ME WILL SHOW THEM UP BY PERSONALLY MAKING GREATEST HORROR MOVIE OF ALL TIME!
GOOD!
ME NOT BE SATISFIED WITH MERELY PUTTING FAKE MAKE-UP ON ACTOR! ME WILL CREATE REAL, LIVE AUTHENTICALLY REVOLTING MONSTER!
BIZARRO NO. 1
THAT RIGHT UP YOUR ALLEY! YOU AM BIG EXPERT ON BEING REVOLTING!
THROUGH OUTER SPACE STREAKS THE IDIOT OF STEEL UNTIL HIS TELESCOPIC VISION REVEALS...
AH-HA! ME SEE JUST WHO ME AM LOOKING FOR! A GOOD-LOOKING, CHARMING CAVE-MAN!
OF COURSE, BIZARRO'S IDEA OF A LOVABLE PERSONALITY IS QUITE DIFFERENT FROM OURS! MOMENTS LATER...
ROARR-RR!
HIM MUST SENSE ME AM GOING MAKE HIM A STAR! HIM SHOWING GRATITUDE!
BOINGG!
BOING!
BOINGG!
CONSTRUCTING A TRANSPARENT GLOBE, BIZARRO NO. 1 SWIFTLY TRANSPORTS HIS CAPTIVE TO HIS DESERT SANCTUM ON THE BIZARRO WORLD...
NOW TO CREATE MONSTER, LIKE DR. FRANKENSTEIN DID IN EARTH MOVIE!
BIZARRO NO. 1
FOURTRISS UV BIZARRO
MOMENTS AFTERWARD...
GAA!... MY IMPERFECT DUPLICATOR RAY MACHINE HAVE CREATED MONSTROUS DUPLICATE OF BEING ME BROUGHT FROM OTHER WORLD! ME SLIGHTLY ALTERED MACHINE, SO MONSTER AM NOT A BIZARRO! NOW ME PUT COSTUME ON HIM!
3

THEN, AFTER *BIZARRO* USES A LANGUAGE-INSTRUCTION HELMET TO QUICKLY TEACH HIS CREATION...

WHO... AM I, SIR?

YOU AM... *SAPOLLO!* ME ...¡URK!¡... CREATE YOU, FROM *HIM!*

SAPOLLO NOT SPEAK GOOD ENGLISH, LIKE US *BIZARROS!*

AT THAT MOMENT, *BIZARRO-LOIS NO.1* ARRIVES AT THE FORTRESS...

ME CURIOUS TO KNOW WHAT PROGRESS MY HUSBAND AM MAKING ON PROJECT TO CREATE AWFUL MONSTER! WILL HIM SUCCEED, OR FLOP?

FOURTRISS UV BIZARRO

SHORTLY...

YEEEAA-AAGHHHH! H-HE'S AWFUL... TERRIBLE... GHASTLY!!

GOOD! IF HE SCARE *YOU,* HE SHOULD FRIGHTEN *EVERYBODY!* OH, BOY! WITH STAR LIKE THIS, HORROR FILM SURE TO BE HIT!

TO *BIZARRO* EYES, HANDSOME *SAPOLLO* APPEARS ULTRA-UGLY!

AFTER PLACING *SAPOLLO* AND THE SPACE-BEING IN SEPARATE CAGES IN ANOTHER ROOM, *BIZARRO NO.1* RE-ADJUSTS HIS IMPERFECT *DUPLICATOR RAY,* THEN...

LUCY LANE AND *LANA LANG* AM BEING INTERVIEWED ON EARTH TV SHOW!

INSTANTS LATER...

¡GASP!¡... YOU CREATED A *BIZARRO-LUCY* AND A *BIZARRO-LANA* BY SHINING RAY ON TELEVISION SET'S PICTURE TUBE!

RIGHT!... ¡CHUCKLE!¡... NOW THEY CAN BE IN CAST OF MY HORROR MOVIE MASTER-PIECE!

SWIFTLY, AN INSPIRED *BIZARRO NO.1* TYPES THE MOVIE SCRIPT...

SCRIPT AM FINISHED! ME DID SWELL JOB!

FINE! NOW TYPE IT OVER, AND THIS TIME PUT *PAPER* IN TYPEWRITER!

NEXT DAY, IN THE **BIZARRO** FILM STUDIO...

BEHOLD, CAST! OUR STAR! DON'T HIM LOOK **CREEPY**?

YAA-AAA!

HIM... URK! HORRIBLE!

BIZARRO NO. 1

AND WHEN THE SCRIPT CALLS FOR ONE OF THE BIZARRO ACTRESSES TO KISS THE HANDSOME STAR...

BIZARRO-LANA, SCRIPT CALL FOR YOU TO KISS MONSTER TO SHOW AUDIENCE YOU HATE HIM!

ME WOULDN'T KISS HIM IF HE WERE **FIRST** MAN ON THE WORLD!

LATER, AFTER VARIOUS **BIZARRO** ACTRESSES ARE GIVEN THE PART...

EEEE-EEEYAAAH-HH!

US IN BIG, BAD TROUBLE, BOSS, EVERY ACTRESS US TRIED FAINTS AT VERY **THOUGHT** OF THAT UGLY MONSTER KISSING HER!

ME GOT TERRIFICALLY FABULOUS IDEA!

BIZARRO NO. 1

OFF FLASHES **BIZARRO NO. 1** TO THE INSANE ASYLUM OF THE ZANY **BIZARRO** WORLD...

ME GOT BIG TREAT FOR YOU, **BIZARRO-LOIS**! ME TAKE YOU TO MAN OF YOUR DREAMS! YOU BE HIS LEADING LADY!

BIZARRO INSANE ASYLUM

WHEN HE RETURNS, MOMENTS LATER, WITH THE **BIZARRO-LOIS**, AND FILMING RESUMES...

GREAT FRANKENSTEIN! THAT ACTRESS YOU BROUGHT **LOVES** KISSING HIM! HOW YOU MANAGE **MIRACLE**?

EASY!

ME GOT HER FROM **BIZARRO INSANE ASYLUM**! SHE AM IMPERFECT BIZARRO WHO GOT TWISTED MIND AND DON'T THINK LIKE US! TO HER POOR THING... MONSTER LOOKS GOOD!

HOW CLEVER YOU AM!

5

AFTER THE MOVIE IS COMPLETED, THE **IDIOT OF STEEL** RETURNS **SAPOLLO** TO HIS FORTRESS...

IT AM SAFER FOR YOU HERE!

TOMORROW, **BIZARRO WORLD** WILL ENJOY PREVIEW OF GREATEST HORROR MOVIE EVER MADE!

NEXT DAY, AS **BIZARROS** FLOCK TO THE MOVIE OPENING...

SAPOLLO the AWRFUL

AW, MOVIE CAN'T **REALLY** BE AS SCARY AS PUBLICITY SAYS!

HA, HA! SOON THEM GET BIG SHOCK!

BIZARRO NO. 1

PRESENTLY, INSIDE THE THEATER, THE **BIZARRO** AUDIENCE VIEWS A FILM **NEGATIVE**... WHAT IS ORDINARILY BLACK APPEARS WHITE, AND VICE VERSA...

ME COULD SCREAM... FROM BOREDOM!

YAWN! WHEN WE GOING SEE MONSTER?

THIS AM GYP!

ME WORRIED, DARLING! EVERYBODY'S COMPLAINING PICTURE AM NOT HORRIBLE!

RELAX, SOUR-BUN! IF ME MADE IT, YOU CAN BE **SURE** IT'S HORRIBLE!

BIZARRO NO. 1

SUDDENLY, AS **SAPOLLO'S** IMAGE APPEARS ON THE SCREEN, PANIC ERUPTS AMONGST THE CUSTOMERS...

YIPE! TH-THAT M-MONSTER! TH-THAT AWFUL, GHASTLY, H-HORRIBLE **MONSTER**!! HIM EVEN **MORE AWFUL** THAN THEM PROMISED!

YIIIIICCH-HHH!

BIZARRO NO. 1

6

TERRIFIED, THE AUDIENCE FLEES...

NO, NO!...GO BACK!!

:GROAN!:...THEM AM WRECKING THEATER!

MONSTER YOU CREATED AM TOO GOOD! NOBODY DARES LOOK AT IT!

MEANWHILE, BACK AT THE FORTRESS...

I JUST NOTICED! THE CAGE HAS NO LOCK!...I'LL ESCAPE AND ASK BIZARRO NO. 1 TO TAKE ME TO ANOTHER WORLD, WHERE MY FASCINATING PROFILE, BULGING BICEPS, AND WINNING PERSONALITY WILL BE APPRECIATED!

SHORTLY, OUTSIDE THE FORTRESS...

ME...LOST! IF ONLY THERE WAS SOMEONE AROUND TO DIRECT ME!

COULD I POSSIBLY BE OF SERVICE, MADAME?

BIZARRO CITY-- THIZ WAY

ON SECOND THOUGHT GO THIS WAY

NO! THAT WAY!

HAAAAAALP!

:CHOKE!:...

SIGHTING ME, SHE FLED!...I MUST FIND BIZARRO NO. 1 AND BE TAKEN TO ANOTHER PLANET, WHERE I'LL BE LOVED AND ADMIRED FOR MY INNER AS WELL AS MY OUTER QUALITIES!

LATER, AS SAPOLLO REACHES BIZARRO CITY...

I SAY, THERE, FRIENDS...WOULD YOU PLEASE DIRECT ME TO YOUR LEADER, BIZARRO NO. 1?

ERK!!...IT'S SAPOLLO THE AWRFUL, THE SCARIEST MOVIE MONSTER THERE EVER WAS!

EVERYBODY VAMOOSE! SKIDOOOOOO!!!

WHEREVER SAPOLLO TURNS...

THE MONSTER AM LOOSE!!!

WHAT MONSTER?...NOW REALLY, CHAPS, CUT OUT THIS JOSHING! I KNOW YOU AREN'T EXACTLY ENTHRALLED BY ME, BUT DASH IT ALL, YOU AREN'T BEING SPORTING!

7

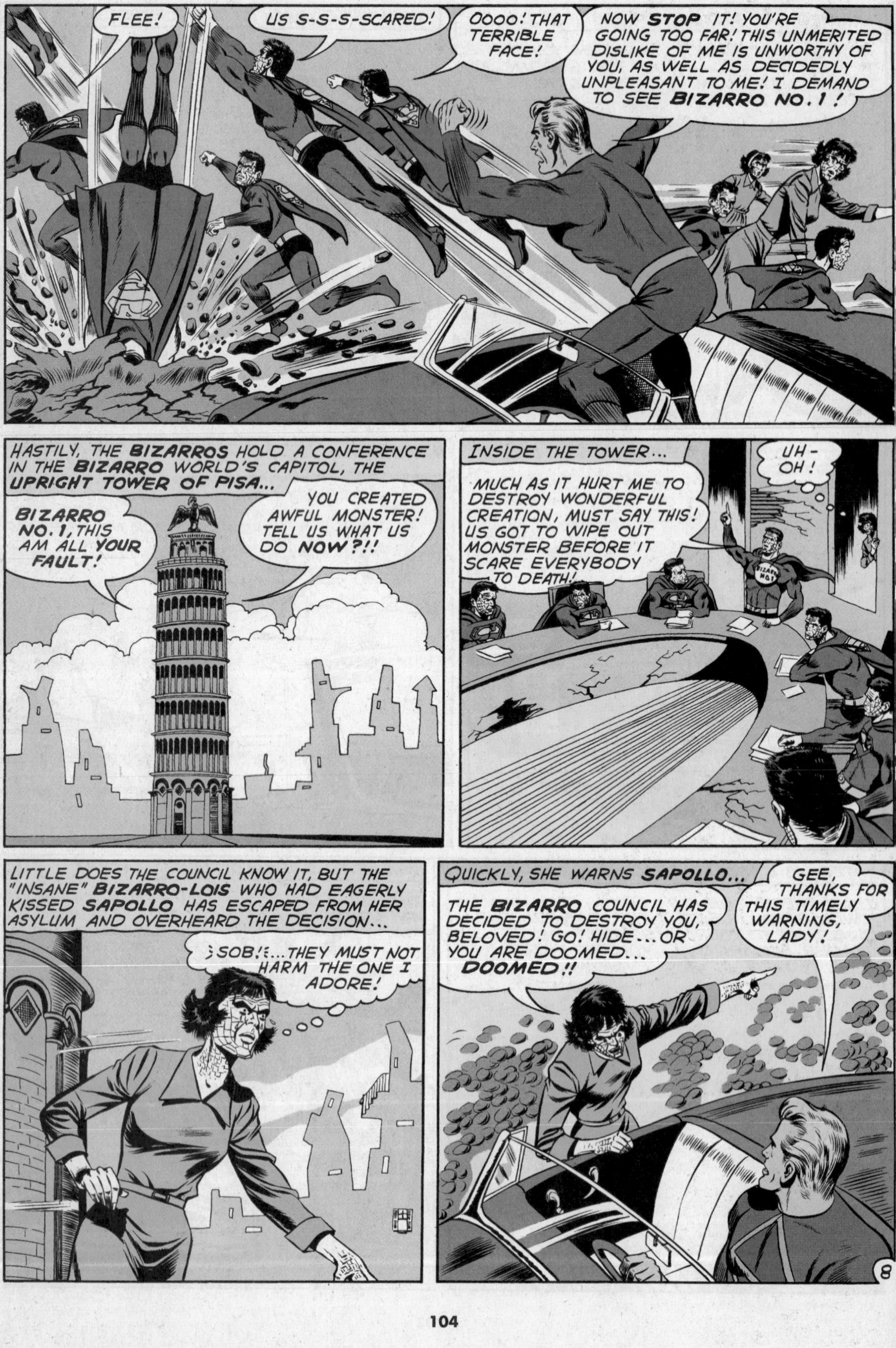
FLEE!
US S-S-S-SCARED!
OOOO! THAT TERRIBLE FACE!
NOW STOP IT! YOU'RE GOING TOO FAR! THIS UNMERITED DISLIKE OF ME IS UNWORTHY OF YOU, AS WELL AS DECIDEDLY UNPLEASANT TO ME! I DEMAND TO SEE BIZARRO NO. 1!
HASTILY, THE BIZARROS HOLD A CONFERENCE IN THE BIZARRO WORLD'S CAPITOL, THE UPRIGHT TOWER OF PISA...
BIZARRO NO. 1, THIS AM ALL YOUR FAULT!
YOU CREATED AWFUL MONSTER! TELL US WHAT US DO NOW?!!
INSIDE THE TOWER...
MUCH AS IT HURT ME TO DESTROY WONDERFUL CREATION, MUST SAY THIS! US GOT TO WIPE OUT MONSTER BEFORE IT SCARE EVERYBODY TO DEATH!
UH-OH!
LITTLE DOES THE COUNCIL KNOW IT, BUT THE "INSANE" BIZARRO-LOIS WHO HAD EAGERLY KISSED SAPOLLO HAS ESCAPED FROM HER ASYLUM AND OVERHEARD THE DECISION...
SOB!...THEY MUST NOT HARM THE ONE I ADORE!
QUICKLY, SHE WARNS SAPOLLO...
THE BIZARRO COUNCIL HAS DECIDED TO DESTROY YOU, BELOVED! GO! HIDE...OR YOU ARE DOOMED... DOOMED!!
GEE, THANKS FOR THIS TIMELY WARNING, LADY!
8

OUT OF THE TOWER POUR THE **BIZARROS**...

SEARCH EVERYWHERE! NO MATTER WHERE HIM HIDE, US FIND HIM!

MONSTER MUST DIE!

DOWN WITH MONSTER!

DESPERATELY, **SAPOLLO** FLEES...

¿GASP!¿...THERE GOES MONSTER!

HIS CAR ALMOST HIT EMPIRE STATE BUILDING, WHICH AM **SMALLEST** BUILDING ON OUR WORLD!

AWAY HE SPEEDS, PAST THE **STATUE OF UNLIBERTY**...

¿GASP!¿...WHAT CHANCE HAVE I AGAINST THESE SUPER-POWERFUL CREATURES, DESPITE MY SUPERB GOOD LOOKS AND HIGH I.Q.? I HATE TO BE PESSIMISTIC, BUT...THIS LOOKS **BAD!!**

RELENTLESSLY, THE **BIZARRO MONSTER-EXTERMINATION COMMITTEE** LOOKS ALMOST EVERYWHERE...

COULD HIM BE HIDING BEHIND MONUMENT US LOVINGLY BUILT TO HONOR TRAITOR **BENNY DICK ARNOLD** FOR BETRAYING OUR COUNTRY?

NOT EVEN MONSTER COULD BE **THAT** MONSTROUS!

FEARFULLY, **SAPOLLO** RETURNS TO BIZARRO'S FORTRESS...

I'LL HIDE IN HERE! MAYBE THEY'LL OVERLOOK SEARCHING IT!

BUT...

AH-HA!...MY SUPER-VISION SHOWS MY...¿UGH!¿ HORRIBLE CREATION AM COWERING INSIDE! HIM TRAPPED!

US GOT HIM WHERE US WANT HIM!...**HAW!**

9

COME OUT OF FORTRESS, **MONSTER**, AND SAVE US TROUBLE OF DRAGGING YOU OUT! ME WILL COUNT UP TO FIVE!...NO, WAIT! ME CAN'T COUNT *THAT* HIGH!...UH...ME WILL COUNT UP TO *TWO!*..."ONE"!!

BIZARRO NO. 1

INSIDE THE FORTRESS...

;CHOKE!... TH-THERE'S NO ESCAPE FOR ME! I-I'M *DOOMED!*

MAYBE YES, AND MAYBE **NO!**

AT THAT MOMENT, AT THE **BIZARRO** JAIL, THE INFURIATED WARDEN RANTS AT **MR. BIZARRO-KLTPZYXM**, WHO IS A **BIZARRO** VERSION OF THE 5TH DIMENSIONAL IMP **MR. MXYZPTLK**...

YOU AM GOING TO BE *PUNISHED!*

WARDEN

BECAUSE YOUR BEHAVIOR HAS BEEN TOO **GOOD**, ME PUNISH YOU BY *RELEASING* YOU! GET OUT!!

ON EARTH, THEY PUNISH MISBEHAVING PRISONERS BY THROWING THEM INTO **SOLITARY CONFINEMENT!** HERE, THEY DO **OPPOSITE!**

AS THE **BIZARRO** IMP STREAKS ALONG, EAGER TO PERFORM GOOD DEEDS...

UH-OH! THAT FELLOW TRAPPED INSIDE **BIZARRO'S** FORTRESS AM IN DANGER! ME MAGICALLY KNOW ALL THAT'S HAPPENED! ME SAVE HIM!... **ALAKAZOOKUS!!**

"TWO"!!

AND SO, AS THE **BIZARROS** CLOSE IN ON **SAPOLLO**...

;GASP!;... **SAPOLLO'S** BODY AM **BLENDING** BACK INTO THE CAGED BODY OF CAVE-MAN ME BROUGHT FROM ANOTHER WORLD! AMAZING!!

GOOD! MY MAGIC RETURNED HIM TO HIS FORMER SELF!

10

NOW *BIZARRO NO. 1*'S PALS ARE CHARMED BY THE UGLY CREATURE THEY CONSIDER HANDSOME...

HIM PLEASANT FELLOW! FREE HIM, *BIZARRO NO. 1!*

OKAY!

GUESS HIM DIDN'T KNOW HIS CAGE WASN'T LOCKED!

GR-RROARR

HA, HA! FRIENDLY, ISN'T HE?

HIM SURE AM! ME ENVY HIS **GOOD LOOKS!!**

IN THE DAYS THAT FOLLOW...

HA, HA! OUR BUDDY-PAL FROM SPACE AM HAVING WONDERFUL TIME WRECKING EVERYTHING HIM CAN!

SHORTLY...

CONGRATULATIONS, *BIZARRO NO. 1,* OLD MAN! NOT ONLY DID YOU CREATE GREATEST HORROR MOVIE OF ALL TIME, BUT YOU'VE BLESSED US WITH THIS **GOOD NEIGHBOR!**

HIM SWEET!

ME GLAD!

A MOMENT LATER...

GR-R-RUNNNG!!!

OH, GOODY! CAVE-MAN **DESTROYED** OUR HOUSE WITH **AVALANCHE!**

THANK GOODNESS WE GOT **HIM** HERE INSTEAD OF THAT AWFUL **SAPOLLO!**

LUCKY US!!

The End.

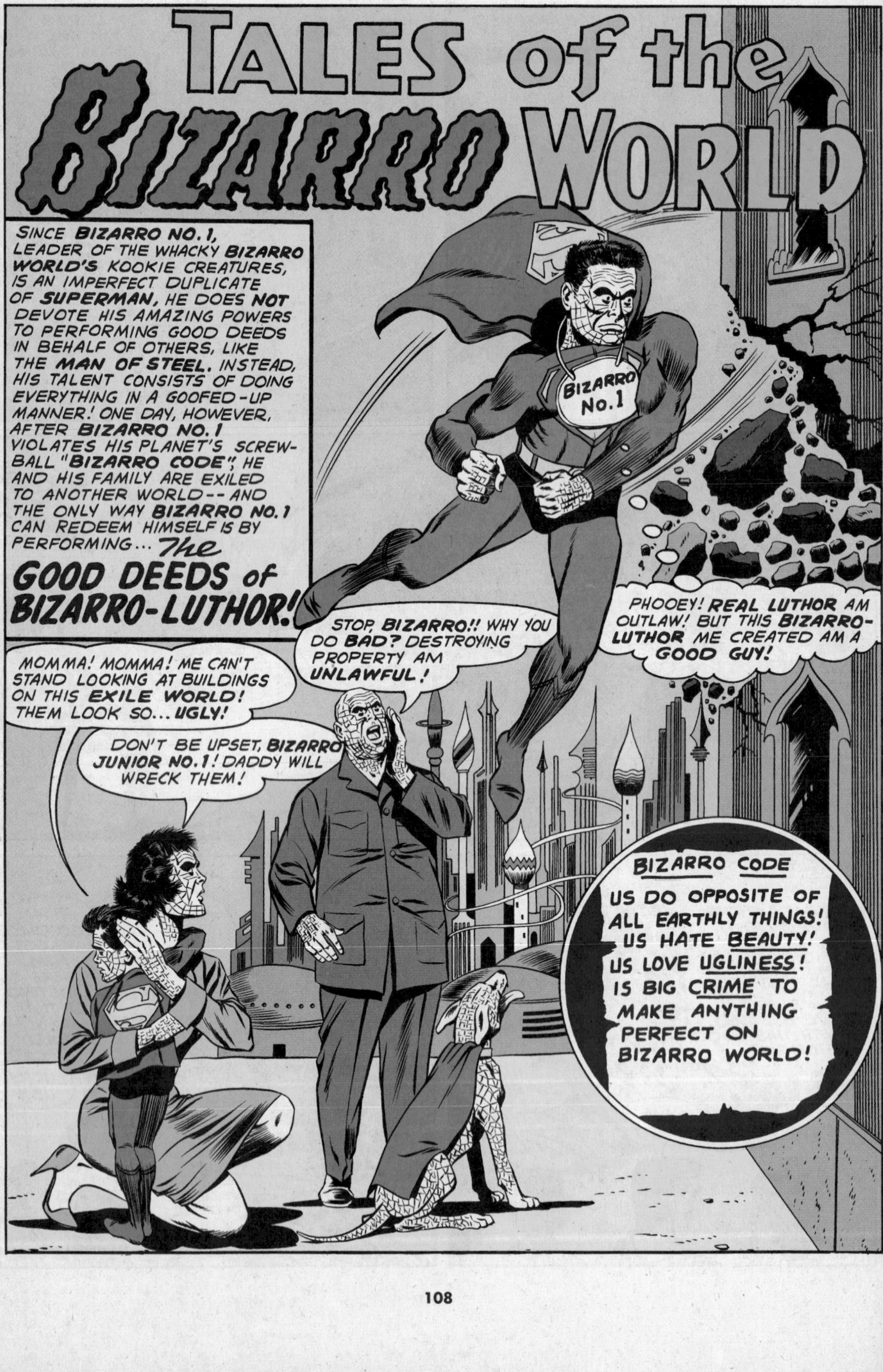

TALES of the BIZARRO WORLD
SINCE BIZARRO NO. 1, LEADER OF THE WHACKY BIZARRO WORLD'S KOOKIE CREATURES, IS AN IMPERFECT DUPLICATE OF SUPERMAN, HE DOES NOT DEVOTE HIS AMAZING POWERS TO PERFORMING GOOD DEEDS IN BEHALF OF OTHERS, LIKE THE MAN OF STEEL. INSTEAD, HIS TALENT CONSISTS OF DOING EVERYTHING IN A GOOFED-UP MANNER! ONE DAY, HOWEVER, AFTER BIZARRO NO. 1 VIOLATES HIS PLANET'S SCREW-BALL "BIZARRO CODE", HE AND HIS FAMILY ARE EXILED TO ANOTHER WORLD-- AND THE ONLY WAY BIZARRO NO. 1 CAN REDEEM HIMSELF IS BY PERFORMING... The
GOOD DEEDS of BIZARRO-LUTHOR!
BIZARRO No. 1
PHOOEY! REAL LUTHOR AM OUTLAW! BUT THIS BIZARRO-LUTHOR ME CREATED AM A GOOD GUY!
STOP, BIZARRO!! WHY YOU DO BAD? DESTROYING PROPERTY AM UNLAWFUL!
MOMMA! MOMMA! ME CAN'T STAND LOOKING AT BUILDINGS ON THIS EXILE WORLD! THEM LOOK SO... UGLY!
DON'T BE UPSET, BIZARRO JUNIOR NO. 1! DADDY WILL WRECK THEM!
BIZARRO CODE
US DO OPPOSITE OF ALL EARTHLY THINGS! US HATE BEAUTY! US LOVE UGLINESS! IS BIG CRIME TO MAKE ANYTHING PERFECT ON BIZARRO WORLD!

FAR OFF IN OUTER SPACE EXISTS THE WEIRDEST, ZANIEST PLANET IN THE ENTIRE UNIVERSE... THE SQUARE *BIZARRO WORLD!* IT IS THE HOME OF THE PATHETIC, STUPID *BIZARRO* CREATURES WHO ARE IMPERFECT DUPLICATES OF *SUPERMAN* AND HIS FRIENDS...

ON THIS CRAZY WORLD, EVERYTHING IS A MAD, REVERSED VERSION OF EARTHLY CUSTOMS, FOR INSTANCE, *"NO SMOKING"* SIGNS MEAN THE *REVERSE...!*

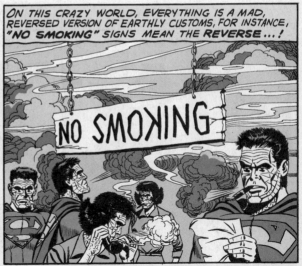

NO SMOKING

BIZARRO HISTORY IS RATHER *DIFFERENT* FROM OURS! LET US PEEK INTO A TYPICAL *BIZARRO* SCHOOLROOM AS THE CLASS' BRIGHTEST PUPIL ANSWERS THE INSTRUCTOR'S QUESTION...

COLUMBUS HIM SAID WORLD AM *SQUARE!*

ABSOLUTELY *RIGHT!!!!*

AND WHEN *BIZARRO* FISHERMEN INDULGE IN THEIR FAVORITE SPORT...

BAH! ME THROW BACK FISH ME CAUGHT! IT *TOO BIG!*

HA, HA! ME LUCKIER THAN YOU! ME CAUGHT *LITTLE FISH!!*

HERE ON THIS LUNATIC PLANET, *BIZARROS* ROLLER SKATE ON *ICE*, AND ICE-SKATE ON *SIDEWALKS...!*

AND INSTEAD OF SLIDING *DOWN* SLIDES!

IT AM *MY* TURN TO SLIDE *UP* SLIDE NEXT!!

BIZARRO SCHOOLE NO. 1

2

EACH EVENING, *BIZARRO* MILKMEN DELIVER EMPTY MILK BOTTLES TO THEIR CUSTOMERS...!

ME GOING ON DIET! STARTING TOMORROW, LEAVE THREE MORE EMPTY BOTTLES DAILY!

MORE BOTTLES YOU TAKE, MORE ME GOT PAY *YOU!*

AND NOW, LET US OBSERVE THE NUMBER ONE *BIZARRO* FAMILY IN THE *FORTRESS UV BIZARRO...*

ME CREATED *BIZARRO* VERSION OF BOTTLE CITY OF *KANDOR!*

GOSH, HOW'D YOU DO IT, DADDY?

EASY! ME AIMED IMPERFECT *DUPLICATOR RAY,* WHICH COULD PENETRATE LEAD-LINING OF *SUPERMAN'S FORTRESS OF SOLITUDE* ON EARTH, AT REAL *KANDOR* CITY THERE, AND MATERIALIZED THIS HERE! LOOK INTO IT!!

;GASP!;...*BIZARRO-KANDOR* CITY AM FULL OF *BIZARROS!*

THAT AM BECAUSE *DUPLICATOR RAY* CREATED IMPERFECT DUPLICATES OF *KANDOR'S* PEOPLE!

;CHUCKLE!; CORRECT, SON!

SUDDENLY, AN UNEXPECTED INTERRUPTION...

BIZARRO NO. 1, YOU AND FAMILY AM UNDER *ARREST* BECAUSE OF YOUR *AWFUL CRIME!*

AWP!!--*BIZARRO POLICE!!* WHY YOU GIVING ME THIS HONOR?

WHAT HIM DID??!

HIM BROKE *BIZARRO CODE* BY MAKING SOMETHING *PERFECT!*

WHEN HIM CREATED US *BIZARRO* DUPLICATES, HIM MADE *PERFECT* IMITATION OF *SUPERMAN'S* UNIFORM! SEE? LETTER "S" AM FORMED *PERFECTLY!*

;GURGLE!;... WHAT A *TERRIBLE ERROR!*

AWFUL CRIME DESERVE AWFUL PUNISHMENT! THIS RAY GIVE YOU AND FAMILY FATE SO GHASTLY ME WON'T DESCRIBE IT!

;CHOKE!;...D-DOES HIM MEAN PHANTOM ZONE??!

BZZ-ZZST!

INSTANTLY, THE RAY CAUSES THE NUMBER ONE BIZARRO FAMILY TO STREAK THROUGH OUTER SPACE TOWARD THEIR DESTINATION IN IMMATERIAL FORM...

YAAGH!--US AM GONNA BE EXILED ON AN...;UGH!;... PERFECTLY ROUND PLANET! HOW H-HORRIBLE!!

AS THEY MATERIALIZE ON THE ROUND WORLD...

;MOAN!;--CIRCULAR PLANET AM SURROUNDED BY BLUE KRYPTONITE AURA! US NEVER WILL BE ABLE TO GET OFF BECAUSE BLUE KRYPTONITE AM AS DEADLY TO US AS GREEN KRYPTONITE AM TO SUPERMAN!

YII-IICHH--THEM BUILDINGS AREN'T BEAUTIFUL LIKE BIZARRO WORLD BUILDINGS!...;URK!;-- IT MAKE ME SICK TO LOOK ON THEM!....DO SOMETHING! PLEASE!!

THEM AM... UGLY!!

GR-RR!... ME SMASH THEM!

BUT... STOP-- OR ME PUSH BUTTON ON MY BELT THAT WILL SHRINK BLUE AURA AND KILL YOU!

HMM... MY X-RAY VISION SHOWS THEM BIZARRO GUARDS AM ROBOTS! NO WONDER THEM CAN STAND SIGHT OF THESE UGLY BUILDINGS!

OKAY!

REJOINING HIS FAMILY, BIZARRO NO.1 SWIFTLY BUILDS AN IMPERFECT DUPLICATOR RAY WITH MACHINERY TAKEN FROM NEARBY BUILDINGS. THEN...

ME NEED HELP! AH, MY TELESCOPIC VISION SEE THE CRIMINAL LUTHOR ON EARTH! ME FOCUS RAY ON HIM!

MEANWHILE, ON EARTH, IN THE COURTYARD OF *METROPOLIS PRISON*, AS SUPERMAN'S GREATEST FOE, CONVICT *LEX LUTHOR*, ENJOYS A RECREATION BREAK...

A RAY FROM SPACE IS ENGULFING *LUTHOR!* IS THIS A WEIRD *ESCAPE* SCHEME?

UNFORTUNATELY... *NO!* I'VE NOTHING TO DO WITH THIS RAY!

AS THE ASTOUNDING RAY CAUSES A *BIZARRO* DUPLICATE OF *LUTHOR* TO MATERIALIZE ON THE EXILE PLANET, *BIZARRO NO. 1* EXPLAINS HIS PREDICAMENT...

ME IN TROUBLE WITH POLICE OF *BIZARRO WORLD!* PLEASE SQUARE ME WITH THEM!

ME DO IT ONLY *IF YOU* DO FOUR *GOOD DEEDS* ON EARTH!

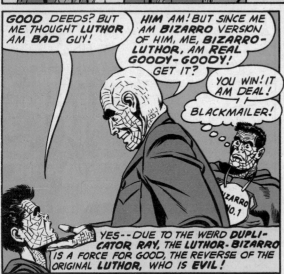

GOOD DEEDS? BUT ME THOUGHT *LUTHOR* AM *BAD GUY!*

HIM AM! BUT SINCE ME AM *BIZARRO* VERSION OF HIM, ME, *BIZARRO-LUTHOR*, AM *REAL GOODY-GOODY!* GET IT?

YOU WIN! IT AM DEAL!

BLACKMAILER!

YES-- DUE TO THE WEIRD *DUPLI-CATOR RAY*, THE *LUTHOR-BIZARRO* IS A FORCE FOR GOOD, THE REVERSE OF THE ORIGINAL *LUTHOR*, WHO IS *EVIL!*

RAPIDLY, *BIZARRO-LUTHOR* CONSTRUCTS A STRANGE MACHINE, AND THEN...

THERE! ME AM DE-ATOMIZING THE *BLUE KRYPTONITE AURA* IMPRISON-ING US ON THIS ROUND PLANET! NOW WE CAN ESCAPE!

BON VOYAGE, *BIZARRO NO. 1!*

HOW *NICE* OF GUARDS TO WAVE BYE-BYE WHEN WE BREAK OUT!

UNLIKE EARTH GUARDS, *BIZARRO* GUARDS GLADLY *LET* PRISONERS ESCAPE!!

MEANWHILE, ON THE *BIZARRO WORLD*, INSIDE THE *BIZARRO-KANDOR* BOTTLE CITY IN *BIZARRO'S* FORTRESS...

OUR MONITOR REVEALED EVERY-THING! *BIZARRO NO. 1* AM FLYING *BIZARRO-LUTHOR* TOWARD EARTH! *BIZARRO-LUTHOR* CAN SURVIVE IN SPACE, THOUGH HIM NOT GOT SUPER-POWERS, BECAUSE HIM SYNTHETIC MAN!

⑤

HURRY! DON UNIFORMS US PREPARE FOR EMERGENCY LIKE *THIS*! BIZARRO NO. 1 AM BEING FORCED TO AID *GOOD* LUTHOR! US FORM *BIZARRO EMERGENCY SQUAD* AND GO HELP BIZARRO!

SWIFTLY, A GROUP OF *BIZARRO-KANDORIANS* DON CHEMICALLY RESISTANT *SUPERMAN* UNIFORMS, THEN FLY ALOFT ON GREAT BIRDS WHICH ARE *BIZARRO* VERSIONS OF EVERYTHING INSIDE THE ORIGINAL *KANDOR* BOTTLE CITY...

TRAINED BIRDS FLY US TO BOTTLE'S CORK! AFTER US PUSH SIDE OF CORK AND EMERGE, US WILL GAIN SUPER-POWERS!

US WEAR MEDALLIONS LIKE OUR HERO, BIZARRO NO. 1!

SECONDS LATER...

NOW US FLY LIKE BIZARRO! *SUPERMAN* EMERGENCY SQUAD AM SUCH GOOD IDEA, US SWIPE IT! US AM *BIZARRO EMERGENCY SQUAD*!!

ONE OF THESE DAYS US WILL BATTLE *SUPERMAN EMERGENCY SQUAD*! THEM UGLY! US HANDSOME!

QUICKLY, THE SQUAD JOINS *BIZARRO NO. 1* IN SPACE...

;CHOKE!: --THEM TAGGING ALONG TO HELP ME OUT! WHAT FRIENDS! WHAT COMRADES!

PRESENTLY, ON EARTH...

UH-OH! MASKED BANDITS GOING ROB BANK! QUICK! I ORDER YOU TO RESCUE BANK!

OKAY, YOU GUYS! IT'S TIME FOR FIRST GOOD DEED! ME FIGURE OUT HOW US'LL WORK IT! LISTEN...

IMMEDIATELY, THE *BIZARRO EMERGENCY SQUAD* FLASHES TO A ROCKY AREA, THEN...

BIZARRO SAID HURL BOULDERS TO HIM!

WHAT BIZARRO SAY, US DO!!

CATCHING THE HURTLING ROCKS, **BIZARRO NO. 1** BEGINS TO ENCLOSE THE MENACED BANK AT SUPER-SPEED...

YIPES! AM I GOING *CRAZY?!*

A F-FLYING SUPER-MONSTER IS SAVING THE BANK! IT'S ENOUGH TO MAKE ME WANNA GO *STRAIGHT!*

SPLIT-SECONDS LATER...

HA, HA! CROOKS CAN'T GET INTO BANK TO ROB IT, *NOW!*

IDIOT!! NEITHER CAN EMPLOYEES OR CUSTOMERS GET *OUT!*...SOME *GOOD DEED!!*...ALL RIGHT! ME GIVE YOU ANOTHER CHANCE!

GOSH, ME HAPPY TO DO *GOOD* INSTEAD OF *EVIL,* OPPOSITE FROM *REAL LUTHOR!*

SHORTLY, AT THE WATERFRONT...

¿CHOKE!¿...MY BUSINESS WENT BUST! I'M BROKE! I-I'VE NOTHING TO LIVE FOR! I'LL DROWN MYSELF, AND END MY MISERY!

AS **BIZARRO** ALIGHTS...

FOR YOUR NEXT GOOD DEED, SAVE THAT POOR, UNFORTUNATE MAN!

NO! DON'T SAVE ME! I *WANT* TO DIE! I'VE LOST ALL MY MONEY!...¿SOB!¿

OKAY! ME SAVED HIM! AM THAT GOOD ENOUGH DEED?

NOT QUITE! NOW YOU MAKE HIM RICH!

HOW ME GOING MAKE THIS GUY RICH LIKE ROCKEFELLER? AH, X-RAY VISION GIVE ME IDEA! ON CRAZY EARTH, PEOPLE THINK DIAMONDS VALUABLE!

SWIFTLY, *BIZARRO* BURROWS INTO THE GROUND, THEN REAPPEARS...

ME SEE *IT*, BELOW!

ME FOUND COAL!

ARE MY EYES P-PLAYING TRICKS?

CHEER UP! YOU *SOON* BE RICH AGAIN!

SPLITTING THE GIANT COAL CHUNK INTO NUMEROUS PIECES, *BIZARRO NO. 1* IS THEN AIDED BY HIS TINY HELPERS...

TH-THEY'RE SQUEEZING THE COAL INTO D-DIAMONDS!

THANKS FOR HELP, LITTLE BUDDIES!

STUPIDLY *BIZARRO* FAILS TO REALIZE HE DOESN'T NEED THE SQUAD'S AID...THAT HE COULD HAVE PERFORMED THE FEAT BY HIMSELF!

AFTERWARD...

THERE YOU AM! BOATLOAD OF DIAMONDS AM *ALL* YOURS!

MINE?...THANKS TO YOU NOBLE, GALLANT MONSTERS, I'LL BE THE *RICHEST* MAN IN THE WORLD!

AND AS THE HAPPY CHAP SPEEDS OFF WITH HIS NEW-FOUND RICHES...

BIZARRO, ME AM *PROUD* OF YOU! THAT WAS *SPLENDID GOOD DEED!*

OH-OH!...TH-THE WEIGHT OF THE GEMS IS S-SINKING THE BOAT!

IT SANK! THE BOAT SANK!!... GOOD DEED?? BAH!!

LATER...

I WANNA GO THERE!

FORGET IT, DANNY! THE ZOO ISN'T WORTH VISITING SINCE MOST OF ITS ANIMALS CAUGHT A MYSTERIOUS JUNGLE FEVER!

HM-MM... ME GETTING FABULOUS IDEA!

METROPOLIS ZOO

8

ME KNOW! FOR NEXT GOOD DEED, YOU WANT ME SHOULD RESTOCK ZOO!... LET'S GO, SQUAD!

RIGHT! BUT FOR GOSH-SAKES MAKE IT INTERESTING ANIMALS PEOPLE WOULD NEVER FORGET SEEING!

METROPOLIS ZOO

BIZARRO NO.1

OFF INTO SPACE STREAK BIZARRO NO.1 AND THE BIZARROS EMERGENCY SQUAD, THEN THEY QUICKLY RETURN...

GOOD LI'L FELLERS! LIKE ME, THEM AM BRINGING FASCINATING CREATURES FROM DIFFERENT WORLDS!

QUICKLY, THE BIZARROS PLACE THE SPACE CREATURES IN ZOO CAGES...

YOU CAN BE PROUD OF THIS SPLENDID GOOD DEED, BIZARRO NO.1!

STOP RUBBING IT IN!... ON TO FOURTH AND FINAL DEED!

A LUTHOR WHO DO GOOD AM PAIN IN NECK!

AS THE BIZARROS DEPART...

¡GULP!¡ ...WH- WHERE'D THESE WEIRD CREATURES COME FROM?

THEY'RE BREAKING OUT! ONE'S EATING THE METAL BARS... ANOTHER'S DWINDLING IN SIZE AND SQUEEZING THROUGH THE BARS... AND ANOTHER'S BLASTING THE BARS OFF!... RUN!! TH-THEY'RE WRECKING THE ZOO!

AND SO ANOTHER BIZARRO "GOOD DEED" ENDS UP AS A BOO-BOO!

LATER, MANY MILES AWAY, AS THE BIZARROS ALIGHT ATOP A MOUNTAIN RANGE...

BIZARRO NO.1, ME SAW THEM CREATURES DESTROYING ZOO! YOU GOOFED AGAIN!!

STOP FLATTERING ME WITH PRAISE! WHAT AM FINAL... ¡UGH!¡... GOOD DEED YOU WANT DONE?

FOURTH GOOD DEED AM TO BE ONE THAT'LL BENEFIT SUPERMAN!

SUPERMAN?!... GR-RR! AM YOU CRAZY? ME HATE HIM TO PIECES! ME HATE HIM THE MOST! GOOD DEED FOR HIM? NO! NO!!! ANYTHING BUT THAT!... ¡ROARRRR!¡

9

ME POSOLUTELY, ABSITIVELY WON'T DO *GOOD DEED* FOR HIM!!

IF YOU WANT ME HELP YOU BE FORGIVEN BY POLICE OF *BIZARRO WORLD*, DO WHAT ME *ORDER*, OR OUR DEAL AM *OFF!*

⋮CHOKE!⋮...YOU WIN!... HM-MM! WHAT AM BEST THING ME COULD DO FOR THAT *SUPER-CREEP*?...PUNCH LOIS LANE FOR BEING SO NOSEY? *NO!*... *EAT* JIMMY OLSEN'S SIGNAL-WATCH SO HIM STOP PESTERING *SUPER-MAN* FOR HELP? *NO!*...

ME GOT IT!!...SUPERMAN AM ALWAYS WORRIED HIS SECRET IDENTITY BE FOUND OUT, *RIGHT?* ME FIX IT SO HIM *NEVER* GOT TO WORRY THAT AGAIN!!

WONDERFUL!... ⋮PANT!⋮ BUT HOW YOU GOING ACCOMPLISH THAT??

SIMPLE! WATCH!

ME ORDERED BIZARRO EMERGENCY SQUAD TO HELP ME!

⋮GASP!⋮...THEM AM CARVING TWO GIANT STONE HEADS OUT OF MOUNTAINSIDE! WHAT AM *BIZARRO NO. 1's* CLEVER SCHEME??

SECONDS LATER...

BEHOLD! STONE HEADS OF *CLARK KENT* AND *SUPERMAN!* AND LOOK WHAT ME CARVED UNDER HEAD OF KENT!

YOU *SUPER-SAP!!* THE MEN IN THAT HELICOPTER WILL SOON FLY OVER THE HUGE FACES AND SEE YOUR INSCRIPTION! *SUPERMAN'S* SECRET WILL BE BETRAYED TO THE WORLD!! YOU CALL *THIS* A GOOD DEED?!

CLERK KENT AM SECRUT IDENTITEE UV SOUPERMANN

10

AT THIS CRUCIAL MOMENT, **SUPERMAN**, RETURNING TO EARTH, SIGHTS...

BIZARRO IS LOOSE AGAIN ON EARTH, CREATING TROUBLE WHICH I'LL HAVE TO FIX!...≥GASP!≤... THOSE TWO GREAT STONE FACES!

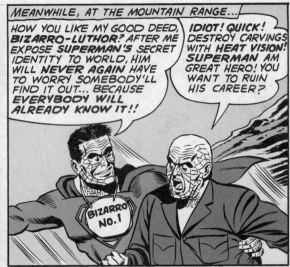

MEANWHILE, AT THE MOUNTAIN RANGE...

HOW YOU LIKE MY GOOD DEED, **BIZARRO-LUTHOR?** AFTER ME EXPOSE **SUPERMAN'S** SECRET IDENTITY TO WORLD, HIM WILL **NEVER AGAIN** HAVE TO WORRY SOMEBODY'LL FIND IT OUT... BECAUSE EVERYBODY WILL ALREADY KNOW IT!!

IDIOT! QUICK! DESTROY CARVINGS WITH **HEAT VISION!** SUPERMAN AM GREAT HERO! YOU WANT TO RUIN HIS CAREER?

BIZARRO No.1

AND AS **BIZARRO** OBEYS...

HIM DESTROYED FACES AND LETTERING JUST IN TIME, BEFORE MEN IN PLANE COULD SEE IT!

FLY ME BACK TO **EXILE PLANET**, STUPID!!

AS THE **BIZARROS** STREAK UP INTO SPACE...

WHEW! WHAT A CLOSE CALL! TO THINK MY SECRET WAS SAVED BY A...**BIZARRO-LUTHOR**...WELL, I'LL QUICKLY UNDO ALL THE MISCHIEF DONE ELSEWHERE BY THOSE ZANY **BIZARRO** CREATURES!

PRESENTLY, AS **BIZARRO NO.1** FLIES PAST THE **BIZARRO WORLD**...

LITTLE PALS AM FLYING BACK TO **BIZARRO-KANDOR** BOTTLE CITY! THEM WAS BIG HELP!... NOW TO JOIN FAMILY ON **EXILE PLANET**!

BIZARRO

SHORTLY AFTERWARD, AS **BIZARRO** REACHES HIS DESTINATION...

ME DID THEM--≥ERK!≤... FOUR GOOD DEEDS! NOW CLEAR MY REPUTATION WITH **BIZARRO WORLD**, LIKE YOU PROMISE!

ME TELL YOU WHAT TO DO!

BIZARRO LOIS NO.1

BIZARRO JUNIOR

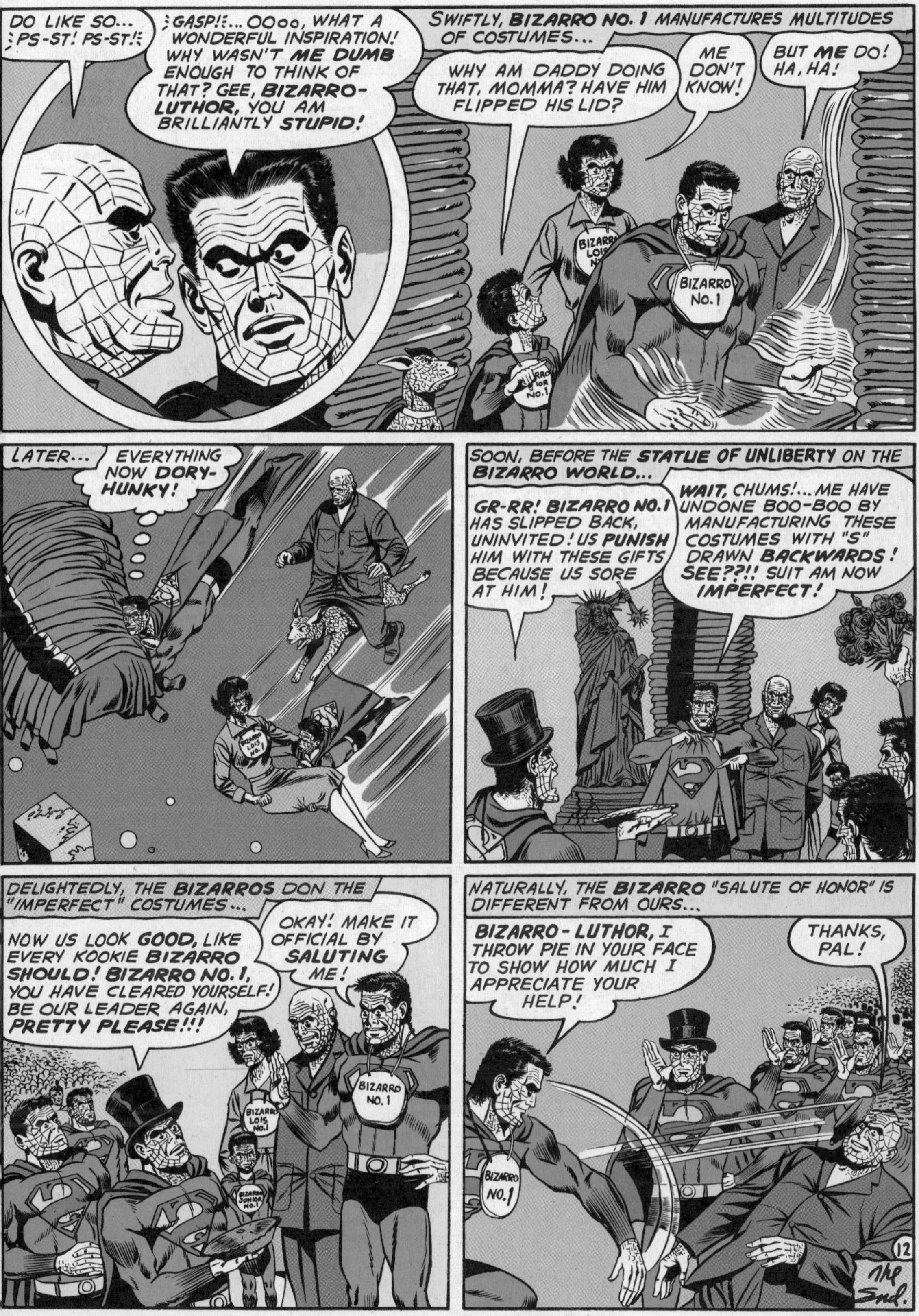
DO LIKE SO... PS-ST! PS-ST!
GASP!... OOoo, WHAT A WONDERFUL INSPIRATION! WHY WASN'T ME DUMB ENOUGH TO THINK OF THAT? GEE, BIZARRO-LUTHOR, YOU AM BRILLIANTLY STUPID!
SWIFTLY, BIZARRO NO. 1 MANUFACTURES MULTITUDES OF COSTUMES...
WHY AM DADDY DOING THAT, MOMMA? HAVE HIM FLIPPED HIS LID?
ME DON'T KNOW!
BUT ME DO! HA, HA!
BIZARRO NO. 1
LATER...
EVERYTHING NOW DORY-HUNKY!
SOON, BEFORE THE STATUE OF UNLIBERTY ON THE BIZARRO WORLD...
GR-RR! BIZARRO NO. 1 HAS SLIPPED BACK, UNINVITED! US PUNISH HIM WITH THESE GIFTS BECAUSE US SORE AT HIM!
WAIT, CHUMS!... ME HAVE UNDONE BOO-BOO BY MANUFACTURING THESE COSTUMES WITH "S" DRAWN BACKWARDS! SEE??!! SUIT AM NOW IMPERFECT!
DELIGHTEDLY, THE BIZARROS DON THE "IMPERFECT" COSTUMES...
NOW US LOOK GOOD, LIKE EVERY KOOKIE BIZARRO SHOULD! BIZARRO NO. 1, YOU HAVE CLEARED YOURSELF! BE OUR LEADER AGAIN, PRETTY PLEASE!!!
OKAY! MAKE IT OFFICIAL BY SALUTING ME!
BIZARRO NO. 1
BIZARRO LOIS NO. 1
BIZARRO JUNIOR NO. 1
NATURALLY, THE BIZARRO "SALUTE OF HONOR" IS DIFFERENT FROM OURS...
BIZARRO-LUTHOR, I THROW PIE IN YOUR FACE TO SHOW HOW MUCH I APPRECIATE YOUR HELP!
THANKS, PAL!
BIZARRO NO. 1
12
THE END.

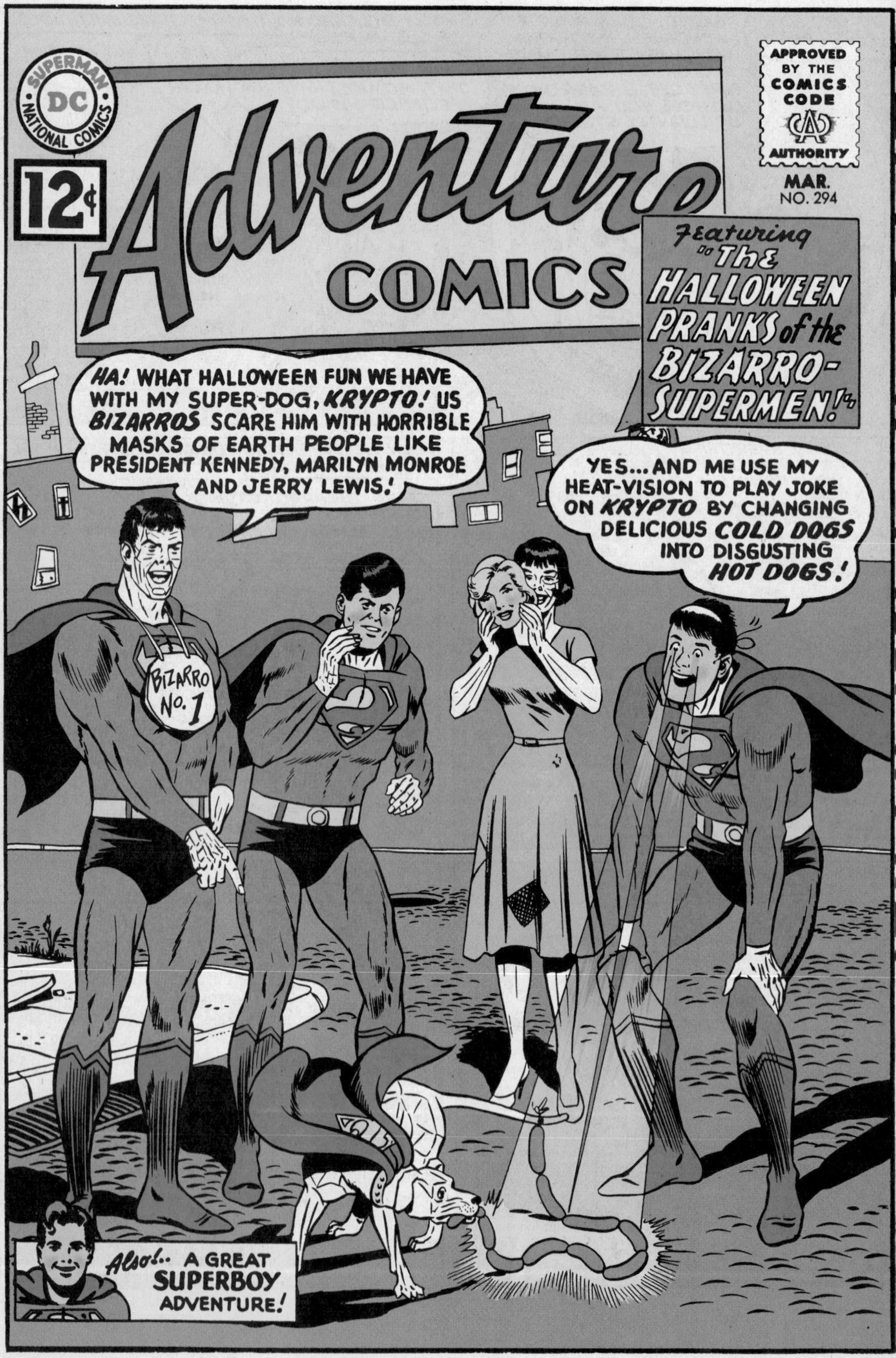

SUPERMAN
DC
NATIONAL COMICS
12¢
Adventure
COMICS
APPROVED BY THE COMICS CODE AUTHORITY
MAR.
NO. 294
Featuring "THE HALLOWEEN PRANKS of the BIZARRO-SUPERMEN!"
HA! WHAT HALLOWEEN FUN WE HAVE WITH MY SUPER-DOG, KRYPTO! US BIZARROS SCARE HIM WITH HORRIBLE MASKS OF EARTH PEOPLE LIKE PRESIDENT KENNEDY, MARILYN MONROE AND JERRY LEWIS!
YES... AND ME USE MY HEAT-VISION TO PLAY JOKE ON KRYPTO BY CHANGING DELICIOUS COLD DOGS INTO DISGUSTING HOT DOGS!
BIZARRO No. 1
Also!.. A GREAT SUPERBOY ADVENTURE!

TALES of the BIZARRO WORLD

HALLOWEEN IS ONE OF THE GAYEST, WACKIEST, AND FUN-FILLED OF ALL EARTH HOLIDAYS! AND SO YOU CAN WELL IMAGINE HOW UTTERLY CRAZY THE *BIZARRO WORLD'S* GOOFED-UP VERSION OF EARTH'S MADCAP HALLOWEEN CELEBRATION MUST BE! HOLD TIGHT, SO YOU WON'T FALL DOWN LAUGHING, WHILE WE GIVE YOU A HOWLARIOUS, UNFORGETTABLE PEEK AT...

The HALLOWEEN PRANKS *of the* BIZARRO SUPERMEN!

YOU ASK FOR *TRICK*, SO US GIVE YOU *TREAT*, HA, HA!

DOGGONIT! *STOP* GIVING US CANDY AND TOYS! YOU GOING *TOO FAR* WITH *MEAN* HALLOWEEN PRANKS!

BIZARRO CODE

US DO OPPOSITE OF ALL EARTHLY THINGS! US HATE BEAUTY! US LOVE UGLINESS! IS BIG CRIME TO MAKE ANYTHING PERFECT ON BIZARRO WORLD!

121

FAR OUT IN SPACE EXISTS THE WACKIEST PLANET IN THE ENTIRE UNIVERSE... IT IS THE SQUARE **BIZARRO WORLD**, HOME PLANET OF THE STUPID **BIZARRO** CREATURES WHO ARE IMPERFECT DUPLICATES OF **SUPERMAN** AND HIS FRIENDS...

EVERYTHING ON THIS ZANY WORLD IS THE EXACT OPPOSITE OF EARTH! FOR INSTANCE, DANCING...

IMAGINE EARTH IDIOTS DOING **SQUARE DANCE**! THEM CRAZY!

THEM SHOULD DO **CIRCLE DANCE** LIKE **US**!!

TO PUT IT MILDLY, THEIR AUTO RACES ARE... **PECULIAR**...

CONGRATULATIONS! YOU WIN RACE! TROPHY AM YOURS BECAUSE YOU CAME IN **LAST**!

AND WHEN THEY TAKE **BATHS**...

MUCH BETTER TO USE **DIRT** THAN WATER! NOT **WET**!

BIZARRO WORLD TELEVISION COMMERCIALS ARE QUITE **DIFFERENT** FROM OURS...

DON'T USE MY SPONSOR'S PRODUCT! ME TRIED IT! UGH! IT AM **AWFUL**!

MALE **BIZARROS** SHOW THEIR RESPECT FOR **BIZARRO** WOMEN IN THE STRANGEST WAYS...

ME GALLANTLY PULL CHAIR OUT FROM UNDER HER!

NOW ME KNOW HIM AM REAL GENTLEMAN!

YES, THE THINKING OF THESE PITIFUL, YET POWERFUL CREATURES, IS CRAZILY SCRAMBLED...

SINCE IT AM EARLY IN MORNING, ME FLY AT SUPER-SPEED TO BUY TICKET FOR EVENING MOVIE SO ME WON'T BE LATE FOR SHOW!

NOW SHOWING

ADMISSHUN PRICCES...
AFTERNOON ZHOW—2 PIECES COAL
KNITE ZHOW—1 PIECE COAL

TICXETS

AND NOW LET US LOOK IN ON THE **NUMBER ONE BIZARRO FAMILY**, ON MAY 24, WHEN THEY CELEBRATE HALLOWEEN...

HA, HA! ME PUT ON SCARY MASK OF MICKEY MANTLE, THEN JOIN MY BUDDY-PALS!

MAYE

16	5	24 HALLOWENE	3	9	12
7	31	14	6		5
29	2	8		19	
10	1			27	

BIZARRO 1

ME SURE WILL!

BIZARRO NO. 1

HAVE FUN PULLING HALLOWEEN PRANKS, DARLING!

SHORTLY, AS THE **IDIOT OF STEEL** JOINS HIS MASK-WEARING FRIENDS...

HELLO, **BIZARRO NO. 1**! ME LOOK LIKE MARILYN MONROE! GRUESOME, EH?

A JERRY LEWIS MASK! **URK!**

WHAT AN AWFUL MICKEY MANTLE MASK! YIIIIII!

BIZARRO NO. 1

YES...ON THE DAFFY **BIZARRO WORLD**, IT'S THE **ADULTS**, NOT THE KIDS, WHO COMMIT HALLOWEEN MISCHIEF!

YOW-WWW! EARTH MONSTERS!

RUN! RUN!

US SURE AM SCARING EVERYBODY! HA, HA!

BIZARRO NO. 1

3

NEXT, THE FUNSTERS RING DOORBELLS...

HELP! EEEEE!

HA, HA! US FOOLED YOU! US AM REALLY GOOD-LOOKING BIZARROS, WEARING FALSE MASKS OF UGLY EARTH PEOPLE!

As the masked pranksters continue their holiday mischief...

STOP watering my lawn, you vandals!

HA, HA! BOY, AM **HE** HAPPY!

Soon, at another broken-down **BIZARRO** house...

WHY YOU IMPS REPAIR MY BEAUTIFUL ROOF? GO AWAY!

HA, HA! US KNEW SHE WOULD HATE US FOR FIXING HOLES IN HER ROOF!

Presently, outside **BIZARRO NO.1**'s home...

SH-HH! MY PET **BIZARRO-KRYPTO** AM FAST ASLEEP! ME PLAY TERRIFIC PRANK ON HIM WITH COLD DOGS ME HID IN CAPE'S POUCH!...HERE, TAKE THIS BOX MADE OF IMPERFECT LEAD!

HA, HA! THIS GOING BE FUNNIER THAN WHEN EARTH KIDS TIE CANS TO A DOG'S TAIL...OOPS—MY MASK FALL OFF AND **BIZARRO-KRYPTO** AM WAKING UP!

??—WHAT AM MY MASTER DOING?

BIZARRO-KRYPTO, TOAST THEM COLD DOGS WITH **HEAT VISION,** OR ME OPEN LEAD BOX! RADIATIONS FROM **BLUE KRYPTONITE** INSIDE CAN KILL YOU, THOUGH THEM CAN'T HURT US LADY **BIZARROS!**

ME MUST DO LIKE SHE SAY!

HA, HA, HA, HA!

NOW **EAT THEM** DELICIOUS HOT DOGS!

HOW **CRUEL** THEM ARE!—¡CHOKE¡—MY MASTER AM HELPING HIS PALS PULL MEAN PRANK ON ME!— ¡SNIFF!¡... ¡SOB!¡

4

US GO PULL MORE HALLOWEEN PRANKS!

¡CHOKE!— ME NOT LOVE **BIZARRO NO.1** ANYMORE! ME GET NEW MASTER WHO APPRECIATE WHAT A SWELL DOG ME AM!

AND **BIZARRO-KRYPTO** DOES INDEED SOON FIND A NEW HOME...

OH, HOW DARLINGLY STUPID YOU LOOK! BE MY PET!

BIZARRO-LANA LANG LIKE ME! ME ADOPT HER!

SHORTLY, INSIDE...

ME NOT HUNGRY, SO IT'S TIME TO EAT! ME MAKE MEAL FOR US OVER KITCHEN BONFIRE! IMAGINE DUMB EARTH PEOPLE USING **OVENS**! HA, HA!

SOMEONE KNOCKING IN DOOR! **BIZARRO-LANA** GOT COMPANY!

THE CALLER IS A **BIZARRO** SUITOR...AND, AS IS THE CUSTOM ON THIS KOOKY WORLD, THE GIRLS GIVE GIFTS TO **BOYS**...!

FOR **ME**?!... GOSH, THANKS! THESE STINKWEEDS SMELL LOVELY... LIKE GARBAGE!

SECOND GIFT EVEN **BETTER**!!

INSIDE THIS BOX OF IMPERFECT LEAD AM GIFT OF **BLUE KRYPTONITE**!

AWRK! IT C-CAN KILL ME!!

5

TOSSING AWAY HIS GIFT, THE SUITOR FLEES...

ME NOT WANT IT! GOODBYE FOREVER!

ME ONLY WANTED TO DESTROY YOU TO **PROVE MY LOVE**!—¡SOB!!

GOOD RIDDANCE! HIM NOT **WORTHY** OF SUCH GREAT LOVE!!

PROMPTLY FORGETTING HER SHATTERED ROMANCE, **BIZARRO-LANA LANG** FINISHES PREPARING THE MEAL--BUT TO HER DOG'S ANGUISH...

HOW SELFISH SHE AM! SHE EATING THEM **DELICIOUS SCRAPS** AND EXPECTS ME TO EAT THIS JUICY **SIRLOIN STEAK!** WELL, **ME WON'T DO IT!**

PHOOIE ON HER! SHE BIG DISAPPOINTMENT TO ME! ME FIND ANOTHER MASTER, ONE WHO TRULY DESERVE A LAZY, GOOD-FOR-NOTHING **BIZARRO** MUTT LIKE ME!

SUDDENLY **BIZARRO-KLTPZYXM**, WHO IS A **GOOD BIZARRO** VERSION OF THE MISCHIEVOUS 5TH DIMENSIONAL IMP, **MR. MXYZPTLK**, STREAKS IN...

HI, **BIZARRO-KRYPTO!** ME KNOW WHAT MAKES YOU SAD! ME WILL BECOME YOUR NEW MASTER!

BEHOLD, ME USE MY MAGIC TO CAUSE MONSTER PLAYMATES TO POP INTO EXISTENCE! ENJOY YOURSELF PLAYING WITH THEM!

AT LAST! A NEW MASTER WHO GOT MY BEST INTERESTS AT HEART! HOW LUCKY ME AM!!

POP

POP

POP

DELIGHTED, THE **MUTT OF STEEL** ROMPS WITH THE MATERIALIZED CREATURES...

HA, HA, HA! FIRE-BREATHING CHUM TRYING TO GIVE ME HOTFOOT, NOT KNOWING FLAMES CAN'T BOTHER ME!

6

BUT AS **BIZARRO-KRYPTO** PLAYFULLY RESPONDS TO THE FIRE-BREATH WITH HIS OWN **HEAT VISION**...

HIM BURN UP! ME NOT KNOW MY RAYS WOULD BE **TOO** MIGHTY FOR HIM!

As another "PLAYMATE" blasts away at the BIZARRO pooch with its ultra-frigid breath...

EVERYTHING HIM BREATHING AT, FREEZE... EXCEPT ME! —≩CHOKE≨— NOW ME SHOW HIM WHAT ME CAN DO WITH MY BREATH!

But as BIZARRO-KRYPTO puffs with his SUPER-BREATH...

UH-OH! HIM BEING BLOWN INTO OUTER SPACE! ME FORGET MY OWN STRENGTH! WELL, THAT END OF HIM!

OH, WELL! ME STILL GOT ANOTHER PLAYMATE! HIM KNOCKING DOWN BIG TREES! HIM NOT ONLY SUPER-STRONG, HIM GOT EXTRA-HARD HEAD! WHAT A NICE, FRIENDLY CREATURE!

But as the BIZARRO dog's "FRIEND" deliberately rams into the invulnerable BIZARRO-KRYPTO...

WHAT A SHAME! HIM MET HEAD HARDER THAN HIS... NAMELY MINE! HIM EXPLODING! AH--SO! HIM HAD A FINE HEAD ON HIM!

Presently...

PLAYMATES ALL GONE! ME LONESOME!

BIZARRO-KRYPTO NEEDS AN ANIMAL PLAYMATE WHO AM STRONG LIKE HIMSELF! HM-MM! ME KNOW WHO TO GET! ME USE MY MAGIC TO MATERIALIZE AN ANIMAL PLAYMATE TOO STRONG FOR HIM TO DESTROY!

Simultaneously, on earth, as SUPERMAN'S SUPER-PET KRYPTO... THE VERY DOG OF WHOM BIZARRO-KRYPTO IS AN IMPERFECT IMITATION... IS FLYING OVER METROPOLIS...

≩GASP!≨ LOOK! KRYPTO IS... VANISHING!!

7

A SPLIT-INSTANT LATER...

?! --HOLY CATS! I--I'M NOW ON THAT CRAZY **BIZARRO WORLD** I VISITED ONCE BEFORE!

SUDDENLY, AS THE TWO **DOGS** OF **STEEL** MEET, THEY SENSE EACH OTHER'S THOUGHTS...

CHEAP, ROTTEN IMITATION!

NO ONE CAN **FLATTER** ME AND GET AWAY WITH IT! ME FIX YOU, EARTH FREAK!

OH, NO, THEM FIGHTING! ME THOUGHT THEM BE **GLAD** TO SEE EACH OTHER, LIKE REUNITED TWINS!

STOP!!

HA, HA! **BIZARRO WORLD** AM GOING TO THE DOGS!

AM THEM BUZZARDS?

AM THEM CHOO-CHOO TRAINS??

NO, THEM AM... AM...! OH, WHO CARES?!

UNEXPECTEDLY...

OW-WW!...GIFT BOX **BIZARRO-LANA'S** BOY-FRIEND THREW AWAY DROPPED **HERE** AND **BLUE KRYPTONITE** CHUNK FELL OUT!

THAT **BLUE KRYPTONITE'S** NOT HURTING ME, BUT IT'S AFFECTING **HIM** THE WAY **GREEN KRYPTONITE** WOULD HARM ME!

AOWRRR-RR!

HM-MM! THOUGH HE WAS SCRAPPING WITH ME, I FEEL SORRY FOR THE PATHETIC THING! I JUST CAN'T STAND IDLY BY AND WATCH HIM DIE, AND SO...

8

128

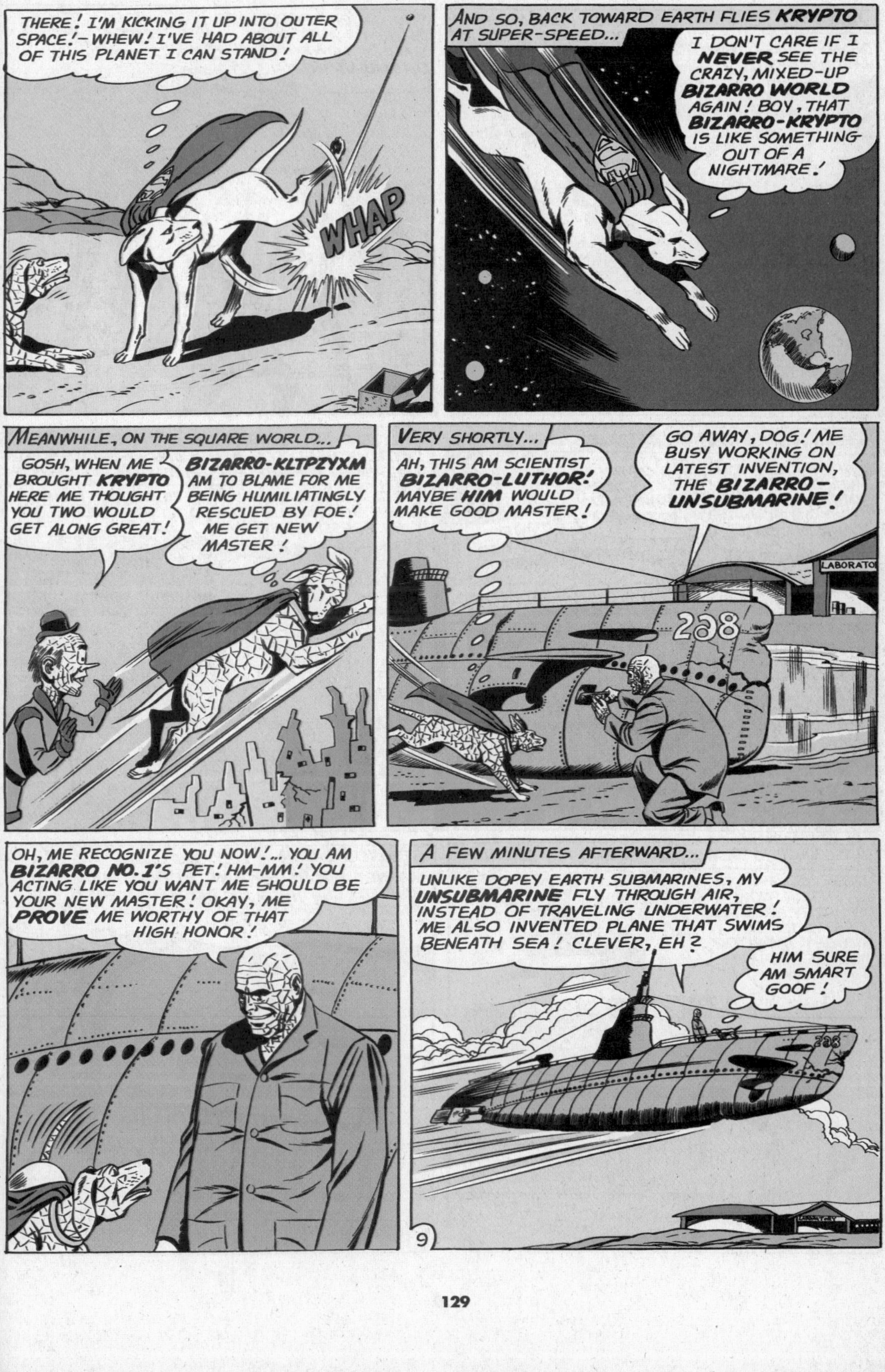
THERE! I'M KICKING IT UP INTO OUTER SPACE!–WHEW! I'VE HAD ABOUT ALL OF THIS PLANET I CAN STAND!
WHAP
AND SO, BACK TOWARD EARTH FLIES KRYPTO AT SUPER-SPEED...
I DON'T CARE IF I NEVER SEE THE CRAZY, MIXED-UP BIZARRO WORLD AGAIN! BOY, THAT BIZARRO-KRYPTO IS LIKE SOMETHING OUT OF A NIGHTMARE!
MEANWHILE, ON THE SQUARE WORLD...
GOSH, WHEN ME BROUGHT KRYPTO HERE ME THOUGHT YOU TWO WOULD GET ALONG GREAT!
BIZARRO-KLTPZYXM AM TO BLAME FOR ME BEING HUMILIATINGLY RESCUED BY FOE! ME GET NEW MASTER!
VERY SHORTLY...
AH, THIS AM SCIENTIST BIZARRO-LUTHOR! MAYBE HIM WOULD MAKE GOOD MASTER!
GO AWAY, DOG! ME BUSY WORKING ON LATEST INVENTION, THE BIZARRO-UNSUBMARINE!
LABORATO
238
OH, ME RECOGNIZE YOU NOW!... YOU AM BIZARRO NO.1'S PET! HM-MM! YOU ACTING LIKE YOU WANT ME SHOULD BE YOUR NEW MASTER! OKAY, ME PROVE ME WORTHY OF THAT HIGH HONOR!
A FEW MINUTES AFTERWARD...
UNLIKE DOPEY EARTH SUBMARINES, MY UNSUBMARINE FLY THROUGH AIR, INSTEAD OF TRAVELING UNDERWATER! ME ALSO INVENTED PLANE THAT SWIMS BENEATH SEA! CLEVER, EH?
HIM SURE AM SMART GOOF!
9

ABRUPTLY...

OH, MY! GREAT INVENTION AM CONKING OUT!

NEVER FEAR! WITH FIRST-CLASS IDIOT LIKE ME AROUND, EVERY — THING SOON BE OKAY!

KLONK!

PLONK...

SQUEEONK!

YOU CAUGHT PERISCOPE IN TEETH AND AM SAFELY LOWERING UNSUBMARINE!

WHY NOT?!

PRESENTLY, IN BIZARRO-LUTHOR'S LAB...

NOW ME SHOW YOU MORE OF MY INVENTIONS!...LOOK! THEM BIZARRO-LOISES ARMED WITH UNSUPER-RAY GUNS AM GONNA ROB BIZARRO BANK OF COAL!

SNOOPY MONITOR

LAST NASHUNAL BANK

THAT'S RIGHT, FOLKS! ON THE BIZARRO WORLD, COAL IS USED FOR MONEY...AND FEMALES ARE THE MOST DANGEROUS CRIMINALS, INSTEAD OF MALES...

ME STOP THEM HOLDING UP BANK, BY PRESSING BUTTON!

HOW THAT GOING TO FOIL CROOKS??

IN RESPONSE TO THE BIZARRO SCIENTIST'S SIGNAL...

THERE GO MY INVENTION! NOW US HURRY BACK INTO LAB, WATCH MY SNOOPY MONITOR, AND SEE WHAT HAPPEN!

GEE, THIS EVEN MORE EXCITING THAN CHASING MYSELF!!

10

SECONDS LATER...

SEE? MY GIANT MAGNET HOLDS UP BANK BEFORE GIRL BANDITS CAN HOLD UP THE BANK! SINCE BIZARRO FEMALES CAN'T FLY, THEM CAN'T STREAK UP AFTER BANK!

LAST NASHUNAL BANK

YES, ON THIS KOOKY WORLD, BIZARRO-LUTHOR, IS GOOD, AND UNLIKE THE REAL LUTHOR, BATTLES CRIME!

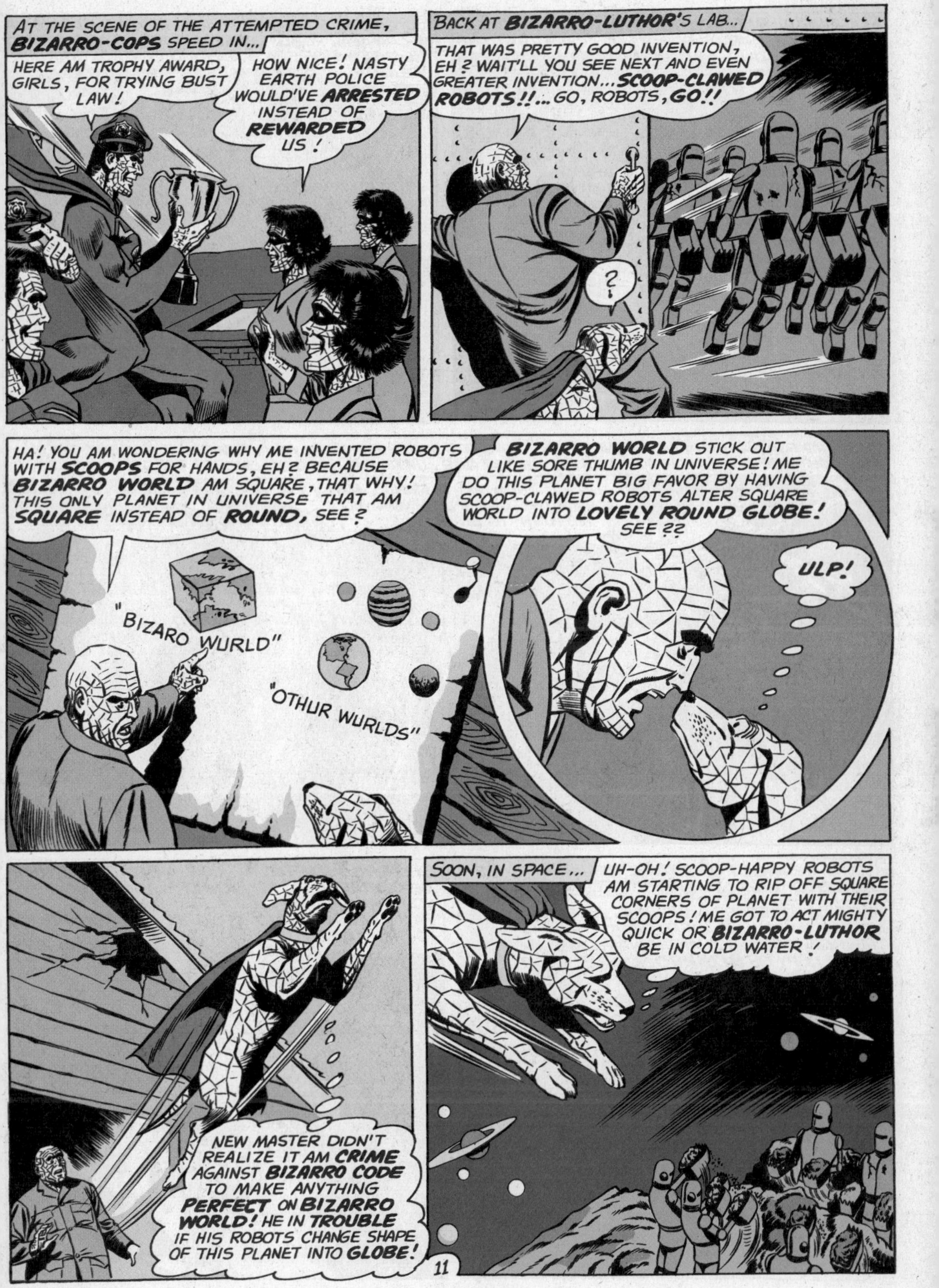
AT THE SCENE OF THE ATTEMPTED CRIME, BIZARRO-COPS SPEED IN...
HERE AM TROPHY AWARD, GIRLS, FOR TRYING BUST LAW!
HOW NICE! NASTY EARTH POLICE WOULD'VE ARRESTED INSTEAD OF REWARDED US!
BACK AT BIZARRO-LUTHOR'S LAB...
THAT WAS PRETTY GOOD INVENTION, EH? WAIT'LL YOU SEE NEXT AND EVEN GREATER INVENTION... SCOOP-CLAWED ROBOTS!!... GO, ROBOTS, GO!!
?
HA! YOU AM WONDERING WHY ME INVENTED ROBOTS WITH SCOOPS FOR HANDS, EH? BECAUSE BIZARRO WORLD AM SQUARE, THAT WHY! THIS ONLY PLANET IN UNIVERSE THAT AM SQUARE INSTEAD OF ROUND, SEE?
"BIZARO WURLD"
"OTHUR WURLDS"
BIZARRO WORLD STICK OUT LIKE SORE THUMB IN UNIVERSE! ME DO THIS PLANET BIG FAVOR BY HAVING SCOOP-CLAWED ROBOTS ALTER SQUARE WORLD INTO LOVELY ROUND GLOBE! SEE??
ULP!
NEW MASTER DIDN'T REALIZE IT AM CRIME AGAINST BIZARRO CODE TO MAKE ANYTHING PERFECT ON BIZARRO WORLD! HE IN TROUBLE IF HIS ROBOTS CHANGE SHAPE OF THIS PLANET INTO GLOBE!
SOON, IN SPACE...
UH-OH! SCOOP-HAPPY ROBOTS AM STARTING TO RIP OFF SQUARE CORNERS OF PLANET WITH THEIR SCOOPS! ME GOT TO ACT MIGHTY QUICK OR BIZARRO-LUTHOR BE IN COLD WATER!
11

FLASHING IN, **BIZARRO-KRYPTO** CRASHES INTO THE DOUBLE LINE OF ROBOTS, QUICKER THAN THE EYE CAN FOLLOW...

MOVE OVER-- GET GOING!!

SO GREAT IS THE IMPACT THAT THE DUAL FLANKS OF MECHANICAL ROBOT DIGGERS HURTLE FAR OUT INTO THE DEPTHS OF SPACE, BEYOND CONTROL OF THEIR CREATOR...

BACK AND FORTH, THEN FORTH AND BACK, MOVE THE SCOOP-HANDS IN AN AUTOMATIC MOVEMENT THAT WILL CONTINUE ON AND ON FOR CENTURIES TO COME, UNTIL THE ROBOTS' ENERGY TUBES GO DEAD...

HA, HA! THEM AM PLAYING... **PATTY-CAKE!** -- CHUCKLE NOW ME RETURN TO MASTER!

AND AS THE **MUTT OF STEEL** RETURNS TO THE **BIZARRO WORLD**...

WATCHING TELESCOPIC VIEWER-SCREEN, ME SAW YOU FLY AT MY ROBOTS--THEN THEM DISAPPEARED! AFTERWARD, ME FOUND COPY OF **BIZARRO-CODE** WHICH EXPLAIN EVERYTHING!!

BIZARRO CODE

BIZARRO-KRYPTO, ME GRATEFUL TO YOU! MIND IF ME PAT YOU ON HEAD TO SHOW GRATITUDE?

HOW **KIND** HIM AM! SIGH

BIZARRO-LUTHOR, THAT DOG MUST LEAVE YOU **FOREVER!!**

12

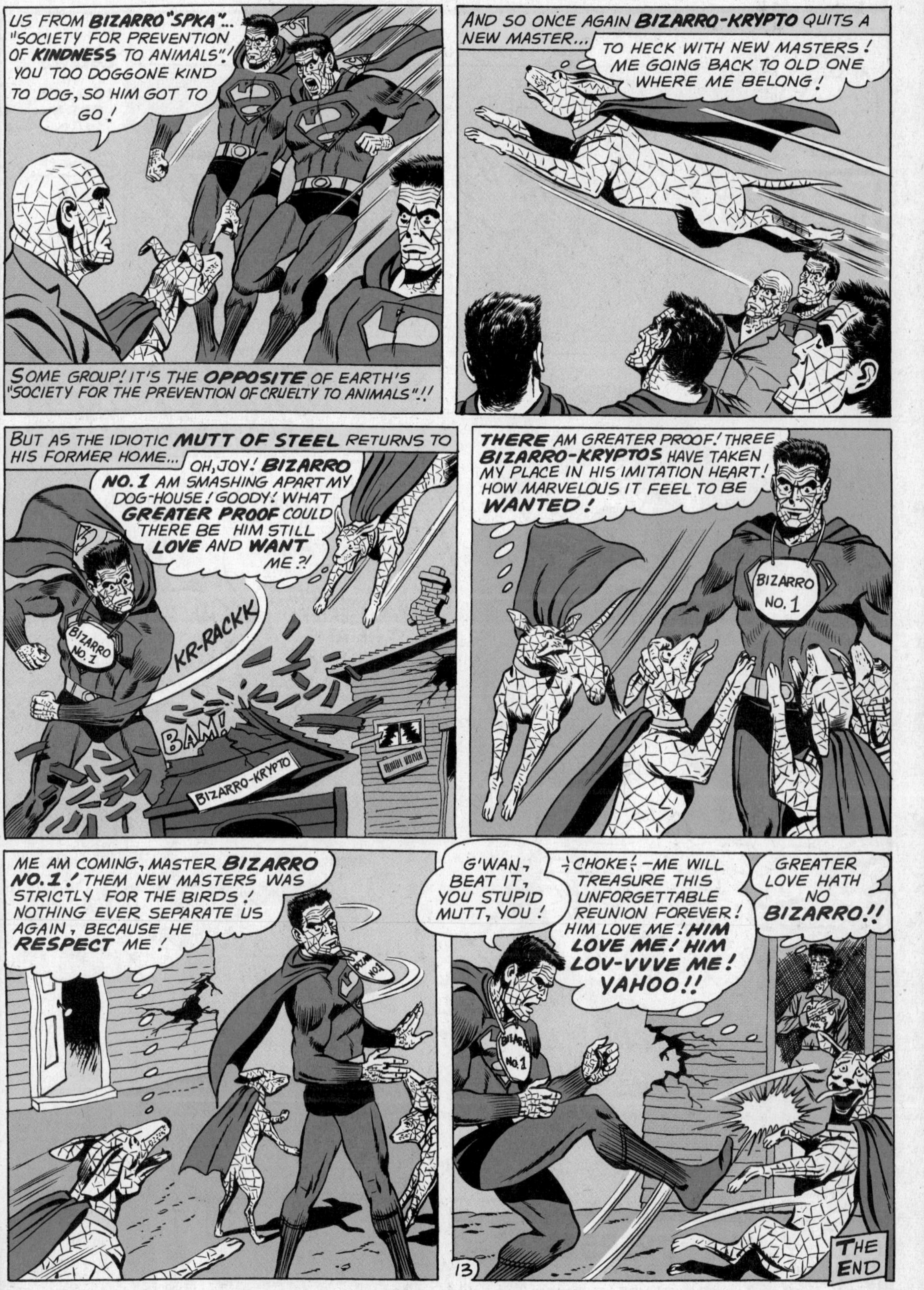
US FROM BIZARRO "SPKA"... "SOCIETY FOR PREVENTION OF KINDNESS TO ANIMALS"! YOU TOO DOGGONE KIND TO DOG, SO HIM GOT TO GO!
SOME GROUP! IT'S THE OPPOSITE OF EARTH'S "SOCIETY FOR THE PREVENTION OF CRUELTY TO ANIMALS"!!
AND SO ONCE AGAIN BIZARRO-KRYPTO QUITS A NEW MASTER...
TO HECK WITH NEW MASTERS! ME GOING BACK TO OLD ONE WHERE ME BELONG!
BUT AS THE IDIOTIC MUTT OF STEEL RETURNS TO HIS FORMER HOME...
OH, JOY! BIZARRO NO. 1 AM SMASHING APART MY DOG-HOUSE! GOODY! WHAT GREATER PROOF COULD THERE BE HIM STILL LOVE AND WANT ME?!
BIZARRO NO. 1
KR-RACKK
BAM!
BIZARRO-KRYPTO
THERE AM GREATER PROOF! THREE BIZARRO-KRYPTOS HAVE TAKEN MY PLACE IN HIS IMITATION HEART! HOW MARVELOUS IT FEEL TO BE WANTED!
BIZARRO NO. 1
ME AM COMING, MASTER BIZARRO NO. 1! THEM NEW MASTERS WAS STRICTLY FOR THE BIRDS! NOTHING EVER SEPARATE US AGAIN, BECAUSE HE RESPECT ME!
G'WAN, BEAT IT, YOU STUPID MUTT, YOU!
-CHOKE- -ME WILL TREASURE THIS UNFORGETTABLE REUNION FOREVER! HIM LOVE ME! HIM LOVE ME! HIM LOV-VVVE ME! YAHOO!!
GREATER LOVE HATH NO BIZARRO!!
BIZARRO NO. 1
13
THE END

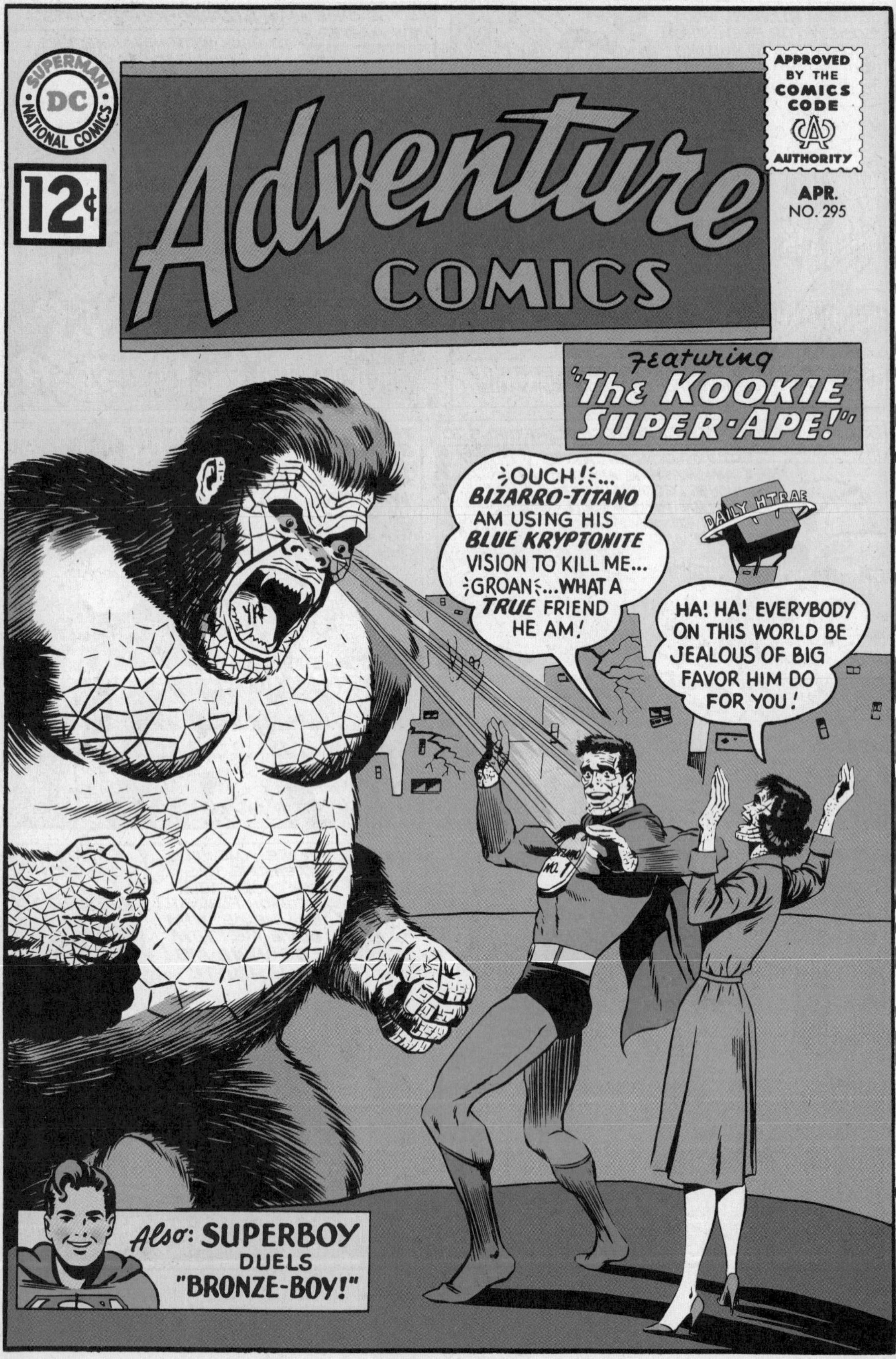
SUPERMAN
DC
NATIONAL COMICS
12¢
Adventure
COMICS
APPROVED BY THE COMICS CODE AUTHORITY
APR.
NO. 295
Featuring "The KOOKIE SUPER-APE!"
OUCH!... BIZARRO-TITANO AM USING HIS BLUE KRYPTONITE VISION TO KILL ME... GROAN... WHAT A TRUE FRIEND HE AM!
DAILY HTRAE
HA! HA! EVERYBODY ON THIS WORLD BE JEALOUS OF BIG FAVOR HIM DO FOR YOU!
BIZARRO NO. 1
Also: SUPERBOY DUELS "BRONZE-BOY!"

TALES of the BIZARRO WORLD

There comes a time in every married man's life when he has to exercise his noodle to help his wife out during a crisis! The same is true on the zany **BIZARRO WORLD**, as dim-witted **BIZARRO NO.1** finds out when his wife, **BIZARRO-LOIS NO.1**, is in danger of being exiled from their crazy planet! However, since everything is whackily mixed up on the **BIZARRO WORLD**, the things **BIZARRO NO.1** dreams up to help his wife are hilariously insane! You'll giggle, you'll howl, you'll flip and yell "UNCLE" when you read how the **IDIOT OF STEEL** enlists the unwitting aid of...

The KOOKIE SUPER-APE!

WHAT SWELL HUSBAND YOU AM! YOU CREATED A **BIZARRO-TITANO** SO HIM COULD WIN WRESTLING CHAMPIONSHIP TITLE AWAY FROM ME! THANK YOU TOO MUCH!

THINK NOTHING OF IT, SOUR-PIE! ME LOVE YOU SO MUCH, THERE AM **NOTHING** IN **BIZARRO WORLD** ME WOULD DO FOR YOU!

BIZARRO LOIS NO. 1

WAY, WAY, WAY, WAY, **WAY OUT** IN THE UNIVERSE EXISTS THE KOOKIEST PLANET IN THE ENTIRE COSMOS...IT IS THE **SQUARE BIZARRO WORLD**, INHABITED BY STRANGE CREATURES WHO ARE IMPERFECT DUPLICATES OF **SUPERMAN**, LOIS LANE, AND OTHER **METROPOLIS** CHARACTERS...

EVERYTHING ON THIS PLANET IS COMPLETELY ZANY, AND ITS DIM-WITTED DENIZENS THINK THE **REVERSE** OF EARTH PEOPLE! FOR INSTANCE, ON **VETERAN'S DAY**, INSTEAD OF OBSERVING A **MINUTE OF SILENCE**...

EVERYBODY MAKING LOUD NOISE FOR ONE MINUTE!

YAHOO!

B-LLEEURPP

ON THE **BIZARRO WORLD**, INSTEAD OF THE MAIL-MAN GIVING **YOU** MAIL, **YOU** GIVE IT TO **HIM**...!

HA, HA! IMAGINE DUMB EARTH MAILMEN **DELIVERING** MAIL, INSTEAD OF **GETTING** IT! HOW NUTTY CAN YOU GET??

IF A **BIZARRO** WANTS GOOD FORTUNE...

EVERYTHING GOING BE OKAY NOW, SOURHEART! BREAKING MIRROR WILL BRING ME **SEVEN YEARS GOOD LUCK!!**

OH, GOODY!

ON EARTH, WE CELEBRATE "**FIRE PREVENTION WEEK**," BUT ON THE WORLD OF **BIZARROS**, THEY CELEBRATE THE SAME WEEK **DIFFERENTLY**...

SINCE THIS AM "**FIRE-STARTING WEEK**" US BURN DOWN FORESTS WITH **HEAT VISION!**

ME SPRINKLE GASOLINE ON FLAMES! ¡CHUCKLE!

GASOLINE

EARTH WOMEN PATRONIZE **BEAUTY PARLORS**--HOW-EVER, **BIZARRO** MEN GO TO..."**UGLY PARLORS**"...

MORE MUD ON FACE, PLEASE! ME WANT TO LOOK **HANDSOME!**

OKAY! WHEN US FINISHED, YOU BE **MESS!** YOU THANK US!

MUD

2

AND IN THE WELL-DECORATED **BIZARRO** HOME, **RUGS** ARE PUT ON THE CEILINGS AND **WALLPAPER** IS PUT ON THE FLOORS!

RUG ON CEILING NEVER WEAR OUT!

WALLPAPER ON FLOOR AM... **PRACTICAL!**

AND WHEN EASTER ARRIVES ON THE **BIZARRO WORLD...**

HA, HA, HA! RABBITS LOOKING FOR **SQUARE** EGGS **US** HID!

ON EARTH, RABBITS HIDE THE EGGS AND **KIDS** DO SEARCHING!

NOW LET'S LOOK AT A CRAZILY-LEANING STRUCTURE ON THIS INSANE WORLD... IS IT A **TREASURE-HOUSE** WHERE DISCARDED CHEWING WADS ARE HOARDED? IS IT AN **ART MUSEUM** WHERE **EMPTY** PICTURE FRAMES ARE PROUDLY HUNG AND EXHIBITED? NO...!!

BIZARRO CITY UNSPORTSMANSHIP ARENA

...IT'S THE **BIZARRO CITY UNSPORTSMANSHIP ARENA** --AND AT THIS VERY MOMENT, INSIDE ITS FIVE-SIDED RING...

WOW!"SNEAKY LANA" AND "TRICKY LOIS-NO.1" AM PUTTING UP GOOD FIGHT FOR WRESTLING CHAMPIONSHIP!

HEY, REFEREE! ME GOT COMPLAINT! **BIZARRO-LANE** HASN'T KICKED MY FACE IN LAST TWO SECONDS!

DON'T BOTHER ME! --SOB!--ME AM READING MY FAVORITE COMIC BOOK... WHICH ALWAYS MAKES ME **CRY!**

PECULIARLY, THE CHOICE RINGSIDE SEATS ARE FILLED WITH **BIZARROS** WHO HAVE LITTLE WEALTH...

BAH! -- WE GOT **WORST SEATS** IN ARENA!

SOME DAY, DARLING, US'LL AFFORD TO SIT IN LAST ROWS WITH THEM **RICH BIZARROS!**

3

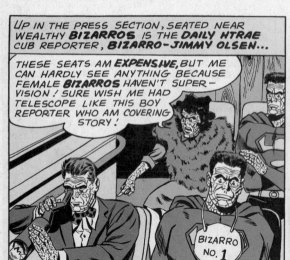

UP IN THE PRESS SECTION, SEATED NEAR WEALTHY *BIZARROS* IS THE *DAILY HTRAE* CUB REPORTER, *BIZARRO-JIMMY OLSEN*...

THESE SEATS AM *EXPENSIVE*, BUT ME CAN HARDLY SEE ANYTHING BECAUSE FEMALE *BIZARROS* HAVEN'T SUPER-VISION! SURE WISH ME HAD TELESCOPE LIKE THIS BOY REPORTER WHO AM COVERING STORY!

BIZARRO NO. 1

YES, THAT'S *BIZARRO NO.1* SEATED NEXT TO HIS FRIEND, *BIZARRO-JIMMY*, WHO IS ALSO NON-SUPER! "NO.1" IS THE *BIZARRO WORLD'S* LEADER AND IS THE HUSBAND OF *BIZARRO-LOIS NO.1*...

÷CHOKE÷---WHAT'LL "*SNEAKY LANA*" D-DO NEXT TO MY WIFE?

BIZARRO NO. 1

YESSIREE, FOLKS, EVERYBODY WONDERING WHAT "*SNEAKY LANA*" NEXT PULL ON "*TRICKY LOIS NO.1*! WILL LANA USE "*HAMMER-UNLOCK HOLD*"... OR "*1½ NELSON GRIP*"?!

ME DREAMED UP SOMETHING EVEN SNEAKIER!

ME USE... "*TICKLE-HOLD*"!

GAA! ME CAN'T *STAND* IT! HA, HA, HA!-REFEREE! MAKE HER *STOP*-- HA, HA!

SHUT UP! SOB, SOB! ME NOW READING MOST *PATHETIC*, HEARTBREAKING PART OF FUNNY BOOK!

OH, BOY! "*TRICKY LOIS*" ESCAPED FROM *TICKLE-HOLD* AND GRABBED *LANA'S* HAIR!-*WAIT!!*"*SNEAKY-LANA*" HAS SNUCK SCISSORS OUT OF BELT AND AM CUTTING HER OWN HAIR! WHAT AM HER STRATEGY ??...*URK!!*-L-LOIS AM *FALLING!!*

"*TRICKY LOIS*" BANGED HER HEAD ON RING FLOOR...GOT KNOCKED OUT! SHE *WIN*... LOIS AM *NEW* CHAMPION!! HOW SMART OF LANA!

BOO, LOIS!!

YEA, LANA!!

THAT'S RIGHT! ON THIS WHACKY WORLD, A *BIZARRO* WHO GETS KNOCKED OUT *WINS* THE FIGHT! AND WINNERS ARE HELD IN *DISGRACE!*

LATER, IN THE HOME OF THE **NUMBER ONE BIZARRO FAMILY,** AS THEY DINE ON A **SUPPER** OF CORNFLAKES AND MILK, WHICH IS A TYPICAL EARTH **BREAKFAST...**

HA, HA, HA, HA-AAAAA!

WHY YOU SO **SAD?**

WHY **SHOULDN'T** ME BE SAD, HA, HA? ME RUINED, NO? EVERYONE HATE A WINNER, YES? ACCORDING TO LAW, IF ME NOT LOSE WRESTLING CHAMPIONSHIP TO SOMEBODY IN 30 DAYS, ME BE EXILED FROM **BIZARRO WORLD** TO...‹UGH!›... EARTH!

GEE, DAD, INSTEAD OF JUST SITTING HERE EATING YOUR MILK AND DRINKING YOUR CORNFLAKES, WHY DON'T YOU **DO** SOMETHING, YOU **BIG APE!**

"BIG APE"!...‹GASP!› **BIZARRO JUNIOR NO. 1,** YOU JUST GAVE ME WONDERFUL IDEA!!

ME **REWARD** YOU, BY MAKING YOU STAND FACING CORNER!

THIS GREAT FUN!...‹CHUCKLE!› LAST TIME, YOU FORGOT AND LEFT ME FACING CORNER A **WHOLE MONTH!**

DEPARTING HASTILY, THE LEADER OF THE **BIZARROS** STREAKS TO HIS DESERT SANCTUM ON THE **BIZARRO WORLD...**

HOT ZIGGETY CAT!! -- FIRST, ME TUNE IN ON PREHISTORIC EARTH WITH MY **TIMESKOPE!**

FOURTRISS UV BIZARRO

SECONDS LATER, INSIDE THE FORTRESS...

AH... **TIMESKOPE** HAVE LOCATED GIANT APE **TITANO** ME ONCE MET IN PAST WHEN ME TRAVELED THROUGH TIME-BARRIER! HIM USE **GREEN KRYPTONITE** VISION WHEN ANGRY!

NEXT...

NOW ME SHINING IMPERFECT **DUPLICATOR RAY** AT **TIME-SKOPE** SCREEN! RAY WILL MATERIALIZE A **BIZARRO-TITANO** HERE IN FORTRESS!!

A SPLIT-MOMENT AFTERWARD...

OOLP! ME FORGOT HOW **BIG** HIM'D BE! FORTRESS AM WRECKED! —OH, WELL! EASY GO, EASY COME!

FORTRESS OF BIZARRO

PRESENTLY, AS **BIZARRO'S** MATE DRIVES CURIOUSLY TOWARD THE SANCTUM...

GREAT FRANKENSTEIN! WHO AM YOU FLYING, DEAR?

MEET MY BUDDY-PAL, **BIZARRO-TITANO!** HANDSOME, ISN'T HIM?

BUT AS THE **IDIOT OF STEEL** ALIGHTS...

¡GASP!¿ HIM SH-SHINING **BLUE KRYPTONITE** VISION AT YOU! HOW COME?

IMPERFECT **DUPLICATOR RAY** CHANGED **TITANO'S GREEN KRYPTONITE** VISION INTO **BLUE KRYPTONITE VISION** IN **BIZARRO-TITANO!** THAT DEADLY TO ME! —OWW!

¡OUCH!¿ —HIM KILLING ME! —¿GROAN¿...WHAT A **TRUE** FRIEND HIM AM!

HA, HA! EVERYBODY BE JEALOUS OF BIG FAVOR HIM DO YOU!

LUCKILY, **BLUE KRYPTONITE** DON'T BOTHER ME BECAUSE ME AM IMPERFECT DUPLICATE OF EARTH GIRL, LOIS LANE!

BIZARRO NO. 1

BIZARRO LOIS NO. 1

THOUGH WEAKENED, **BIZARRO NO. 1** MUSTERS ENOUGH SUPER-STRENGTH TO STOMP LIGHTLY ON THE BEAST'S BIG TOE...

¿¿ HIM NO LONGER SHINING **BLUE KRYPTONITE VISION** ON YOU!

BECAUSE ME HURTING HIS BIG TOE, **BIZARRO-TITANO** GET EVEN BY NOT TRYING KILL ME NO MORE!

6

FUN AM FUN... BUT WHY YOU NOT BUSY SAVING ME FROM BEING EXILED?

ME AM!! ACCORDING TO BIZARRO LAW, NOBODY CAN FIGHT YOU FOR WRESTLING CHAMPION-SHIP UNTIL THEM FIRST WIN THREE MATCHES AGAINST OTHER WRESTLERS!

ME HEREBY APPOINT MYSELF MANAGER OF SENSATIONAL NEW BIZARRO WORLD WRESTLER!-- PRESENTING..."THE BIG APE"!! --GET IT? ME BUILD HIM UP... SO HIM CAN BE MATCHED AGAINST YOU! HIM'LL WIN... BECOME NEW CHAMP... WHICH'LL SAVE YOUR REPUTATION!

ME SHOULD'VE KNOWN TRUE-BLUE YOU WOULD THINK OF SOME STUPID WAY TO SAVE ME! HOW LUCKY ME AM TO HAVE FIRST-CLASS IDIOT FOR HUSBAND!

HAW!-ON EARTH, WRESTLING NOT FIXED! BUT ME FIX WRESTLING HERE!

AT ONCE, BIZARRO NO.1 CONTACTS HIS YOUNG REPORTER CHUM...

BIZARRO-JIMMY, MEET "THE BIG APE"-- MY NEWEST WRESTLING FIND! HIM SUPERB STUMBLE-BUM... WILL TAKE ON ALL COMERS!

JEEPERS! WHAT A STORY!

SO SENSATIONAL IS THE NEWS FLASH THAT THE BIZARRO WORLD VERSION OF METROPOLIS' DAILY PLANET BURIES IT ON THE BACK PAGE... BECAUSE ONLY DULL STORIES MAKE THE FRONT PAGE...

PAGE 32

"BIG APE" AM MERELY GREATEST RASSLER THEM EVER WAS! HONEST!!

IN THE DAILY HTRAE EDITORIAL OFFICE, EDITOR BIZARRO-PERRY WHITE SOUNDS OFF...

LITTLE NAPOLEON'S GHOST! ME WANT MORE, MORE, MORE STORIES ABOUT "BIG APE," BIZARRO-JIMMY!

HERE COLD TIP, JIMMY! "BIG APE" LOVE BANANAS!

ME GOT PLOT!

LATER...

GOLLY, *BIZARRO NO. 1!!* THANKS FOR TELLING ME HOW TO GET IN GOOD WITH *"BIG APE"* SO ME CAN GET PUNK INTERVIEW!

IT'S JUST LIKE I TOLD YOU, KID! ...*BANANAS,* THE KEY TO THAT HAIRY FATHEAD'S HEART IS... *BANANAS!!*

BUT INSTEAD OF GIVING THE BANANAS TO *BIZARRO-TITANO,* AS IS NATURAL ON THIS MAD WORLD, *BIZARRO-JIMMY* EATS THEM *HIMSELF* AND TOSSES THE SKINS TO THE APE...

FEAST, *"BIG APE"!* BE MY GUEST!

OH, HOW THIS WILL MAKE *TITANO* LOVE ME!

NOW TO *FIX* MATCH BETWEEN *OLSEN-BIZARRO* AND *TITANO-BIZARRO* WITH PUFF OF SUPER-BREATH!

AND AS THE WILY *IDIOT OF STEEL* HAD FIGURED...

HA! BANANA PEELS, BLOWN UNDER APE'S FOOTSIES, AM DOING TRICK! HIM *FLOPPING!* GOOD! NOW TO OPEN MY BIG FAT MOUTH AND CREATE WRONG IMPRESSION ABOUT THIS HERE EVENT!

PWONKK

LOOK!! *"THE BIG APE"* GOT KNOCKED OUT BY MERE SKINNY YOUTH *BIZARRO-JIMMY!* AMN'T THAT *TERRIFIC??*

WOW, WHAT A WRESTLER!*"BIG APE"* AM *GREAT!*

FANTABULOUS!

SUPERFULOUS!

ME GREAT MANAGER! *"BIG APE"* WON FIRST MATCH! AFTER HE REVIVE, TWO MORE BOUTS TO GO-- THEN IT'LL BE *"BIG APE"* VS. *"TRICKY LOIS NO. 1"!*--ME MUST SAVE LOIS FROM EXILE AT ANY COST!--PROVIDING IT DON'T COST *TOO MUCH!*

A LITTLE LATER, IN *BIZARRO NO. 1'S* HOME...

OKAY, DADDY! ME WILL DO TO *"BIG APE"* JUST LIKE YOU SAY! BUT WHERE'LL *YOU* BE MEANWHILE?

IN A SEWER, NATURALLY! WHILE YOU FLY IN SKY, ME WILL FOLLOW YOU THROUGH *BIZARRO CITY* STORM DRAINS!

ME LOVE ME

8

SHORTLY, A STARTLING SIGHT IS SEEN IN THE CITY...

HA, HA! YOU AM PUSHOVER FOR MY FINGER-HOLD!!

YEEP!!

;GASP!; AM IT A BIRDHOUSE?

AM IT A PLANE JANE?

NO! IT AM LITTLE BIZARRO JUNIOR NO. 1!!

YIPES!— WHAT AN APE!! BEING KNOCKED OUT BY A BABY AM EVEN GREATER FEAT THAN BEING KNOCKED UNCONSCIOUS BY A BOY REPORTER!

"TRICKY LOIS NO. 1" BETTER WATCH OUT! THIS APE GOT TALENT!

BIZARRO-TITANO WON TWO MATCHES, SO FAR!

FIXING THEM TWO FIGHTS WAS A CINCH! BUT WHO'LL ME FIND WHO AM MEEK ENOUGH, MILD ENOUGH, COWARDLY AND SPINELESS ENOUGH TO DESERVE BEING PITTED NEXT AGAINST "THE BIG APE"?? HMM ... ME GOT IT! ME!!

WHAT UNIMAGINABLE SCHEME HAS BUBBLED UP FROM THE HOLLOW DEPTHS OF THE IDIOT OF STEEL'S PATHETIC INTELLECT? LET US WATCH AS HE CLIMBS FROM CONCEAL-MENT, THEN SLOWLY ADVANCES TOWARD THE "BIG APE," WHO IS RISING DAZEDLY...

OH, NO! THIS...THIS JUST CAN'T BE!; CHOKE, GASP!; RIGHT BEFORE THE EYES OF THE ONLOOKERS...

ME AM CHANGING PUBLICLY TO MY UNSECRET DUAL IDENTITY OF CLARK KENT! NO ONE AM MORE MEEK AND MILD THAN KENT!

BY GEORGE-- COME TO THINK OF IT-- SINCE BIZARRO NO. 1 IS SUPERMAN'S IMPERFECT DUPLICATE WHO DOES THINGS IN REVERSE, HE WOULD SWITCH IDENTITIES PUBLICLY, RATHER THAN PRIVATELY, AS THE MAN OF STEEL DOES...

NOW ME GENTLY USE FLYSWATTER-GRIP!

9

143

ONE INSTANT LATER...

WOW-EE-WOW!!

D-D-DID YOU S-SEE THAT?!—MEEK, MILD, WEAK CLARK KENT HAVE KNOCKED OUT "THE BIG APE"!

"BIG APE" HIM FABULOUS! HIM SURE TO BECOME NEW CHAMPION WRESTLER!

ME TELL LOIS!!

QUICKLY, BIZARRO NO. 1 FLIES HOME...

ME FIXED IT SO "BIG APE" BE MATCHED AGAINST YOU RIGHT AWAY!

WAIT! HIM SO STRONG, HIM WILL BEAT ME BLUE AND BLACK!... ME WILL REMAIN CHAMPION, AND BE EXILED!

HA, HA, HA! DON'T WORRY, SOUR-PIE! YOUR HUSBAND ...THAT ME!... HAVE FIGURED OUT SOLUTION TO YOUR PROBLEM! ME SURPRISE YOU!

WHAT CAN CUTE RASCAL'S BIG SURPRISE BE?

NEXT DAY, AS THRONGS POUR INTO THE ARENA TO WITNESS THE CHAMPIONSHIP MATCH...

WHAT YOU DOING WITH BOTTLE OF KNOCKOUT DROPS!

SINCE IT AM YOUR JOB, REFEREE, TO SEE THAT NOBODY FIGHT FAIR, ME WILL TELL YOU, HA, HA!

AS "BIG APE"'S MANAGER, ME GOING HAVE HIM SWALLOW THIS SO HIM FALL UNCONSCIOUS AND WIN FIGHT!

BRILLIANT!-- ER... YOU SURE THEM DROPS'LL WORK??

NOCKOUT DROPS

GURGLE, GURGLE, GURGLE! ME SWALLOW SOME AND FIND OUT!

IF YOU FAINT, US'LL KNOW DROPS AM OKAY!

10

MINUTES LATER...

SO HOW COME YOU NOT FALL ON FACE, YET?

;GROAN; --CAN BE ONLY ONE REASON!

BIZARRO N°1 NOCKOUT DROPS

GRR-RR! KNOCKOUT DROPS DON'T WORK!

SM-MASHH!

STUPIDLY, *BIZARRO NO.1* DOESN'T REALIZE THE KNOCKOUT DROPS CAN'T HARM *HIS* INVULNERABLE BODY... BUT *WOULD* AFFECT UNSUPER *BIZARRO-LOIS NO.1!*

SHORTLY...

THIS AM IT, FANS! *"THE BIG APE"* VS. *"TRICKY LOIS-NO.1"!* WILL CHAMPION WRESTLER *LOIS* WIN FIGHT AND BE EXILED? THAT WHAT EVERYBODY EXCITEDLY NOT WANT TO KNOW!!

ME NOT AFRAID OF SUPER-APE, DARLING, SINCE YOU GOT BIG SURPRISE DOWN YOUR SLEEVE!

;CHOKE; --LITTLE DOES P-POOR LOIS KNOW MY SURPRISE HAS... ;CHOKE;... FIZZLED! --;CHOKE;!

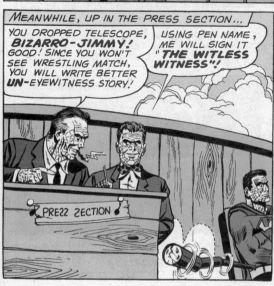

MEANWHILE, UP IN THE PRESS SECTION...

YOU DROPPED TELESCOPE, *BIZARRO-JIMMY!* GOOD! SINCE YOU WON'T SEE WRESTLING MATCH, YOU WILL WRITE BETTER *UN*-EYEWITNESS STORY!

USING PEN NAME, ME WILL SIGN IT *"THE WITLESS WITNESS"!*

PREZZ ZECTION

ALSO MEANWHILE, DOWN IN THE ARENA...

NOW FOR ACTION! AM *"BIG APE"* GOING USE *"COLD CONK GRIP"* ON *"TRICKY LOIS NO.1"*?!

YII! M-ME CAN'T LOOK!...WONDER IF *LOIS* BEING POUNDED INTO PULP WILL *IMPROVE* HER LOOKS??

11

CURIOUSLY, THE COLOSSAL APE GETS *BIZARRO-JIMMY'S* TELESCOPE WHICH HAS FALLEN BEFORE HIM, THEN...

YEEP!

GEE!

GOSH!

GOLLY!

CRIMINEY JICKETS!

WHY AM SPECTATORS YELLING SO WILDLY?-- ME CAN'T STAND SUSPENSE! WILL LOWER HANDS AND FIND OUT!

BIZARRO NO. 1

GREAT FRANKENSTEIN! *"THE BIG APE"* AM RUNNING OFF!

TIME FOR ME TO STOP READING PATHETIC COMIC BOOK! WILL ANNOUNCE MATCH'S DECISION!

SINCE *"THE BIG APE"* RAN AWAY FROM *"TRICKY LOIS"* LIKE SCARED YELLOW DOG... HIM AM *WIN* MATCH! HIM AM NEW WRESTLING CHAMP!

DID YOU *HEAR* THAT, SOUR-BUN?

YES, SOUR-PIE!

ME LOST, DEAREST... *ME LOST!* NOW ME IS A *HAS-BEEN!* EVERYONE WILL ADMIRE ME AND ME WON'T BE EXILED! AMN'T THAT *BORING?!!*

NOW ME STUCK WITH YOU... FOREVER! ME SO *HAPPY*, ME SORRY ME EVER WAS BORNED!

SIMULTANEOUSLY, IN A *BIZARRO WORLD* JUNGLE, *"THE BIG APE"* EATS THE COCONUTS HE'D SIGHTED THROUGH THE TELESCOPE! FOR THE TRUTH IS, HE HADN'T FLED IN *FEAR*... BUT IN *HUNGER*...!

CHOMP! CHOMP!— BLE-ECHH!

A WAY-OUT, KOOKIE ENDING? ARE YOU ANNOYED, IRRITATED, CONFUSED? GO SUE THE *BIZARRO WORLD!*

The End

TALES of the BIZARRO WORLD

EVERY SATURDAY NIGHT, EARTH'S TELEVISION LISTENERS ARE GLUED TO THEIR TV SETS, THRILLING TO THE ADVENTURES OF *PERRY MASON*, THE BRILLIANT ATTORNEY-AT-LAW WHO *NEVER* LOSES A CASE! WHAT HAS THIS TO DO WITH THE ZANY *BIZARRO WORLD*, WHERE EVERYTHING IS EXACTLY THE REVERSE OF EARTHLY THINGS? PLENTY! ONE DAY, REPORTER *BIZARRO-JIMMY OLSEN* IS ARRESTED FOR MURDER! WHO STREAKS IN TO HANDLE THE LAD'S CASE? WHY, NONE OTHER THAN *BIZARRO NO.1*, WHO HAS ABANDONED HIS POSITION AS LEADER OF THE *BIZARRO WORLD* IN ORDER TO ASSUME THE IDENTITY OF *BIZARRO MERRY PASON*, BUNGLING ATTORNEY EXTRAORDINARY. FOLLOW HIS MAD ANTICS IN...

The CASE of the SUPER-LOONEY LAWYER!

YOUR HONOR, ME GOING TO PROVE MY CLIENT, BIZARRO-JIMMY OLSEN, KILLED HIS BOSS, BIZARRO-PERRY WHITE!

BOY, AM ME GLAD BIZARRO NO.1 HAVE BECOME GREAT LAWYER MERRY PASON AND AM DEFENDING ME! NOW ME REALLY AM DOOMED! ;CHUCKLE!

MERRY PASON

STELLA AVENUE

147

FAR OUT IN THE UNIVERSE EXISTS THE STRANGEST, WHACKIEST PLANET IN THE ENTIRE COSMOS... IT IS THE **SQUARE BIZARRO WORLD**, INHABITED BY STRANGE CREATURES WHO ARE IMPERFECT DUPLICATES OF **SUPER-MAN**, LOIS LANE, PERRY WHITE, JIMMY OLSEN AND OTHER **METROPOLIS** CHARACTERS...

EVERYTHING IS UTTERLY ZANY ON THIS WORLD, THE EXACT OPPOSITE OF EARTH! FOR INSTANCE, WHEN **BIZARROS** WANT TO BUY A NEW CAR, THEY GO TO A **JUNKYARD**...

NOTE BEAUTIFUL DENTS... BROKEN STEERING WHEEL...FLAT TIRES! THIS CAR AM REAL **BARGAIN!**

ME BUY IT!!

UNLIKE US, **BIZARROS** VACATION AT THE BEACH IN THE **WINTERTIME** AND STAY HOME DURING THE **SUMMERTIME**...

HAVING A GOOD TIME, DARLING?

A W-W-W-WONDERFUL T-T-T-TIME, D-D-DEAR! --BR-RRR...!

HERE ON EARTH, PEOPLE SIT AT TABLES WHILE DINING, AND THEIR DOGS EAT ON THE FLOOR, BUT ON THE KOOKIE **BIZARRO** PLANET...

WILL **BIZARRO-KRYPTO** TOSS US MORE SCRAPS?

ME SURE HOPE SO, SON!

ON OUR PLANET, WHEN YOU BUY FOOD, YOU'RE GIVEN TRADING STAMPS! BUT IT'S...ER... **DIFFERENT** ON THE **BIZARRO WORLD**...

TRADING STAMPS COST TWO LUMPS COAL! YOU GET THIS CAN OF BEANS **FREE!**

CLERK

BEANS

IN OUR EARTH LIBRARIES AND HOSPITALS, **SILENCE** IS REQUESTED...BUT ON THE TOPSY-TURVY PLANET...

CAN'T YOU READ? GET OUT!! YOU **TOO QUIET!!**

NOISE, PLEASE!

EXIT

LIBRARIAN

2

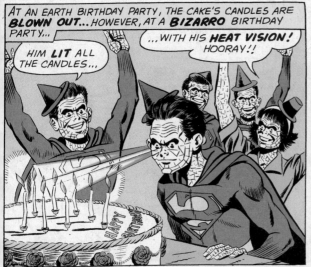

AT AN EARTH BIRTHDAY PARTY, THE CAKE'S CANDLES ARE **BLOWN OUT**... HOWEVER, AT A **BIZARRO** BIRTHDAY PARTY...

HIM **LIT** ALL THE CANDLES...

...WITH HIS **HEAT VISION!** HOORAY!!

ON THE **BIZARRO WORLD**, THE PRICE OF COMIC BOOKS HAS GONE **DOWN** INSTEAD OF **UP** AS HERE ON EARTH...

PRICE OF COMICS HAVE DROPPED FROM 10 LUMPS COAL, TO EIGHT!

TOO BAD!

BIZARRO ROMANTIK HATE KOMIKS

UNSUPER-MANN KOMIKS

DULL KOMIKS

UNFUNNY KOMIKS

EARTH IDIOT KOMIKS

KOMIKS

AND WHEN A **BIZARRO** HOUSEWIFE NEEDS A DISHWASHER MACHINE REPAIRMAN, IT'S BECAUSE...

MACHINE AM WORKING **TOO GOOD**, MR. REPAIRMAN! FIX IT, PLEASE!

DON'T WORRY, LADY! WHEN ME GET FINISHED, IT **WON'T** WORK **AT ALL!!**

WASHER

JUST AS **METROPOLIS** HAS ITS **DAILY PLANET**, THE **BIZARRO WORLD** HAS ITS **NIGHTLY HTRAE!** LET US LOOK INTO THE OFFICE OF EDITOR **BIZARRO-PERRY WHITE** AS HE BAWLS OUT CUB REPORTER **BIZARRO-JIMMY OLSEN**...

WHAT WRONG, BOSS?

GR-RR!... BAH!! ...LITTLE NAPOLEON'S GHOST!!

IDIOT! STOP TURNING IN **EXCITING** SCOOPS! ME NEED **DULL** FRONT-PAGE STORIES!

CHOKE! OKAY!

EXIT

UNLIKE EARTH NEWSPAPERS, THE **NIGHTLY HTRAE** PLAYS UP **UNINTERESTING** NEWS!

PRESENTLY...

WHERE AM **BIZARRO-PERRY WHITE**, THIS PAPER'S DIRTY DOG OF AN EDITOR?

OUR DIRTY DOG OF AN EDITOR AM IN HIS OFFICE, GOOFING OFF!

BOY, THIS **BIZARRO-LOIS** SURE IS ANGRY! ME WONDER WHY?!

3

SECONDS LATER...

WHAT AM MATTER, LADY?

"WHAT AM MATTER?"...YOU PRINTED MY PICTURE ON FRONT PAGE, THAT AM "WHAT AM MATTER"! THAT AM BIG INSULT!

NIGHTLY HTRAE

DON'T TRY WIGGLE OUT OF THIS BY SAYING ALL BIZARRO-LOISES LOOK ALIKE! THAT NO EXCUSE! ME HATE YOU! I WISH YOU WERE DEAD! — GOODBYE!

HM-MM! THAT SOUND SUSPICIOUSLY LIKE THREAT!

SHORTLY, THE EDITOR IS VISITED BY AN IRATE BIZARRO-LANA LANG...

BOO-HOO! YOU RIGGED STRAIGHTWORD PUZZLE CONTEST, SO ME WON! ME DISGRACED! ME NOT WANT THE LUMPS OF COAL CONTEST-PRIZE! —: SOB!: YOU NOT DESERVE TO LIVE FOR WAY YOU HAVE SHAMED ME!

MINUTES LATER, AS BIZARRO-LANA DEPARTS AND BIZARRO-KRYPTO DROPS IN...

:CHOKE: — YOU REFUSING ACCEPT BEAUTIFUL SWEATER! YOU MAD BECAUSE ME CHOSE YOU TO BE NIGHTLY HTRAE MASCOT!

OTPYRK

BIZARRO DOGS WAG THEIR TAILS WHEN ANGRY... AND BITE YOU WHEN THEY ARE HAPPY!

THEN, AFTER BIZARRO-KRYPTO LEAVES

A SHOT! SOUND CAME FROM EDITOR'S OFFICE! ME BETTER GO SEE WHAT HAPPENED IN THERE!

BANGG!

MOMENTS AFTERWARD...

HEY, BIZARRO-WHITE, BOSS! HOW COME YOU LYING ON FLOOR NEXT TO SMOKING GUN, HAH?...ME CALL A DOCTOR! IF YOU SICK, DOCTOR MAKE YOU WORSE!

4

WHEN THE PHYSICIAN ARRIVES...

HIM... **DEAD!**

¡GASP!¡ -THAT TAG ON GUN IDENTIFY IT AS **MY** GUN WHICH ME USUALLY KEEP IN MY DESK DRAWER 'CAUSE ME DON'T NEED PROTECTION FROM NOTHING! ME GRAB IT, QUICK!

BIZARRO-OLSEN

OFF RACES **BIZARRO-OLSEN**...

ME GOT TO GET RID OF GUN, SO ME WON'T BE SUSPECTED OF KILLING BOSS! AH...**POLICE STATION** AM SAFE PLACE TO HIDE INCRIMINATING EVIDENCE! ME THROW GUN INSIDE POLICE STATION!

KR-RASHH!

POLICE STATION

NEXT INSTANT...

WE GET 'IM!

DOCTOR TELEPHONED US!... **BIZARRO-OLSEN**, YOU AM UNDER ARREST FOR MURDER OF **BIZARRO-WHITE!** GUN INCRIMINATE YOU!

?-- HOW'D THEM EVER FIND GUN AFTER ME SO CAREFUL TO HIDE IT?

SOON, AS **BIZARRO NO.1** AND HIS WIFE **BIZARRO-LOIS NO.1** WATCH EARTH'S **PERRY MASON TV SHOW** ON THEIR ULTRA-POWERFUL TELEVISION SET IN THEIR HOME...

CONGRATULATIONS, MR. MASON! I FIND YOUR CLIENT **NOT GUILTY!**

PHOOEY!

PERRY MASON IS PUNK LAWYER-DETECTIVE! HE ALWAYS WIN CASES, HELPED BY SECRETARY **DELLA STREET!** IF **ME** WAS HIM, INSTEAD OF LEADER OF **BIZARRO WORLD**, ME WOULD CLEVERLY **LOSE** TRIALS!

NEWS FLASH! **BIZARRO-JIMMY OLSEN** HAVE MURDERED **BIZARRO-PERRY WHITE!**

BIZARRO NO. 1

BIZARRO LOIS NO. 1

BIZARRO JUNIOR

BIZARRO-OLSEN IS YOUR PAL, YES, DADDY?

RIGHT!--QUICK AS A FLASH, ME GRAB DETECTIVE CAP AND PIPE! ME BECOME **MERRY PASON**, FAMOUS **BIZARRO** LAWYER! ME WILL REPRESENT OLSEN!

ME'LL BE **STELLA AVENUE**, YOUR SECRETARY!

BIZARRO 1

5

SHORTLY, AT THE **BIZARRO** JAIL...

¡GASP!¡ -- OH, HOW **LUCKY** ME AM TO BE REPRESENTED BY WORST LAWYER ON WHOLE **BIZARRO WORLD**!

REST ASSURED, ME WILL FRAME YOU!

CHEER UP! YOU AS GOOD AS DEAD!

NEXT DAY, IN THE **BIZARRO** COURTROOM...

DISORDER IN THE COURT! JUDGE AM GOING ENTER!

JUDGE? WHO HIM?

OH, JUST SOME NUT WHOSE JOB AM TO MAKE SURE PRISONER GET **UNFAIR** TRIAL!

ON EARTH, EVERYONE STANDS RESPECTFULLY WHEN THE JUDGE ENTERS...BUT ON THE **BIZARRO WORLD** THINGS ARE **REVERSED**...

EVERYBODY SITTING AND EATING... JURY AM FAST ASLEEP! YES, INDEEDY... ME SURE AM A **GOOD GROUP**!

HOKAY, **MERRY PASON**! MAKE OPENING ADDRESS!

THANK YOU, YOUR HONOR!

AS DISTRICT ATTORNEY, ME PROTEST!...SEE, JURY? HIM TRYING TO GET IN GOOD WITH JUDGE BY ANSWERING HIM RESPECTFULLY!

YOU RULED OVER, D.A.!

BUMS OF THE JURY...BEFORE TRIAL OVER, ME PROVE BEYOND SHADOW OF DOUBT THAT MY CLIENT **BIZARRO-OLSEN** AM...**GUILTY**!

SHADDUP, YOU! YOU AM DISTURBING OUR SLEEP!

NOW THE FIRST WITNESS TAKES THE STAND...SHE IS THE **BIZARRO-LOIS** WHO HAD THREATENED **BIZARRO-WHITE** IN HIS OFFICE!

CREEP! HAG!

ON EARTH, WITNESSES ARE **SWORN IN**! ON THE **BIZARRO WORLD**, THEY ARE **SWORN AT**...

6

152

ALSO, ON THE TOPSY-TURVY PLANET, WITNESSES QUESTION THE *LAWYER*, INSTEAD OF THE OPPOSITE, AS ON OUR WORLD!

HAVE YOUR WIFE STOPPED BEATING YOU? *ANSWER*, YOU SNIVELLING *RAT!*

UH...; *URK!* ...!

OO-OOO, WHAT A *BRILLIANT* CROSS-EXAMINATION!

AS THE *BIZARRO-LOIS* WITNESS LEAVES TRIUMPHANTLY...

BIZARRO-KRYPTO, YOU CHIEF SUSPECT, BECAUSE IT *IMPOSSIBLE* FOR YOU TO HAVE HELD GUN THAT KILLED VICTIM!! *TAKE THE STAND!!*

ONE DISMAYING MOMENT LATER...

HEY! ME DIDN'T MEAN FOR YOU TO *TAKE THE STAND* WITH YOU!... FLY IT BACK, WISE-GUY!

THEN, AS THE *MUTT OF STEEL* QUESTIONS THE *BIZARRO* ATTORNEY RUTHLESSLY...

ARF! ARF! WOOF! WOOF!

STOP DOGGING

ME! ME SWEAR ME DON'T KNOW NOTHING! ME CAN *PROVE* ME AM 100% *IMBECILE!* HONEST! -- ; CHOKE ;

BIZARRO-LANA LANG, WHO HAD WON THE PUZZLE CONTEST, IS THE NEXT WITNESS...

CAN YOU PROVE *YOU* DIDN'T KILL *BIZARRO-WHITE?*...CAN YOU PROVE YOU *EXIST?*... WHERE WERE YOU ON *NIGHT OF JANUARY 32ND?* EH, BOY??!!

URP!!!

AFTER *BIZARRO-LANA* DEPARTS, THE LUNATIC LAWYER CONSULTS WITH HIS SECRETARY, *STELLA AVENUE!*

; MOAN! ; --ME WORRIED, STELLA! ME NOT FRAMING MY CLIENT GOOD ENOUGH!

HAVE NO FEAR, BOSS! ME AM LOADED WITH SNEAKY INSPIRATIONS! DO *THIS!*...PPS-ST! PS-ST!;

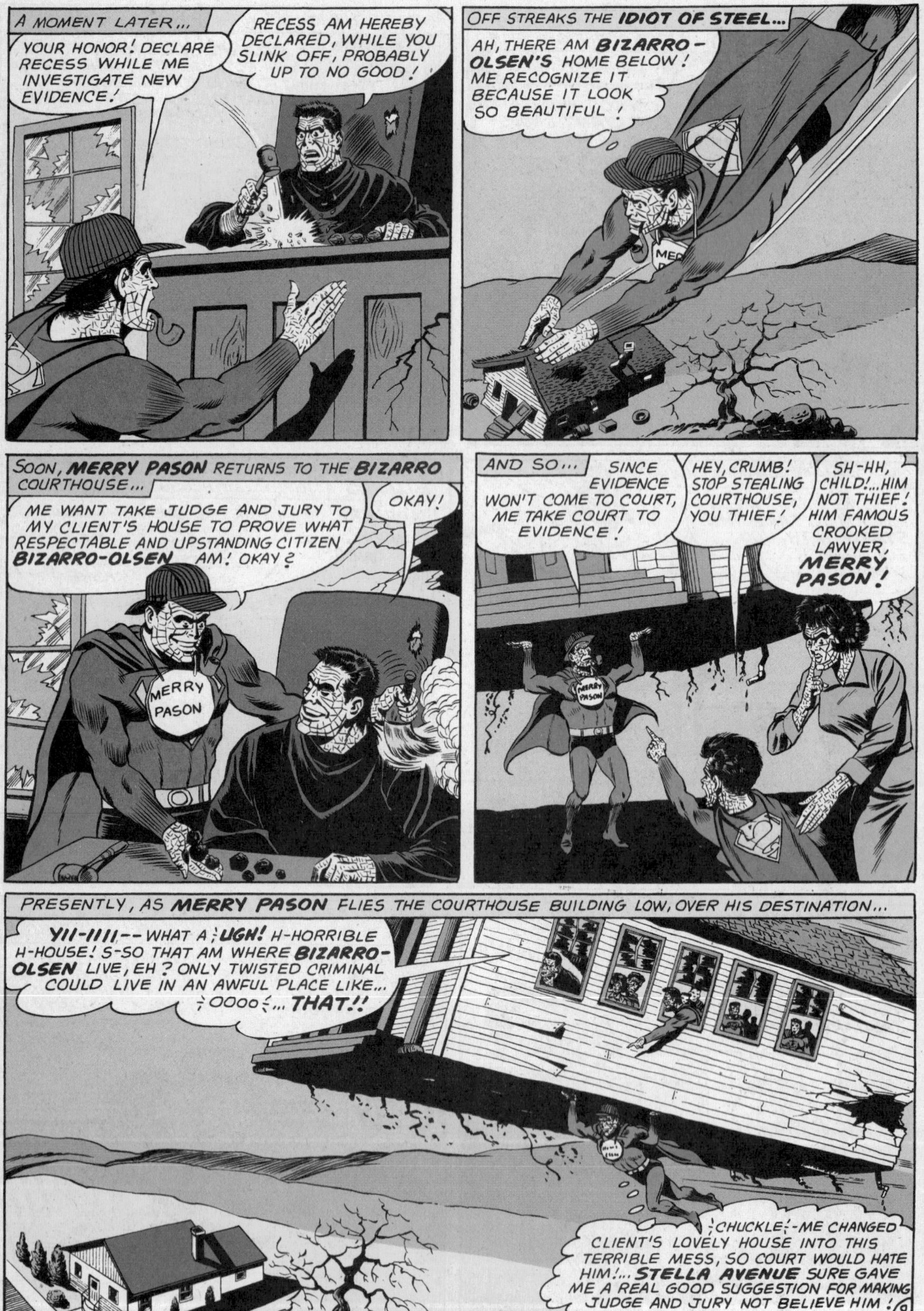
A MOMENT LATER...
YOUR HONOR! DECLARE RECESS WHILE ME INVESTIGATE NEW EVIDENCE!
RECESS AM HEREBY DECLARED, WHILE YOU SLINK OFF, PROBABLY UP TO NO GOOD!
OFF STREAKS THE IDIOT OF STEEL...
AH, THERE AM BIZARRO-OLSEN'S HOME BELOW! ME RECOGNIZE IT BECAUSE IT LOOK SO BEAUTIFUL!
SOON, MERRY PASON RETURNS TO THE BIZARRO COURTHOUSE...
ME WANT TAKE JUDGE AND JURY TO MY CLIENT'S HOUSE TO PROVE WHAT RESPECTABLE AND UPSTANDING CITIZEN BIZARRO-OLSEN AM! OKAY?
OKAY!
MERRY PASON
AND SO...
SINCE EVIDENCE WON'T COME TO COURT, ME TAKE COURT TO EVIDENCE!
HEY, CRUMB! STOP STEALING COURTHOUSE, YOU THIEF!
SH-HH, CHILD!...HIM NOT THIEF! HIM FAMOUS CROOKED LAWYER, MERRY PASON!
MERRY PASON
PRESENTLY, AS MERRY PASON FLIES THE COURTHOUSE BUILDING LOW, OVER HIS DESTINATION...
YII-IIII,--WHAT A ;UGH! H-HORRIBLE H-HOUSE! S-SO THAT AM WHERE BIZARRO-OLSEN LIVE, EH? ONLY TWISTED CRIMINAL COULD LIVE IN AN AWFUL PLACE LIKE... ;OOOO;... THAT!!
;CHUCKLE;-ME CHANGED CLIENT'S LOVELY HOUSE INTO THIS TERRIBLE MESS, SO COURT WOULD HATE HIM!... STELLA AVENUE SURE GAVE ME A REAL GOOD SUGGESTION FOR MAKING JUDGE AND JURY NOT BELIEVE HIM!
8

AFTER THE **BIZARRO** LAWYER RETURNS THE COURT-HOUSE WHERE IT BELONGS...

HEY! WHAT AM THAT MACHINERY YOU CARRYING INTO COURTROOM, MR. PASON?

MACHINERY AM A LIE DETECTOR, YOUR HONOR, SIR!

ME SUSPECT MY CLIENT AM GUILTY AS SIN! ME GOING PUT HIM ON WITNESS STAND AND TEAR TRUTH OUT OF HIS LYING MOUTH!

SHORTLY... ANSWER QUICKLY! DON'T HESITATE! **WHAT AM YOUR NAME, BIZARRO-OLSEN?!**

UH... ER... I THINK..., WAIT, NO... IT ISN'T,... I MEAN, I'M NOT SURE...

SEE, YOUR HONOR, AND JURY? POINTER ON LIE DETECTOR REVEAL HIM TELLING **TRUTH!** ...NOW FOR TOUGHER QUESTIONS!

AWRIGHT NOW, CLIENT! THINK CAREFULLY BEFORE ANSWERING! DID YOU HAVE **MOTIVE** FOR KILLING **BIZARRO-WHITE?**

ME RUBBING COMB ME BORROWED FROM STELLA, ON COSTUME!

A MOTIVE? **ME?**

NO, ME DIDN'T!

LOOK! LIE DETECTOR'S POINTER INDICATES **BIZARRO-OLSEN LYING!**

⁚CHUCKLE⁚-- FRICTION OF COMB AGAINST COSTUME MANUFACTURED STATIC ELECTRICITY WHICH MADE COMB TEMPORARY **MAGNET,** CAUSING METAL POINTER TO AIM **UPWARD**... WHERE ME WANT IT TO!

⑨

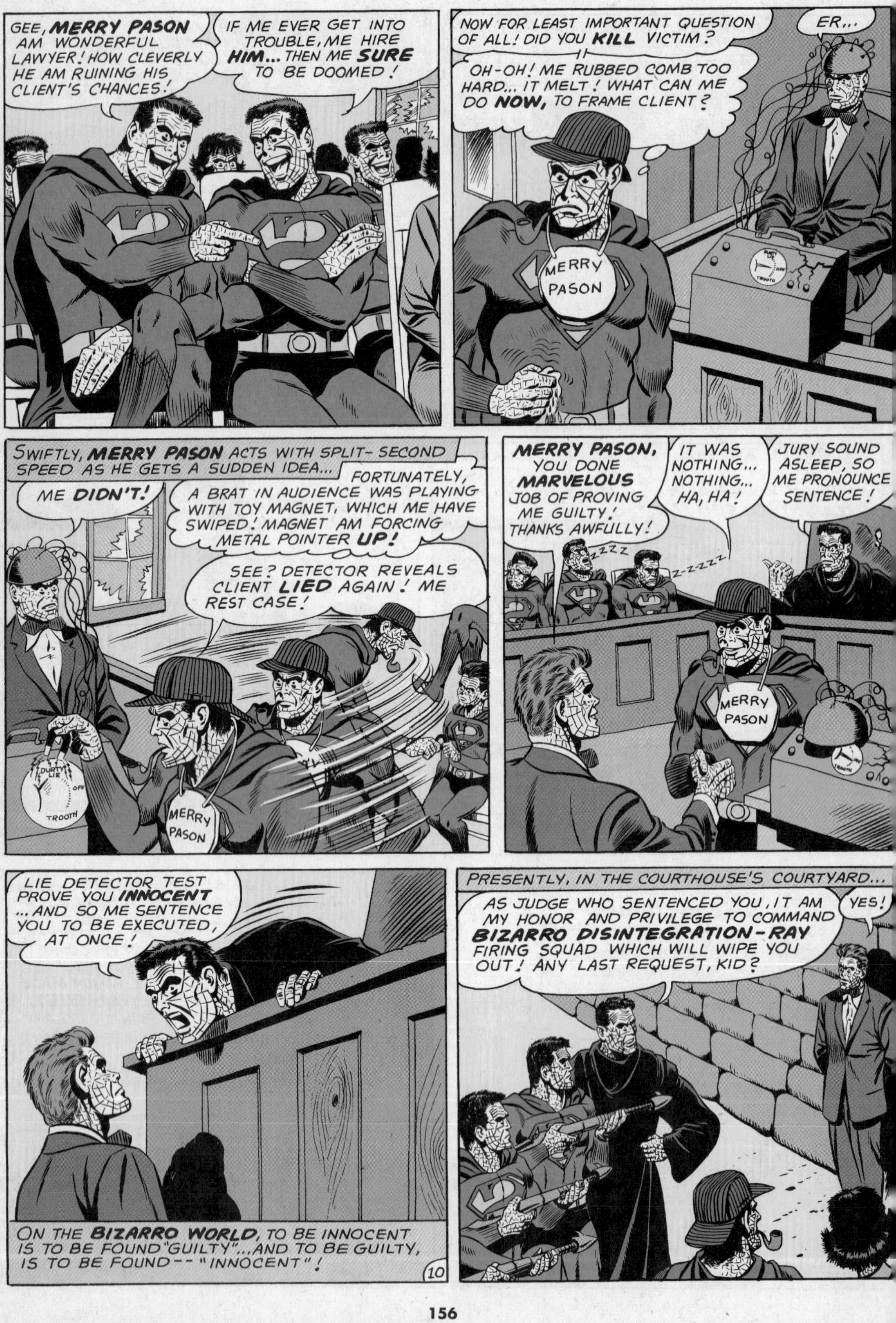

GEE, MERRY PASON AM WONDERFUL LAWYER! HOW CLEVERLY HE AM RUINING HIS CLIENT'S CHANCES!
IF ME EVER GET INTO TROUBLE, ME HIRE HIM... THEN ME SURE TO BE DOOMED!
NOW FOR LEAST IMPORTANT QUESTION OF ALL! DID YOU KILL VICTIM?
ER...
OH-OH! ME RUBBED COMB TOO HARD... IT MELT! WHAT CAN ME DO NOW, TO FRAME CLIENT?
MERRY PASON
TROOTH
SWIFTLY, MERRY PASON ACTS WITH SPLIT-SECOND SPEED AS HE GETS A SUDDEN IDEA...
ME DIDN'T!
FORTUNATELY, A BRAT IN AUDIENCE WAS PLAYING WITH TOY MAGNET, WHICH ME HAVE SWIPED! MAGNET AM FORCING METAL POINTER UP!
SEE? DETECTOR REVEALS CLIENT LIED AGAIN! ME REST CASE!
DURTY LIE
OFF
TROOTH
MERRY PASON
MERRY PASON, YOU DONE MARVELOUS JOB OF PROVING ME GUILTY! THANKS AWFULLY!
IT WAS NOTHING... NOTHING... HA, HA!
JURY SOUND ASLEEP, SO ME PRONOUNCE SENTENCE!
Z-Z-Z-Z
Z-Z-Z-Z-Z
MERRY PASON
LIE DETECTOR TEST PROVE YOU INNOCENT ...AND SO ME SENTENCE YOU TO BE EXECUTED, AT ONCE!
ON THE BIZARRO WORLD, TO BE INNOCENT IS TO BE FOUND "GUILTY"...AND TO BE GUILTY, IS TO BE FOUND-- "INNOCENT"!
10
PRESENTLY, IN THE COURTHOUSE'S COURTYARD...
AS JUDGE WHO SENTENCED YOU, IT AM MY HONOR AND PRIVILEGE TO COMMAND BIZARRO DISINTEGRATION-RAY FIRING SQUAD WHICH WILL WIPE YOU OUT! ANY LAST REQUEST, KID?
YES!

LET'S CHANGE PLACES, JUDGE! ME ALWAYS WANTED LEAD A FIRING SQUAD! LIFELONG AMBITION! PLEASE GRANT LITTLE WHIM OF MINE!

WHIM RULED OVER! BIZARRO CODE 84 B-- SAY "NUTS TO WHIMS"!

BUT IT'S ONLY A TEENSIE-WEENIE LITTLE WHIM!

EXECUTION WILL PROCEED! ATTENTION, FIRING SQUAD! READY... AIM...

...DON'T FIRE! HA, HA, HA, HEE HEE, HEE, HO, HO!

HE S-SAID, "DON'T FIRE"!!

HEY! CUT OUT HORSEPLAY, JUDGE, AND KILL MY CLIENT! AFTER ALL, WHAT'S RIGHT IS WRONG, RIGHT?

US CAN'T REALLY GO THROUGH WITH EXECUTION!...WHY?... ME REMOVE PLASTIC MASK, AND SHOW YOU WHY!!

GASP! ...Y-YOU AM R-REALLY BIZARRO-PERRY WHITE!

THEN MY BOSS WAS NOT REALLY MURDERED, AFTER ALL... DARN IT!

BUT THE DOCTOR PRONOUNCED YOU...DEAD!

RIGHT!--DOCTOR SAID ME WAS DEAD, BECAUSE ME WAS ALIVE!

IF THE BIZARRO DOCTOR HAD SAID BIZARRO-WHITE WAS "ALIVE," HE'D HAVE MEANT HE WAS "DEAD"! BUT HE DIDN'T! SEE!...???

"AFTER THOSE VISITORS RAISED A RUCKUS IN MY OFFICE, ME GOT IDEA FOR DULL NEWS STORY! WHILE BIZARRO-OLSEN WAS IN STUPID DAZE, ME STOLE HIS GUN, SHOT IT OUT MY OFFICE WINDOW..."

⑪

157

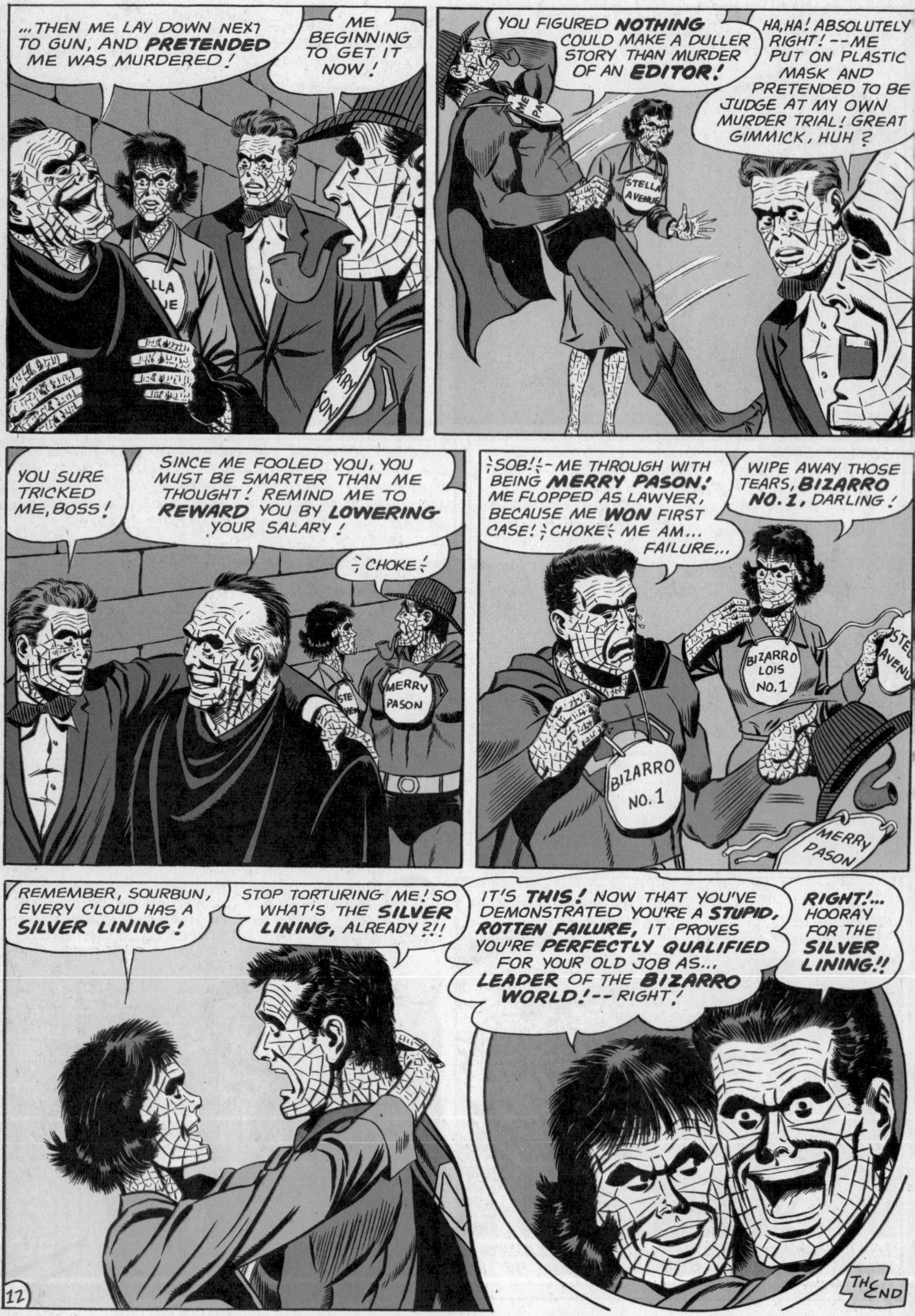

...THEN ME LAY DOWN NEXT TO GUN, AND PRETENDED ME WAS MURDERED!
ME BEGINNING TO GET IT NOW!
YOU FIGURED NOTHING COULD MAKE A DULLER STORY THAN MURDER OF AN EDITOR!
HA, HA! ABSOLUTELY RIGHT! --ME PUT ON PLASTIC MASK AND PRETENDED TO BE JUDGE AT MY OWN MURDER TRIAL! GREAT GIMMICK, HUH?
STELLA AVENUE
YOU SURE TRICKED ME, BOSS!
SINCE ME FOOLED YOU, YOU MUST BE SMARTER THAN ME THOUGHT! REMIND ME TO REWARD YOU BY LOWERING YOUR SALARY!
-CHOKE-
MERRY PASON
-SOB!- ME THROUGH WITH BEING MERRY PASON! ME FLOPPED AS LAWYER, BECAUSE ME WON FIRST CASE! -CHOKE- ME AM... FAILURE...
WIPE AWAY THOSE TEARS, BIZARRO NO. 1, DARLING!
BIZARRO LOIS NO. 1
BIZARRO NO. 1
MERRY PASON
REMEMBER, SOURBUN, EVERY CLOUD HAS A SILVER LINING!
STOP TORTURING ME! SO WHAT'S THE SILVER LINING, ALREADY?!!
IT'S THIS! NOW THAT YOU'VE DEMONSTRATED YOU'RE A STUPID, ROTTEN FAILURE, IT PROVES YOU'RE PERFECTLY QUALIFIED FOR YOUR OLD JOB AS... LEADER OF THE BIZARRO WORLD! -- RIGHT!
RIGHT!... HOORAY FOR THE SILVER LINING!!
12
THE END

TALES of the BIZARRO WORLD

PRESIDENT ABE!!! ACCORDING TO HISTORY, JOHN WILKES BOOTH GOING TO SHOOT YOU DEAD! TAKE THIS GUN! ASSASSINATE BOOTH BEFORE HE SHOOT YOU! MAKE BUM OUT OF HISTORY! OKAY?!

HAVE YOU EVER WISHED YOU COULD GO INTO THE PAST TO CHANGE THINGS? WELL, THAT'S JUST WHAT THAT WHACKY, IMPERFECT DUPLICATE OF SUPERMAN... BIZARRO NO. 1... DECIDES TO DO IN THIS CRAZY, MIXED-UP STORY! ZANILY, THE IDIOT OF STEEL STREAKS HERE AND THERE IN THE PAST, TURNING HISTORY UPSIDE-DOWN, INSIDE-OUT, AND THOROUGHLY FRACTURING GREAT EVENTS THAT HAPPENED LONG AGO, IN THIS LOONIEST TALE OF THEM ALL... *The* BIZARRO WHO GOOFED UP HISTORY!

BIZARRO NO. 1

¿GASP!¿...WHAT? A FAMOUS, RESPECTED ACTOR LIKE JOHN BOOTH ASSASSINATE ME, PRESIDENT LINCOLN? YOU'RE MAD, YOU MONSTER!

BIZARRO CODE
US DO OPPOSITE OF ALL EARTHLY THINGS! US HATE BEAUTY! US LOVE UGLINESS! IS BIG CRIME TO MAKE ANYTHING PERFECT ON BIZARRO WORLD!

FAR OUT IN SPACE, THERE ONCE EXISTED A PLANET WHICH WAS LIKE THE OTHER WORLDS IN THE COSMOS, EXCEPT THAT IT WAS INHABITED BY PATHETIC, WITLESS *BIZARRO* BEINGS WHO HATE PERFECTION, AND DO EVERYTHING THE REVERSE OF EARTHLY CUSTOMS...

SINCE THIS PLANET WAS *PERFECTLY* ROUND, THE *BIZARROS* GOT BUSY AND CHANGED ITS SHAPE, TRANSFORMING IT INTO THE ONLY *SQUARE* WORLD IN THE UNIVERSE...

DUE TO AN AMAZING *DUPLICATOR RAY,* TODAY THE *BIZARRO WORLD* IS INHABITED BY IMPERFECT DUPLICATES OF SUCH METROPOLIS CHARACTERS AS *SUPERMAN,* LOIS LANE, JIMMY OLSEN, PERRY WHITE, ETC....

WHAT A SHAME UGLY EARTH LANA LANG *ISN'T* **PRETTY,** LIKE *ME!*

ME CAN'T UNDERSTAND WHY EARTH LUCY LANE THINK JIMMY OLSEN AM PAIN IN FOOT!

| BIZARRO NO. 1 | BIZARRO-LOIS NO. 1 | BIZARRO-JUNIOR NO. 1 | BIZARRO-JIMMY OLSEN | BIZARRO-PERRY WHITE | BIZARRO-LANA LANG | BIZARRO-LUCY LANE | BIZARRO-KRYPTO | BIZARRO MR. KLTPZYXM | BIZARRO LUTHOR |

YES, EVERYTHING ON THE *BIZARRO WORLD* IS A CRAZY, MIXED-UP VERSION OF EARTH! FOR INSTANCE, *BIZARRO* FEMALES SWIM IN... *EVENING GOWNS...*

IMAGINE EARTH IDIOTS SWIMMING IN -- BIKINI *BATHING SUITS!* HA, HA!

AND INSTEAD OF "WELCOME MATS" IN FRONT OF EACH DOOR!

AREN'T WE LUCKY TO HAVE FRIENDLY NEIGHBORS LIKE THESE?!

2

HERE ON THE *BIZARRO WORLD*, RATHER THAN MAKE YOU LAUGH, CIRCUS CLOWNS MAKE YOU CRY...!

BAWW-WWW!

WAH-HH!

WHAT A *MARVELOUS CLOWN!* HIM BREAKING MY HEART!--SOBBB!

AND AS FOR *BIZARRO* DOGS...WELL...*THEY,* INSTEAD OF CATS, GET CHASED UP TREES!

YOU BULLY, YOU!

SCAREDY-DOG!!

BIZARRO ROCKET SCIENTISTS LAUNCH THEIR MISSILES IN A MANNER WE WOULD CONSIDER...ER...PECULIAR...

DUMB EARTH SCIENTISTS! THEY SHOOT ROCKETS INTO OUTER SPACE, INSTEAD OF INTO GROUND!

ON THIS KOOKIE PLANET, *GIRLS* PLAY FOOTBALL, AND *MEN* PLAY... *HOPSCOTCH!*

FOOTBALL IS FOR SISSIES!

NEXT, US'LL PLAY REAL TOUGH GAME... *JACKS!!*

IN *BIZARRO* FACTORIES, THE *BOSSES,* INSTEAD OF THE WORKERS, DO THE WORK...

SLOWER, BOSS, OR US FIRE YOU!

FOR WORKING TOO HARD, YOU GET CUT IN SALARY!

ON THE *BIZARRO WORLD,* MT. EVEREST IS THE SMALLEST MOUNTAIN, AND A MOLEHILL IS THE LARGEST-- THE EXACT OPPOSITE OF EARTH!

READY TO START CLIMBING MT. EVEREST, LADS?

YES, GUIDE! US NOT SCARED! LEAD ON!

MT. EVEREST

3

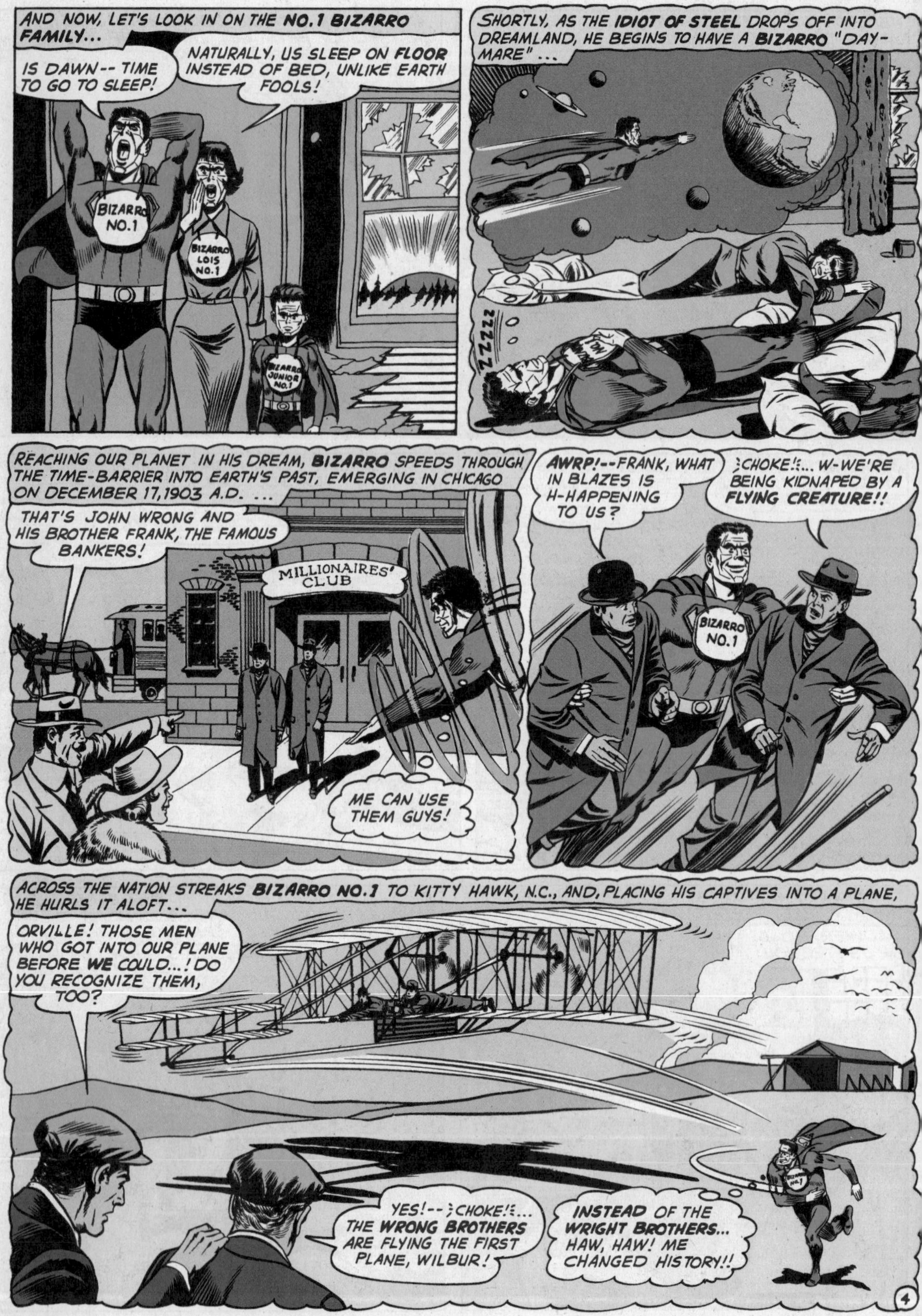
AND NOW, LET'S LOOK IN ON THE NO.1 BIZARRO FAMILY...
IS DAWN-- TIME TO GO TO SLEEP!
NATURALLY, US SLEEP ON FLOOR INSTEAD OF BED, UNLIKE EARTH FOOLS!
BIZARRO NO.1
BIZARRO LOIS NO.1
BIZARRO JUNIOR NO.1
SHORTLY, AS THE IDIOT OF STEEL DROPS OFF INTO DREAMLAND, HE BEGINS TO HAVE A BIZARRO "DAY-MARE"...
ZZZZZ
REACHING OUR PLANET IN HIS DREAM, BIZARRO SPEEDS THROUGH THE TIME-BARRIER INTO EARTH'S PAST, EMERGING IN CHICAGO ON DECEMBER 17,1903 A.D. ...
THAT'S JOHN WRONG AND HIS BROTHER FRANK, THE FAMOUS BANKERS!
MILLIONAIRES' CLUB
ME CAN USE THEM GUYS!
AWRP!--FRANK, WHAT IN BLAZES IS H-HAPPENING TO US?
¡CHOKE!¡... W-WE'RE BEING KIDNAPED BY A FLYING CREATURE!!
BIZARRO NO.1
ACROSS THE NATION STREAKS BIZARRO NO.1 TO KITTY HAWK, N.C., AND, PLACING HIS CAPTIVES INTO A PLANE, HE HURLS IT ALOFT...
ORVILLE! THOSE MEN WHO GOT INTO OUR PLANE BEFORE WE COULD...! DO YOU RECOGNIZE THEM, TOO?
YES!--¡CHOKE!¡... THE WRONG BROTHERS ARE FLYING THE FIRST PLANE, WILBUR!
INSTEAD OF THE WRIGHT BROTHERS... HAW, HAW! ME CHANGED HISTORY!!
4

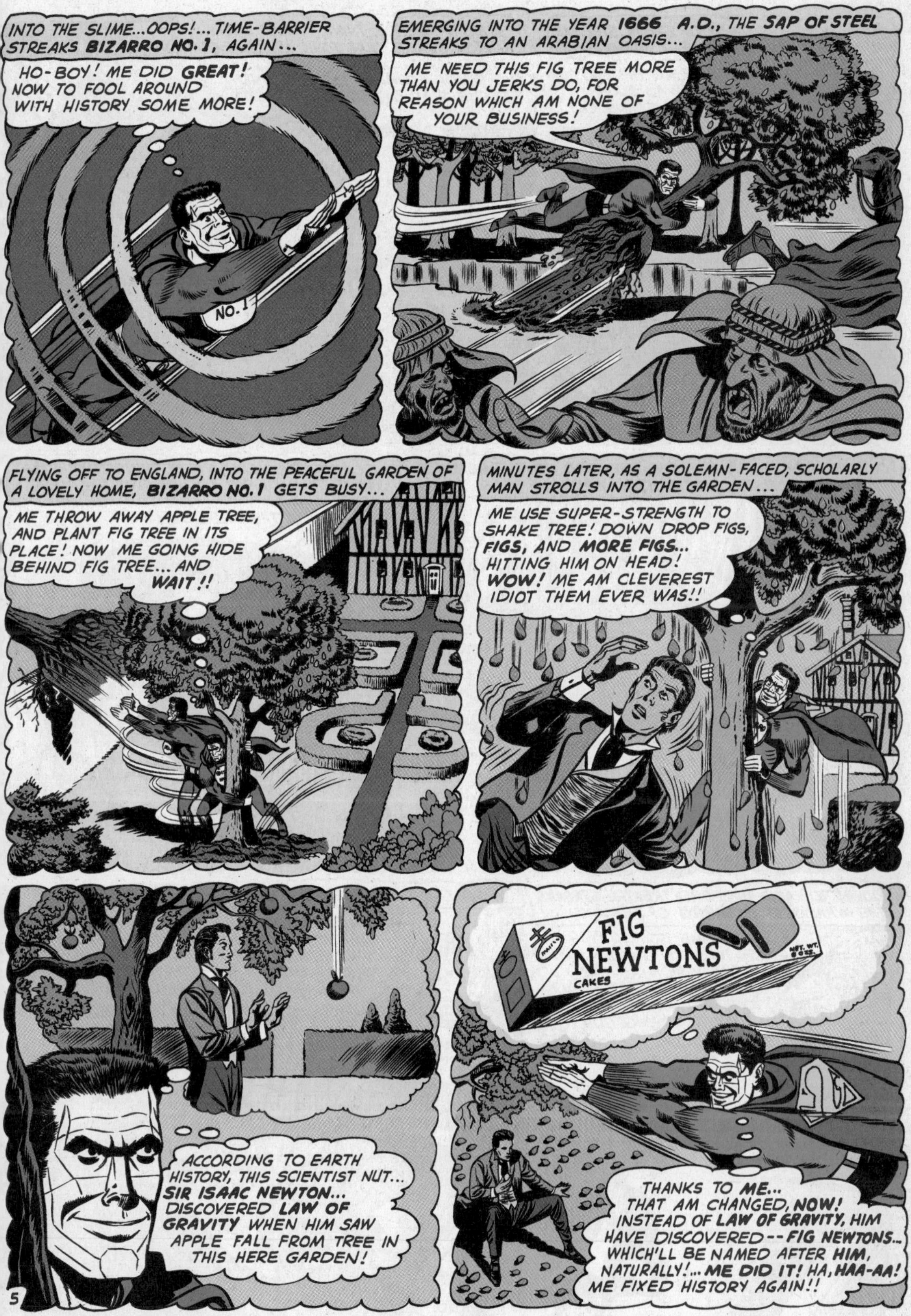
INTO THE SLIME...OOPS!...TIME-BARRIER STREAKS BIZARRO NO.1, AGAIN...
HO-BOY! ME DID GREAT! NOW TO FOOL AROUND WITH HISTORY SOME MORE!
NO.1
EMERGING INTO THE YEAR 1666 A.D., THE SAP OF STEEL STREAKS TO AN ARABIAN OASIS...
ME NEED THIS FIG TREE MORE THAN YOU JERKS DO, FOR REASON WHICH AM NONE OF YOUR BUSINESS!
FLYING OFF TO ENGLAND, INTO THE PEACEFUL GARDEN OF A LOVELY HOME, BIZARRO NO.1 GETS BUSY...
ME THROW AWAY APPLE TREE, AND PLANT FIG TREE IN ITS PLACE! NOW ME GOING HIDE BEHIND FIG TREE... AND WAIT!!
MINUTES LATER, AS A SOLEMN-FACED, SCHOLARLY MAN STROLLS INTO THE GARDEN...
ME USE SUPER-STRENGTH TO SHAKE TREE! DOWN DROP FIGS, FIGS, AND MORE FIGS... HITTING HIM ON HEAD! WOW! ME AM CLEVEREST IDIOT THEM EVER WAS!!
ACCORDING TO EARTH HISTORY, THIS SCIENTIST NUT... SIR ISAAC NEWTON... DISCOVERED LAW OF GRAVITY WHEN HIM SAW APPLE FALL FROM TREE IN THIS HERE GARDEN!
5
FIG NEWTONS
CAKES
THANKS TO ME... THAT AM CHANGED, NOW! INSTEAD OF LAW OF GRAVITY, HIM HAVE DISCOVERED -- FIG NEWTONS... WHICH'LL BE NAMED AFTER HIM, NATURALLY!... ME DID IT! HA, HAA-AA! ME FIXED HISTORY AGAIN!!

ONCE MORE, THE *IDIOT OF STEEL* STREAKS INTO THE TIME-BARRIER...

ALTERING HISTORY TWICE WAS SUCH FUN, ME GOING DO IT AGAIN!

EARTH PEOPLE THINK IT WAS DIRTY ROTTEN SHAME THAT JOHN WILKES BOOTH ASSASSINATED LINCOLN! ME DO EARTH BIG FAVOR...CHANGE HISTORY, AND RESCUE HIM, *BIZARRO* FASHION!

OUT OF THE BARRIER FLASHES *BIZARRO NO.1*, EMERGING IN WASHINGTON, D.C., ON FRIDAY, APRIL 14, 1865...

ACCORDING TO EARTH HISTORY, BOOTH SNEAKED INTO PRESIDENTIAL BOX AT FORD THEATRE, THEN HIM SHOT ABE LINCOLN!

OO, WHAT A MEAN, NASTY THING THAT WAS! BOOTH DIDN'T PAY TO GET INTO THEATERE... AND HIM DIDN'T SAY "PARDON ME" BEFORE HIM SHOT THE PRESIDENT!

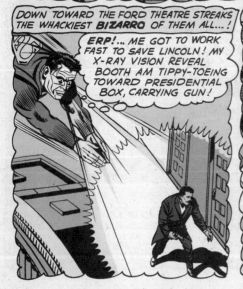

DOWN TOWARD THE FORD THEATRE STREAKS THE WHACKIEST *BIZARRO* OF THEM ALL...!

ERP!... ME GOT TO WORK FAST TO SAVE LINCOLN! MY X-RAY VISION REVEAL BOOTH AM TIPPY-TOEING TOWARD PRESIDENTIAL BOX, CARRYING GUN!

INTO THE THEATRE FLIES *BIZARRO*...

PRESIDENT ABE!! ACCORDING TO HISTORY, JOHN WILKES BOOTH GOING TO SHOOT YOU DEAD! TAKE THIS GUN! SHOOT BOOTH *BEFORE* HE SHOOT YOU! MAKE BUM OUT OF HISTORY! OKAY?

¡GASP!¿

A FAMOUS, RESPECTED ACTOR LIKE BOOTH ASSASSINATE ME? YOU'RE **MAD**, YOU MONSTER!

MAD? **ME**? ME NOT MAD AT YOU! ME NEVER EVEN **MET** YOU 'TIL NOW!

OH-OH! BOOTH AM AIMING GUN INTO BOX!!

SECRET SERVICE MEN! SEIZE THIS BLITHERING, FLYING IDIOT!

HA! ME USE MY **HEAT VISION** TO MELT BULLET FIRED FROM GUN BEFORE IT CAN HIT ABE IN HEAD!

BANG!

SNATCHING UP THE GUNMAN, **BIZARRO NO.1** MAKES OFF WITH HIM...

US FLYING INTO TIME-BARRIER, JOHN WILKES!

?!!!

THEN, OUT OF THE BARRIER INTO PENNSYLVANIA AT DAYBREAK ON JUNE 19, 1778 A.D., SPEED THE TWO...

DEVIL! YOU THWARTED MY SCHEME TO MURDER LINCOLN! NOW **YOU** WILL DIE... WHEN I RELOAD THIS GUN!

NEED ANY HELP?

SHORTLY...

DIE, MONSTER!

YOUR BULLET BOUNCED OFF MY INVULNERABLE BODY AND HIT THAT GUY SLEEPING IN TENT! ME GO SEE HOW HIM AM!

RUNK!

BANG!

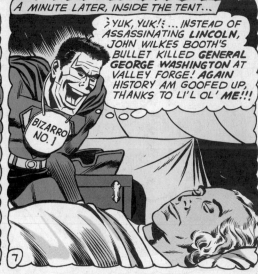

A MINUTE LATER, INSIDE THE TENT...

¿YUK, YUK!¿ ...INSTEAD OF ASSASSINATING **LINCOLN**, JOHN WILKES BOOTH'S BULLET KILLED **GENERAL GEORGE WASHINGTON** AT VALLEY FORGE! AGAIN HISTORY AM GOOFED UP, THANKS TO LI'L OL' **ME**!!!

⑦

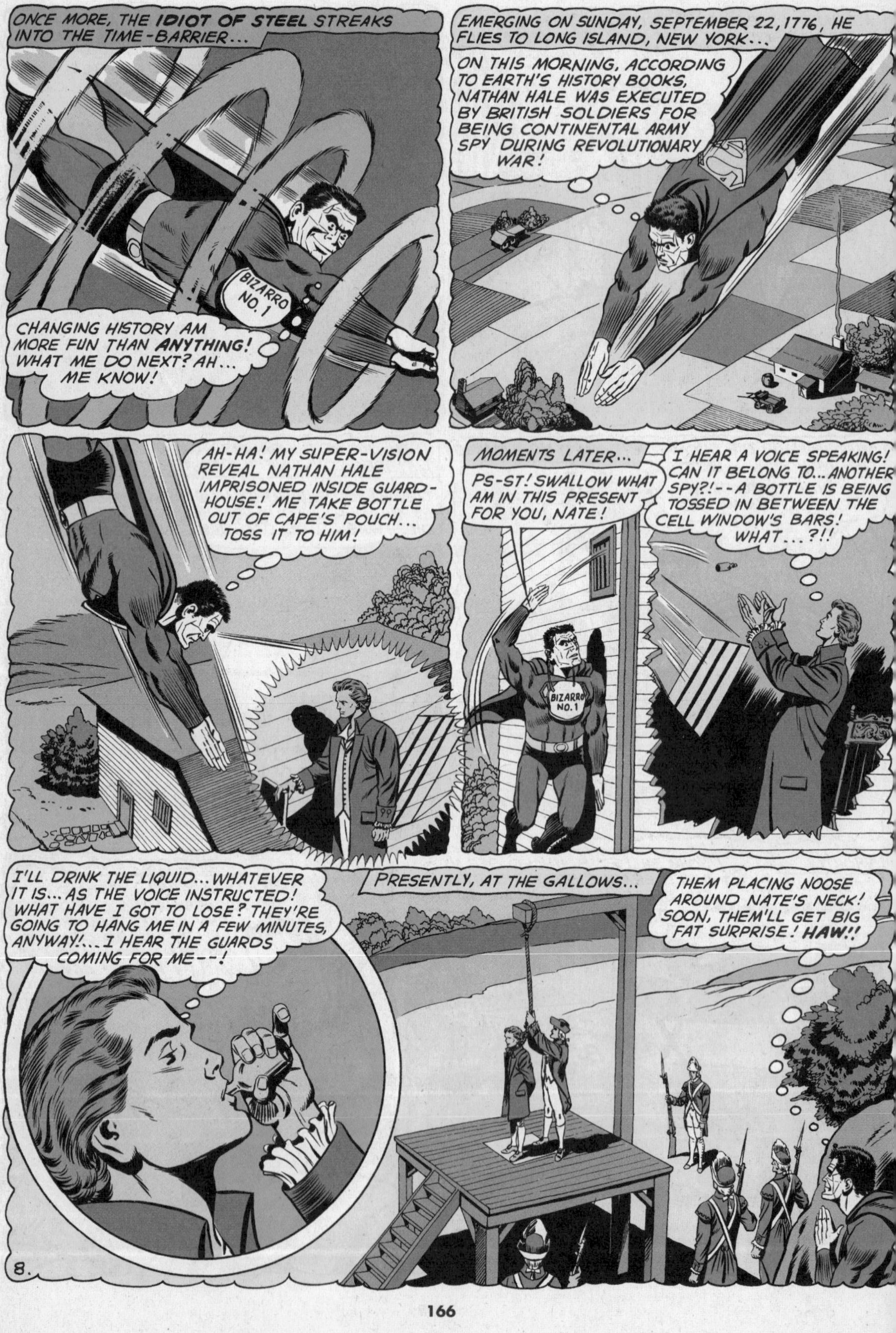
ONCE MORE, THE IDIOT OF STEEL STREAKS INTO THE TIME-BARRIER...
BIZARRO NO. 1
CHANGING HISTORY AM MORE FUN THAN ANYTHING! WHAT ME DO NEXT? AH... ME KNOW!
EMERGING ON SUNDAY, SEPTEMBER 22, 1776, HE FLIES TO LONG ISLAND, NEW YORK...
ON THIS MORNING, ACCORDING TO EARTH'S HISTORY BOOKS, NATHAN HALE WAS EXECUTED BY BRITISH SOLDIERS FOR BEING CONTINENTAL ARMY SPY DURING REVOLUTIONARY WAR!
AH-HA! MY SUPER-VISION REVEAL NATHAN HALE IMPRISONED INSIDE GUARD-HOUSE! ME TAKE BOTTLE OUT OF CAPE'S POUCH... TOSS IT TO HIM!
MOMENTS LATER...
PS-ST! SWALLOW WHAT AM IN THIS PRESENT FOR YOU, NATE!
BIZARRO NO. 1
I HEAR A VOICE SPEAKING! CAN IT BELONG TO... ANOTHER SPY?!--A BOTTLE IS BEING TOSSED IN BETWEEN THE CELL WINDOW'S BARS! WHAT...?!!
I'LL DRINK THE LIQUID... WHATEVER IT IS... AS THE VOICE INSTRUCTED! WHAT HAVE I GOT TO LOSE? THEY'RE GOING TO HANG ME IN A FEW MINUTES, ANYWAY!... I HEAR THE GUARDS COMING FOR ME--!
PRESENTLY, AT THE GALLOWS...
THEM PLACING NOOSE AROUND NATE'S NECK! SOON, THEM'LL GET BIG FAT SURPRISE! HAW!!
8.

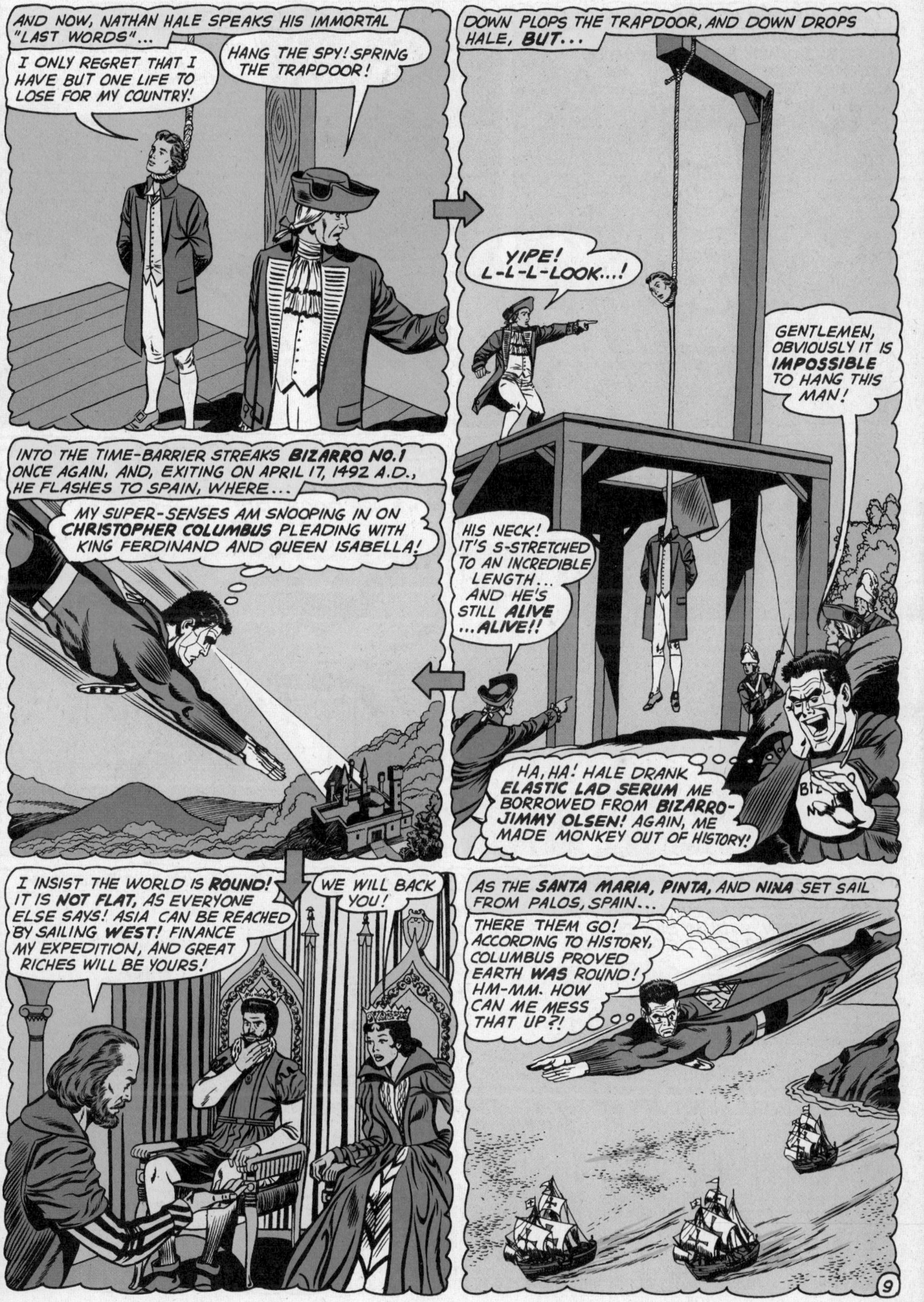
AND NOW, NATHAN HALE SPEAKS HIS IMMORTAL "LAST WORDS"...
I ONLY REGRET THAT I HAVE BUT ONE LIFE TO LOSE FOR MY COUNTRY!
HANG THE SPY! SPRING THE TRAPDOOR!
DOWN PLOPS THE TRAPDOOR, AND DOWN DROPS HALE, BUT...
YIPE! L-L-L-LOOK...!
GENTLEMEN, OBVIOUSLY IT IS IMPOSSIBLE TO HANG THIS MAN!
HIS NECK! IT'S S-STRETCHED TO AN INCREDIBLE LENGTH... AND HE'S STILL ALIVE ...ALIVE!!
HA, HA! HALE DRANK ELASTIC LAD SERUM ME BORROWED FROM BIZARRO-JIMMY OLSEN! AGAIN, ME MADE MONKEY OUT OF HISTORY!
INTO THE TIME-BARRIER STREAKS BIZARRO NO.1 ONCE AGAIN, AND, EXITING ON APRIL 17, 1492 A.D., HE FLASHES TO SPAIN, WHERE...
MY SUPER-SENSES AM SNOOPING IN ON CHRISTOPHER COLUMBUS PLEADING WITH KING FERDINAND AND QUEEN ISABELLA!
I INSIST THE WORLD IS ROUND! IT IS NOT FLAT, AS EVERYONE ELSE SAYS! ASIA CAN BE REACHED BY SAILING WEST! FINANCE MY EXPEDITION, AND GREAT RICHES WILL BE YOURS!
WE WILL BACK YOU!
AS THE SANTA MARIA, PINTA, AND NINA SET SAIL FROM PALOS, SPAIN...
THERE THEM GO! ACCORDING TO HISTORY, COLUMBUS PROVED EARTH WAS ROUND! HM-MM. HOW CAN ME MESS THAT UP?!
9

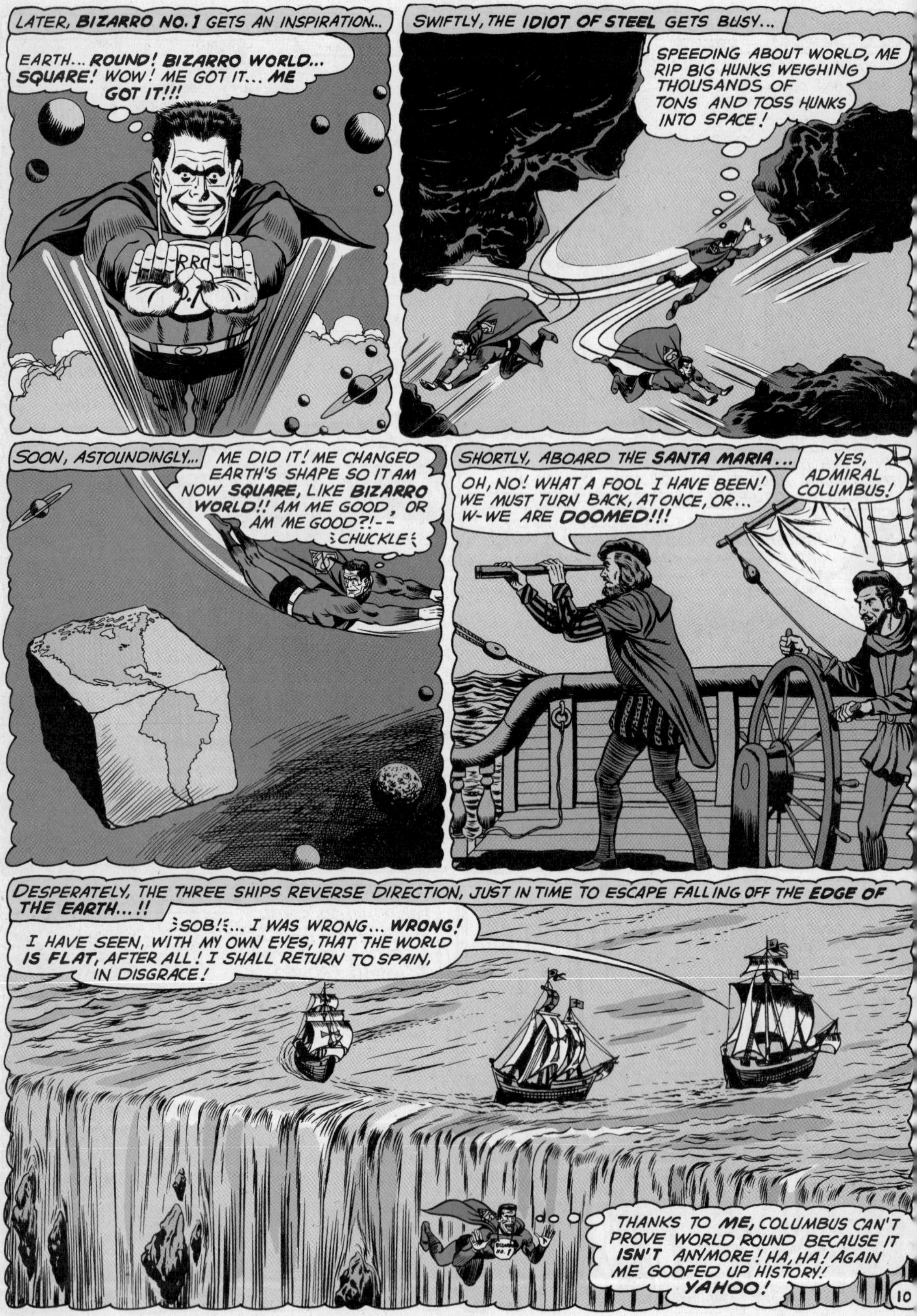
LATER, **BIZARRO NO. 1** GETS AN INSPIRATION...
EARTH... **ROUND! BIZARRO WORLD... SQUARE!** WOW! ME GOT IT... **ME GOT IT!!!**
SWIFTLY, THE **IDIOT OF STEEL** GETS BUSY...
SPEEDING ABOUT WORLD, ME RIP BIG HUNKS WEIGHING THOUSANDS OF TONS AND TOSS HUNKS INTO SPACE!
SOON, ASTOUNDINGLY...
ME DID IT! ME CHANGED EARTH'S SHAPE SO IT AM NOW **SQUARE**, LIKE **BIZARRO WORLD!!** AM ME GOOD, OR AM ME GOOD?!-- ⸗CHUCKLE⸗
SHORTLY, ABOARD THE **SANTA MARIA**...
OH, NO! WHAT A FOOL I HAVE BEEN! WE MUST TURN BACK, AT ONCE, OR... W-WE ARE **DOOMED!!!**
YES, ADMIRAL COLUMBUS!
DESPERATELY, THE THREE SHIPS REVERSE DIRECTION, JUST IN TIME TO ESCAPE FALLING OFF THE **EDGE OF THE EARTH**...!!
⸗SOB!⸗... I WAS WRONG... **WRONG!** I HAVE SEEN, WITH MY OWN EYES, THAT THE WORLD **IS FLAT**, AFTER ALL! I SHALL RETURN TO SPAIN, IN DISGRACE!
THANKS TO **ME**, COLUMBUS CAN'T PROVE WORLD ROUND BECAUSE IT **ISN'T** ANYMORE! HA, HA! AGAIN ME GOOFED UP HISTORY! **YAHOO!**
10

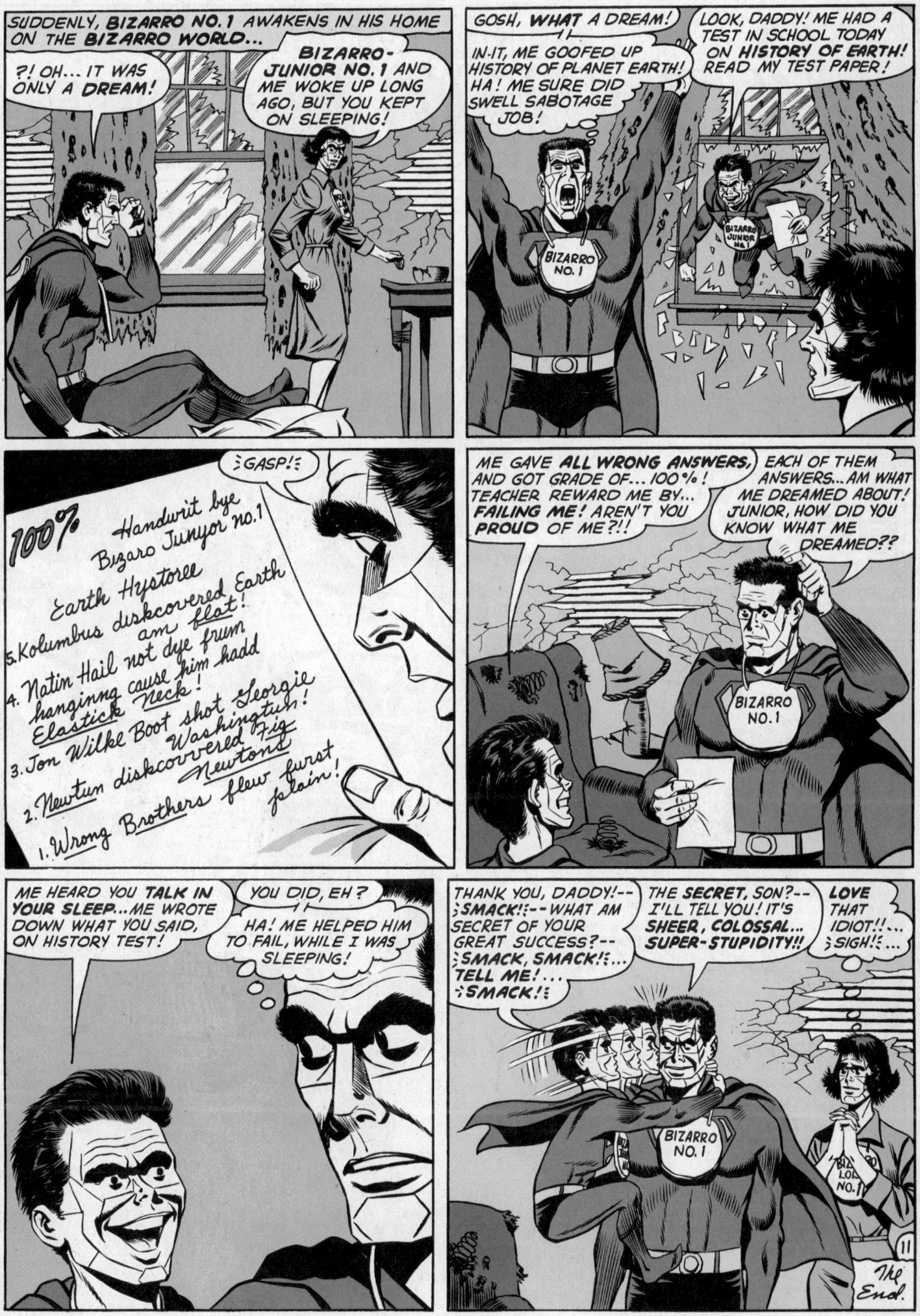
SUDDENLY, BIZARRO NO. 1 AWAKENS IN HIS HOME ON THE BIZARRO WORLD...
?! OH... IT WAS ONLY A DREAM!
BIZARRO-JUNIOR NO. 1 AND ME WOKE UP LONG AGO, BUT YOU KEPT ON SLEEPING!
GOSH, WHAT A DREAM!
IN-IT, ME GOOFED UP HISTORY OF PLANET EARTH! HA! ME SURE DID SWELL SABOTAGE JOB!
LOOK, DADDY! ME HAD A TEST IN SCHOOL TODAY ON HISTORY OF EARTH! READ MY TEST PAPER!
BIZARRO JUNIOR NO. 1
BIZARRO NO. 1
;GASP!;
100%
Handwrit bye Bizaro Junyor no.1
Earth Hystoree
5. Kolumbus diskcovered Earth am flat!
4. Natin Hail not dye frum hanginng cause him hadd Elastick Neck!
3. Jon Wilke Boot shot Georgie Washingtun!
2. Newtun diskcovvered Fig Newtons
1. Wrong Brothers flew furst plain!
ME GAVE ALL WRONG ANSWERS, AND GOT GRADE OF... 100%! TEACHER REWARD ME BY... FAILING ME! AREN'T YOU PROUD OF ME?!!
EACH OF THEM ANSWERS... AM WHAT ME DREAMED ABOUT! JUNIOR, HOW DID YOU KNOW WHAT ME DREAMED??
BIZARRO NO. 1
ME HEARD YOU TALK IN YOUR SLEEP... ME WROTE DOWN WHAT YOU SAID, ON HISTORY TEST!
YOU DID, EH?
HA! ME HELPED HIM TO FAIL, WHILE I WAS SLEEPING!
THANK YOU, DADDY!-- ;SMACK!;-- WHAT AM SECRET OF YOUR GREAT SUCCESS?-- ;SMACK, SMACK!;... TELL ME!... ;SMACK!;
THE SECRET, SON?-- I'LL TELL YOU! IT'S SHEER, COLOSSAL... SUPER-STUPIDITY!!
LOVE THAT IDIOT!!... ;SIGH!;...
BIZARRO NO. 1
11
The End.

TALES of the BIZARRO WORLD

ONE DAY, ON THE **BIZARRO WORLD**, A TERRIBLE CALAMITY BEFALLS **BIZARRO NO. 1**, THE SQUARE PLANET'S LEADER! HE IS TOSSED INTO A **BIZARRO** INSANE ASYLUM BECAUSE OF THE "TERRIBLE" ACCUSATION THAT HE IS ACTING IN A WAY EARTH PEOPLE WOULD CONSIDER SENSIBLE...THEREFORE, ACCORDING TO THE **BIZARRO'S** TWISTED THINKING, HE HAS FLIPPED HIS LID! FOR THE WILDEST, WHACKIEST, NUTTIEST TALE OF THE YEAR, SEE WHAT HAPPENS WHEN...

BIZARRO GOES SANE!

¿GASP!¿ ISN'T **TROOP LEADER BIZARRO NO. 1 WONDERFUL?** HIM RUBBING TWO **BIZARRO BOY SCOUTS** TOGETHER, TO MAKE A FIRE! FRICTION OF BOYS' BODIES CREATE... SPARKS!!

¿CHUCKLE¿ --ON EARTH, DUMB BOY SCOUTS START FIRE BY RUBBING **TWO STICKS** TOGETHER! HA, HA!

BIZARRO CODE
US DO OPPOSITE OF ALL EARTHLY THINGS! US HATE BEAUTY! US LOVE UGLINESS! IS BIG CRIME TO MAKE ANYTHING PERFECT ON **BIZARRO WORLD!**

FAR OUT IN SPACE EXISTS THE ZANIEST PLANET IN THE UNIVERSE...IT IS THE **SQUARE BIZARRO WORLD,** HOME PLANET OF THE STUPID **BIZARRO** CREATURES WHO ARE IMPERFECT DUPLICATES OF **SUPERMAN** AND HIS FRIENDS...

EVERYTHING ON THIS WHACKY WORLD IS THE OPPOSITE OF EARTH! FOR INSTANCE, THE INMATES OF ORPHAN-AGES ARE **ADULTS** INSTEAD OF CHILDREN...

YOU GOING ADOPT ME? OH, THANK YOU, THANK YOU!

SHUT UP! ADULTS SHOULD BE SEEN, NOT HEARD!

ORFUNAG STUPORINTENDUNT

AND WHEN **BIZARRO** GIRLS BUY PERFUME...

WEAR THIS AWFUL-SMELLING PERFUME AND ME GUARANTEE NO BOY WILL DARE GO NEAR YOU!

JUST WHAT ME WANT!... HYUK! HYUK!

DISGUSTNIK Per-fume

AT **BIZARRO WORLD** ZOOS, MONKEYS THROW PEANUTS TO PEOPLE, INSTEAD OF VICE VERSA, AS ON EARTH...

DON'T NOT FEED THE PEOPLE

ON THIS LOONY PLANET, WHEN A BOY AND GIRL BECOME BETROTHED, **SHE** GIVES THE ENGAGEMENT RING TO **HIM!**

A C-COAL RING? GULP! M-ME AM **UNDERWHELMED!**

CHUCKLE! EARTH CHEAPSKATES GIVE **DIAMONDS** TO SWEETHEARTS INSTEAD OF VALUABLE **COAL!**

BIZARRO PARENTS SLEEP IN CRADLES, AND THEIR BABIES SLEEP IN BIG BEDS...!

WAHH-HH!

MOAN!- BABY'S CRYING KEEPING ME AWAKE... SO ME'LL ROCK MYSELF TO SLEEP!

2

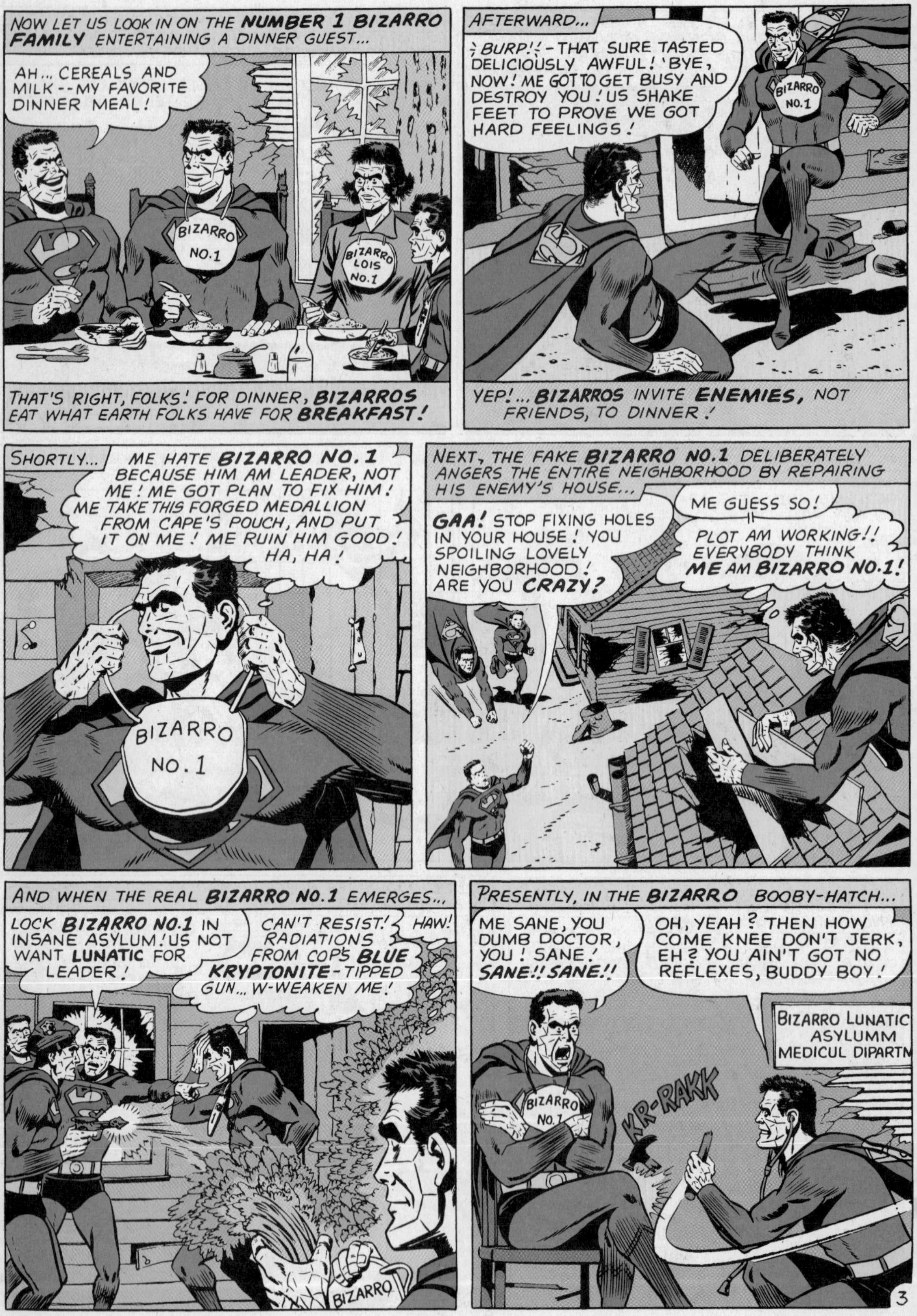

NOW LET US LOOK IN ON THE NUMBER 1 BIZARRO FAMILY ENTERTAINING A DINNER GUEST...
AH... CEREALS AND MILK--MY FAVORITE DINNER MEAL!
BIZARRO NO.1
BIZARRO LOIS NO.1
THAT'S RIGHT, FOLKS! FOR DINNER, BIZARROS EAT WHAT EARTH FOLKS HAVE FOR BREAKFAST!
AFTERWARD...
BURP!! -THAT SURE TASTED DELICIOUSLY AWFUL! 'BYE, NOW! ME GOT TO GET BUSY AND DESTROY YOU! US SHAKE FEET TO PROVE WE GOT HARD FEELINGS!
BIZARRO NO.1
YEP!... BIZARROS INVITE ENEMIES, NOT FRIENDS, TO DINNER!
SHORTLY...
ME HATE BIZARRO NO.1 BECAUSE HIM AM LEADER, NOT ME! ME GOT PLAN TO FIX HIM! ME TAKE THIS FORGED MEDALLION FROM CAPE'S POUCH, AND PUT IT ON ME! ME RUIN HIM GOOD! HA, HA!
BIZARRO NO.1
NEXT, THE FAKE BIZARRO NO.1 DELIBERATELY ANGERS THE ENTIRE NEIGHBORHOOD BY REPAIRING HIS ENEMY'S HOUSE...
GAA! STOP FIXING HOLES IN YOUR HOUSE! YOU SPOILING LOVELY NEIGHBORHOOD! ARE YOU CRAZY?
ME GUESS SO!
PLOT AM WORKING!! EVERYBODY THINK ME AM BIZARRO NO.1!
AND WHEN THE REAL BIZARRO NO.1 EMERGES...
LOCK BIZARRO NO.1 IN INSANE ASYLUM! US NOT WANT LUNATIC FOR LEADER!
CAN'T RESIST! RADIATIONS FROM COP'S BLUE KRYPTONITE-TIPPED GUN... W-WEAKEN ME!
HAW!
BIZARRO
PRESENTLY, IN THE BIZARRO BOOBY-HATCH...
ME SANE, YOU DUMB DOCTOR, YOU! SANE! SANE!! SANE!!
OH, YEAH? THEN HOW COME KNEE DON'T JERK, EH? YOU AIN'T GOT NO REFLEXES, BUDDY BOY!
BIZARRO LUNATIC ASYLUMM MEDICUL DIPARTM
BIZARRO NO.1
KR-RAKK
3

THE OTHER INMATES OF THE *BIZARRO* INSANE ASYLUM ARE FREAK *BIZARROS* WHO, BECAUSE THE *DUPLICATOR MACHINE* DIDN'T AFFECT THEIR MINDS, CAN THINK AND SPEAK NORMALLY, THOUGH THEY STILL HAVE SUPER-POWERS...

URK! THEM POOR SICK NUTS AM *MAKING* THINGS INSTEAD OF *BREAKING* THINGS, 'CAUSE THEM DON'T KNOW NO BETTER! *; CHOKE;*

I SURE WISHED I LIVED ON *EARTH,* DON'T YOU?

YES, THINGS ARE SENSIBLE THERE!

HOW PATHETICALLY TWISTED THEM ARE! ME MUST GET OUT OF HERE BEFORE LISTENING TO THEM DRIVE *ME* INSANE, TOO!

"BIZARRO WURLD"   "URTH"

BIZARRO NO. 1

LATER, IN HIS CELL, *BIZARRO NO.1* GETS AN IDEA...

ME ESCAPE BY TUNNELING DOWN THROUGH CELL FLOOR! OTHER INMATES NOT THINK OF THIS 'CAUSE THEM ISN'T BRILLIANTLY STUPID LIKE ME!

HOORAY! NOW THAT ME AM FREE LIKE BIRDIE, ME FLY FAR AWAY AND DO CRAZY THINGS WHICH PROVE THAT ME AM SANEST IDIOT ON *BIZARRO WORLD!*

OFF HE STREAKS TO THE SQUARE PLANET'S "TAME EAST", HIS WORLD'S VERSION OF EARTH'S WILD WEST...

HEY! WHY YOU RIPPING PIECES OUT OF STORES, STRANGER?

ME BUILDING SALOON, THAT WHY!

FRIENDLY SORT, ISN'T HIM?!

4

SHORTLY...

OH, BOY! JUST WHUT THIS TOWN NEEDED! ANOTHER SALOON! IT'LL GIVE THIS BURG *CLASS!*

WONDER WHY IT'S CALLED THE "BROKEN BAR X"?

OPIN FOR BIZNESS
"BROKEN BAR X SALOON"
VARMINTS CORJIALLY UNVITED

SALOON AM CALLED *"BROKEN BAR X"* BECAUSE ITS BAR AM *BROKEN,* SEE?... WHAT YOU HAVE, COWPOKES?

THE USUAL, BARTENDER! AND MAKE IT QUICK! ME AM *SLOWEST GUN* IN THE EAST!

PROMPTLY, *BIZARRO NO. 1* OBLIGES...

HERE YOU AM, GENTS! *GIANT MALTEDS!*

CRAZY EARTH BARTENDERS SELL WHISKEY! SERVING *PROPER BIZARRO* SALOON DRINKS AM PART OF CLEVER PLAN TO PROVE MYSELF *SANE!*

PRESENTLY, TROUBLE ERUPTS...

BIG GYP! GAME AM *CROOKED!* IT *FIXED* SO US *ALWAYS WIN!*

PS-ST! LET PLAYERS LOSE A FEW TIMES, SO THEM NOT GET WISE!

AND IN ANOTHER CORNER OF THE SALOON...

YAHOO! ME GOT THREE *DIFFERENT* PICTURES LINED UP ON SLOT MACHINE... ME *HIT JACKPOT!*

EARTH SLOT-MACHINE PLAYERS WIN IF GET THREE *SAME* PICTURES! WOW! WOTTA JACKPOT!! STALE CIGAR BUTTS! OLD, BENT BOTTLE-TOPS! YIPPEE!

AND WHEN **BIZARRO NO.1** PLAYS POKER WITH SOME OF HIS PATRONS...

CUT THE CARDS! AND DON'T DEAL HONESTLY, OR ME CHALLENGE YOU TO A SHOWDOWN... I MEAN "SHOW-UP"!

OKAY!

THEN... HA, HA! ME PEEK THROUGH BACK OF THEIR CARDS WITH X-RAY VISION... AND NOW SWIPE ONES ME WANT--SLOW ENOUGH SO OTHER PLAYERS SEE WHAT ME DOING!

GREAT CHEATING, PARD!

WISH **ME** COULD CHEAT THAT GOOD!

ME WIN 'CAUSE ME GOT "EMPTY HOUSE"... **LOWEST** CARDS IN DECK!

ON EARTH, **HIGHEST** CARDS WIN--AND A "**FULL HOUSE**" IS CONSIDERED ONE OF THE GREATEST. BUT ON THE **BIZARRO WORLD**, IT'S DIFFERENT!

SUDDENLY...

EVERYBODY MOVE! THIS AM HOLD-UP--QUICK, GALS,.. DUMP VALUABLES AND LET'S **GIT**!

ER... ON THE SQUARE PLANET, THE OUTLAWS ARE **GIRLS**, AND INSTEAD OF **ROBBING** VICTIMS, THEY FORCE THEM TO ACCEPT LOOT!

AS THE NON-SUPER **BIZARRO** FEMALES FLEE ON THEIR STEEDS, **BIZARRO NO.1** ORGANIZES A POSSE...

SLOW DOWN, HOMBRES! US GOT MAKE SURE THEM GET AWAY! THREE-- TWO-ONE--**GO**!

NO, YOU AREN'T SEEING HALLUCINATIONS! ON THE **BIZARRO WORLD**, THE HORSES RIDE ON THE **BIZARRO** COWBOYS...

HI-YO, SILVERWARE! AWAA-AAAY!

WHO YOU?

ME FLYALONG CASSIDY!

6

POLITELY, **BIZARRO NO. 1** SUPER-SHOUTS TOWARD THE FLEEING OUTLAWS...

WHY YOU SO DANGED SLOW, YOU CLEVER, PRETTY DAMES? WANT GIT CAPTURED? RIDE THEM MUSTANGS FASTER!!

ABRUPTLY, HIS TELESCOPIC VISION SIGHTS...

OH-OH! VIBRATIONS FROM MY SUPER-LOUD YELL LOOSE GREAT BOULDER ATOP **STEVE CANYON!** IF BOULDER FALL INTO NARROW CANYON, IT WILL BLOCK OUTLAWS' ESCAPE! ME ACT QUICK! DO ROPE TRICK!

FASTER THAN MOLASSES, ME TOSS TRUSTY LARIAT LOOP **TWO MILES** TO CATCH AND YANK ASIDE FALLING BOULDER SO OUTLAW GALS CAN GET PAST! PRETTY GOOD, HAH?

WOW! SOME TOSS! IT EVEN GREATER THAN A TOSSED SALAD!

HIM GREATEST COWBOY HERO THEM NEVER WAS!

BUT DISMAYINGLY...

BAW!--US LASSOED!

URK! WIND BLEW LARIAT DOWN ON OUTLAWS! ME CATCH **THEM** INSTEAD OF BOULDER!

ONLY **LUNATIC** WOULD CAPTURE OUTLAWS! THIS **BIZARRO** AM PLUM **LOCO!** ME CALL POLICE SO THEY CAN TAKE HIM AWAY TO **INSANE** ASYLUM!

AND SO, PRESENTLY...

;CHOKE;--THE POLICE THROWED ME BACK IN INSANE ASYLUM! BUT ME FOOL THEM ALL! AGAIN ME WILL ESCAPE FROM COZY CELL INTO HARSH, CRUEL **BIZARRO WORLD** AND **UNCLEAR MYSELF!!** ME **PROVE** ME NOT CRAZY!

SWIFTLY BURROWING TO FREEDOM, THE **IDIOT OF STEEL** EMERGES IN FRONT OF A **BIZARRO** BOY SCOUT TROOP...

WANT CROSS STREET **AGAINST** TRAFFIC, LADY?

NO!

I SAID... **NO!!**

SORRY, US BOY SCOUTS **GOT** DO BAD-DEED-A-DAY-- SO US **HELP** YOU ACROSS STREET WHETHER YOU WANT CROSS OR NOT! SHADDUP OR US BELT YOU!

ME GETTING IDEA!

HIS ADDLED BRAIN AFIRE WITH INSPIRATION, **BIZARRO NO.1** TRAILS THE YOUTHS...

CLOCK ON TOWER RAN DOWN, SO **BIZARRO BOY SCOUT** AM WINDING CLOCK-- ANOTHER BAD DEED!... HMM! ME USE THEM BRATS TO PROVE SELF SANE!

BOY SKOUT KLUBHOWSE

SHORTLY... ME HEREBY DECLARE MYSELF **TROOP LEADER!** ME BEAT UP ANYBODY WHO NOT WANT ME! THAT INCLUDE YOU, TOO, **BIZARRO-JIMMY OLSEN!** ANY OBJECTIONS?

OF COURSE NOT! CLEAN-LIVING, UPRIGHT HOODLUM LIKE YOU WOULD MAKE REALLY **DANDY TROOP LEADER!**

BIZARRO NO.1

AS THE MEETING RESUMES... RECITE SCOUT OATH, **BIZARRO-JIMMY OLSEN!**

ME BE UNTRUSTWORTHY, DISLOYAL, UNHELPFUL, UNFRIENDLY, DISCOURTEOUS, UNKIND, DISOBEDIENT, UNCHEERFUL, A SPENDTHRIFT, COWARDLY, SLOPPY AND IRRELEVANT!

SKOUT MOTTO "BE UNPREPARED"

BIZARRO

AFTERWARD, **BIZARRO NO.1** LEADS HIS TROOP ON A LONG "HIKE"...

ME BE TERRIFIC TROOP LEADER! TRUST ME, IDIOTS, AND US'LL **NEVER** FIND WAY BACK TO UNCIVILIZATION! WE **GET LOST** FOREVER!

GEE!

GREAT!

8

177

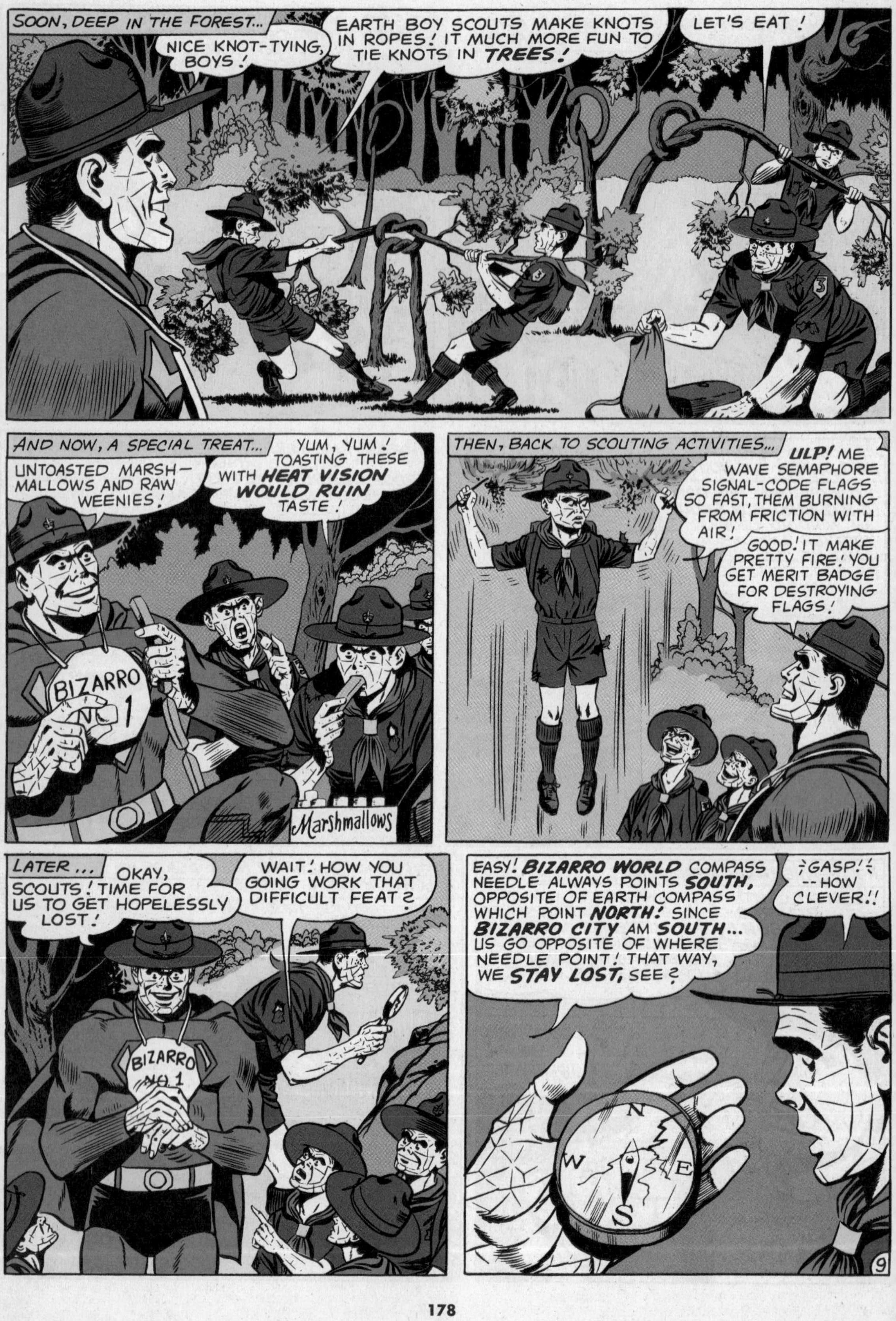

SOON, DEEP IN THE FOREST...
NICE KNOT-TYING, BOYS!
EARTH BOY SCOUTS MAKE KNOTS IN ROPES! IT MUCH MORE FUN TO TIE KNOTS IN TREES!
LET'S EAT!
AND NOW, A SPECIAL TREAT...
UNTOASTED MARSH-MALLOWS AND RAW WEENIES!
YUM, YUM! TOASTING THESE WITH HEAT VISION WOULD RUIN TASTE!
BIZARRO No 1
Marshmallows
THEN, BACK TO SCOUTING ACTIVITIES...
ULP! ME WAVE SEMAPHORE SIGNAL-CODE FLAGS SO FAST, THEM BURNING FROM FRICTION WITH AIR!
GOOD! IT MAKE PRETTY FIRE! YOU GET MERIT BADGE FOR DESTROYING FLAGS!
LATER...
OKAY, SCOUTS! TIME FOR US TO GET HOPELESSLY LOST!
WAIT! HOW YOU GOING WORK THAT DIFFICULT FEAT?
BIZARRO No 1
EASY! BIZARRO WORLD COMPASS NEEDLE ALWAYS POINTS SOUTH, OPPOSITE OF EARTH COMPASS WHICH POINT NORTH! SINCE BIZARRO CITY AM SOUTH... US GO OPPOSITE OF WHERE NEEDLE POINT! THAT WAY, WE STAY LOST, SEE?
¿GASP!¿ --HOW CLEVER!!
N
W
E
S
9

GLEEFULLY, THE **IDIOT OF STEEL** CARRIES OUT HIS SCHEME...

HA! HA! KEEPING TROOP LOST ON PURPOSE PROVE HOW **SANE** I AM! POLICE APOLOGIZE FOR PUTTING ME IN LOONY BIN WHEN THEY HEAR OF THIS!

US SURE LUCKY TO HAVE **YOU** FOR TROOP LEADER INSTEAD OF INCOMPETENT FOOL!

BUT SHORTLY...

OOooLP! **B-BIZARRO CITY!** WE **NOT LOST!**

ME SEE IT ALL NOW! YOU PROMISED KEEP US LOST... BUT LED US BACK HERE... BECAUSE YOU AM **STARK RAVING NUTS!**

HELP! POLICE! SAVE US FROM **LUNATIC!!**

TO **INSANE ASYLUM** WITH YOU!

WAIT! ME GET IT, NOW! **BIZARRO-JIMMY OLSEN'S** SIGNAL-WATCH **MAGNETIZED** MY COMPASS SO DUMB NEEDLE POINT **NORTH** INSTEAD OF **SOUTH** LIKE ANY SENSIBLE NEEDLE SHOULD!

OUCH-- THE BLUE KRYPTONITE'S RADIATIONS W-WEAKEN ME!

ME WENT SOUTH, THINKING ME WAS GOING NORTH...**NOT** BECAUSE ME WANTED TO GO EAST OR WEST, BUT BECAUSE SOUTH WAS NORTH AND NORTH WAS SOUTH! UNDER-STAND?

US UNDER-STAND... YOU AM **MAD!!**

SOON, BACK IN HIS SAME, OLD FAMILIAR CELL IN THE ASYLUM...

THIS AM GETTING MONOTONOUS! IN, OUT...OUT, IN! GAA! IF ME DON'T SOON PROVE ME SANE, ME'LL GO INSANE!

BIZARRO NO.1

AND SO...QUICK AS A TURTLE...DOWN THROUGH CELL FLOOR ME BURROW! **DOWN, DOWN** AND **AWAA-AAYY!!**

A SPLIT-INSTANT LATER, OUTSIDE THE ASYLUM...

MY MEDALLION AM GONE!...? OH, ME KNOW WHAT HAPPENED!

MOMENTS AFTERWARD, AS THE BOOBY-HATCH'S DOCTORS ANSWER A KNOCK ON THE DOOR...

BEGGING YOUR PARDON, KIND SIRS, BUT CAN ME COME IN? ME DROPPED SOMETHING WHEN ME BROKE OUT OF MY CELL...NAMELY MY MEDALLION!

BIZARRO LUNATICK ASY

COULD ME HAVE IT BACK, DOC? PRETTY PLEASE!

GREAT FRANKENSTEIN! DO YOU REALIZE WHAT THIS MEANS? YOU AM CURED! ÷SPUTTER÷ -- YOU NOT CRAZY ANYMORE! YOU AS SANE AS REST OF US IDIOTS!

ONLY SANE BIZARRO WHO ESCAPED FROM CELL WOULD BE SMART ENOUGH TO COME TO ASYLUM DOOR OPENLY AND RISK RECAPTURE! AN INSANE BIZARRO WOULDV'E TUNNELLED BACK INTO HIS CELL AFTER MEDALLION AND WOULD NEVER HAVE BEEN CAUGHT... SEE!

BIZARRO LUNATICK ASYLUMM

HOORAY! ME AM SANE, SANE!! WHOOPEE! MERRY CHRISTMAS! HAPPY NEW YEAR! GESUNDHEIT!

÷CHUCKLE÷ --JUST LOOK AT HIM! COULD ANYONE DOUBT HIM SANE NOW?!!

AFTER BIZARRO NO.1 RETURNS HOME...

YOU NOW BIZARRO WORLD'S LEADER AGAIN! WHAT AN HONOR!

ME GOT EVEN GREATER HONOR, DARLING... GRADUATION DIPLOMA FROM BIZARRO INSANE ASYLUM!

GEE, DAD, THAT'S KEEN! EVERYBODY WILL ENVY US!!

The End

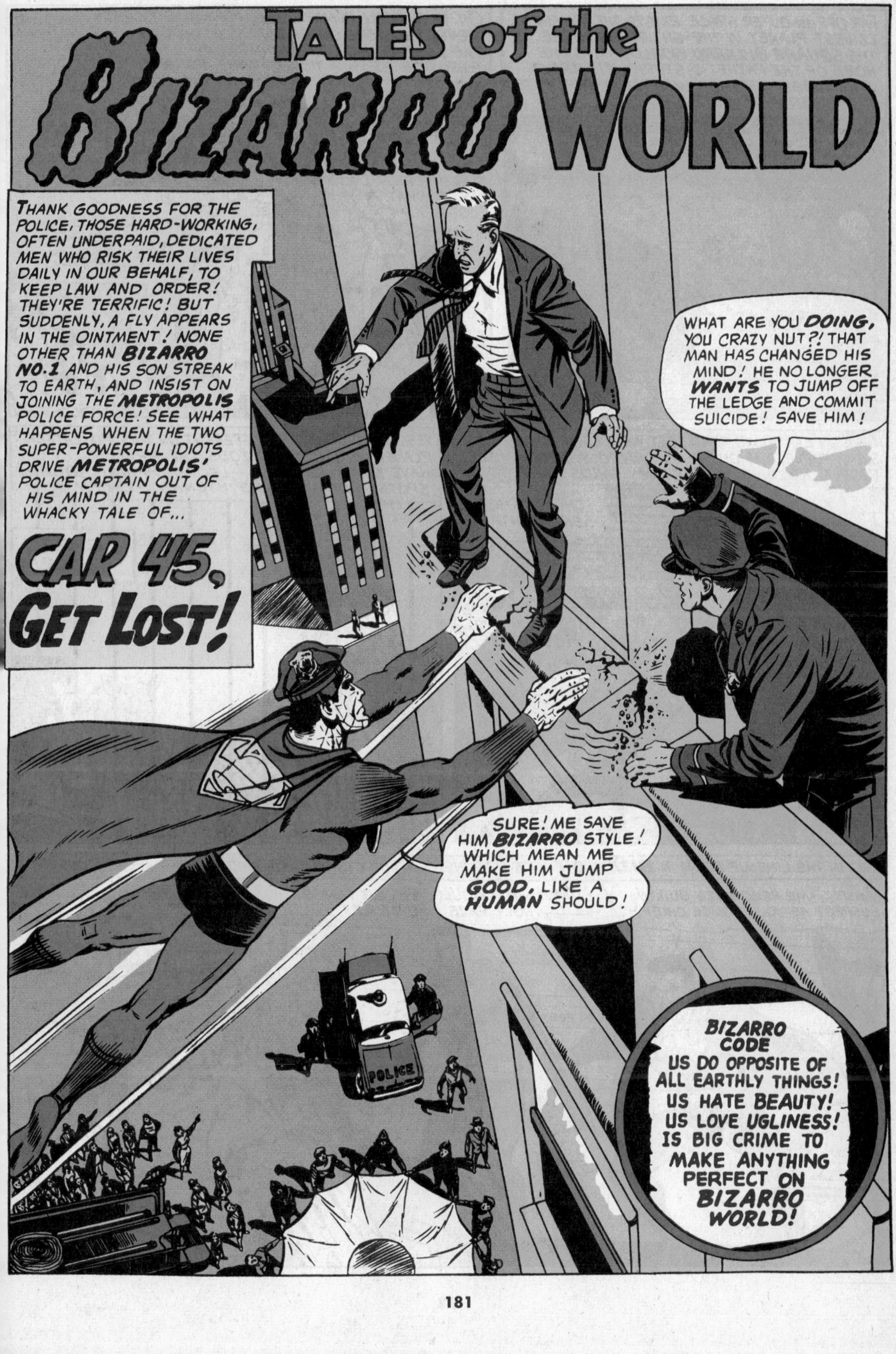
TALES of the BIZARRO WORLD
THANK GOODNESS FOR THE POLICE, THOSE HARD-WORKING, OFTEN UNDERPAID, DEDICATED MEN WHO RISK THEIR LIVES DAILY IN OUR BEHALF, TO KEEP LAW AND ORDER! THEY'RE TERRIFIC! BUT SUDDENLY, A FLY APPEARS IN THE OINTMENT! NONE OTHER THAN BIZARRO NO.1 AND HIS SON STREAK TO EARTH, AND INSIST ON JOINING THE METROPOLIS POLICE FORCE! SEE WHAT HAPPENS WHEN THE TWO SUPER-POWERFUL IDIOTS DRIVE METROPOLIS' POLICE CAPTAIN OUT OF HIS MIND IN THE WHACKY TALE OF...
CAR 45, GET LOST!
WHAT ARE YOU DOING, YOU CRAZY NUT?! THAT MAN HAS CHANGED HIS MIND! HE NO LONGER WANTS TO JUMP OFF THE LEDGE AND COMMIT SUICIDE! SAVE HIM!
SURE! ME SAVE HIM BIZARRO STYLE! WHICH MEAN ME MAKE HIM JUMP GOOD, LIKE A HUMAN SHOULD!
POLICE
BIZARRO CODE
US DO OPPOSITE OF ALL EARTHLY THINGS! US HATE BEAUTY! US LOVE UGLINESS! IS BIG CRIME TO MAKE ANYTHING PERFECT ON BIZARRO WORLD!

FAR OFF IN OUTER SPACE EXISTS THE WEIRDEST, ZANIEST PLANET IN THE ENTIRE UNIVERSE... THE *SQUARE BIZARRO WORLD!* IT IS THE HOME OF THE PATHETIC, STUPID *BIZARRO* CREATURES WHO ARE IMPERFECT DUPLICATES OF *SUPERMAN* AND HIS FRIENDS...

ON THIS LOONY PLANET, EVERYTHING IS A CRAZY, REVERSED VERSION OF EARTHLY CUSTOMS--FOR INSTANCE, THE *LOSER... NOT* THE WINNER... OF A PRESIDENTIAL ELECTION GETS A TICKER TAPE PARADE...

HOORAY FOR INFERIOR CREEP WHAT LOST!'...

HERE ON EARTH, WE SEND "GET WELL SOON" CARDS TO SICK PEOPLE, BUT ON THE *BIZARRO WORLD,* WELL PEOPLE RECEIVE *"GET SICK"* CARDS!

YOUR NAME AM FREDDIE --

SO GET SICK, ALREADY!

;CHOKE; - HOW... SENTIMENTAL...

YES, THINGS ARE VERY DIFFERENT ON THIS PIXILATED PLANET. IN *BIZARRO* ZOOS, THE GIRAFFES HAVE *SMALL* NECKS--LEOPARDS HAVE *SQUARE* SPOTS...AND LAUGHING HYENAS --*CRY!!*

BIZARRO ZOOE

AND IN THE LINE-UP ROOM IN *BIZARRO* POLICE STATIONS, IT IS THE *CRIMINALS* WHO IDENTIFY THEIR ACCUSER...

;GASP!; --ME RECOGNIZE GUILTY SUSPECT AS YOU...POLICE CHIEF.!!

;URK!; --ME WOULD *NEVER* FORGET UGLY FACE LIKE *THAT!*

AND NOW LET'S LOOK IN ON **BIZARRO NO. 1** AND HIS SON **BIZARRO JUNIOR NO. 1,** AS THEY FLY AWAY FROM THE GOOFY PLANET...

US GOING SPEND VACATION ON EARTH! THAT MEAN WE GOT TO GET JOBS AND WORK HARD! STUPID EARTH PEOPLE *LOAF* DURING VACATION!

BIZARRO NO. 1

SHORTLY...

YII-IICHH! WHAT A DISGUSTING WORLD EARTH AM!

EARTH LOOK QUEER! IT *ROUND* INSTEAD OF *SQUARE!*

LATER, AT **METROPOLIS** POLICE HEADQUARTERS, CAPTAIN BLOKE GETS THE SHOCK OF HIS LIFE...

GREAT SCOTT! FLYING MONSTERS!

GO AWAY-- OR I'LL SHOOT!

YOU GIVE US JOBS ON POLICE FORCE, SO WE CAN ENJOY VACATION FROM **BIZARRO WORLD!**

BIZARRO NO. 1

ME TRIPLE-- DARE YOU TO SHOOT US!

--ERK! MY B-BULLETS ARE BOUNCING OFF THEM!

GEE, DADDY, CAPTAIN AM SURE GIVING US WARM WELCOME!

THAT BECAUSE HIM SO *THRILLED* US WANT TO BECOME *FLATFEET!*

CAPTAIN BLOKE SUMMONS HELP...

¡PUFF!¡-- WE CAN'T BUDGE 'EM, SIR!

IT'S IMPOSSIBLE TO THROW THEM OUT!

BIZARRO NO. 1

ER... LEAVE ME ALONE WITH THESE TWO CREATURES!

SUPERMAN'S AWAY ON A SPACE MISSION, SO I CAN'T SUMMON HIM TO GET RID OF THESE MONSTERS! HMM... I'LL ACCOMPLISH IT BY *USING MY HEAD!!!*

3

AND SO... BIZARROS, YOU ARE NOW MEMBERS OF THE METROPOLIS POLICE FORCE AND I'M ASSIGNING YOU BOTH TO SQUAD CAR 45! BUT IF YOU FAIL ANY ASSIGNMENT, YOU'LL HAVE TO QUIT THE FORCE, AGREED?

OKAY, EARTH SLOB!

BIZARRO No. 1

NOW GO CAPTURE A PICKPOCKET, OFFICERS--OR YOU'RE FIRED!

MY PICKPOCKET SQUAD HAS CAUGHT ALL THE CITY'S PICKPOCKETS! THE MONSTERS WILL FAIL THEIR ASSIGN-MENT AND QUIT--I'M USING MY HEAD...HA, HA!!

SOON, IN THE POLICE STATION'S PARKING LOT...

URK! THOSE CREATURES WERE GIVEN CAR 45! BUT LOOK HOW THEY'RE CHANGING IT! SQUARE WHEELS!

CAPT. BLOKE SAYS NOT TO RESIST THEM! HE SAYS HE'LL GET RID OF THEM BY USING HIS HEAD!

POLICE 45

POLIC PARKIN ONLY

PRESENTLY, AS CAR 45 WHIZZES ALONG, LOADED WITH EQUIPMENT FASHIONED BY THE BIZARRO COPS...

WITH SQUARE WHEELS AND A PROPELLER ON BACK, CAR NOW LOOK GOOD, LIKE A CLASSY JUNKHEAP SHOULD!

POLICE 45

PRESENTLY, AT THE ZOO...

ZOO AM GOOD PLACE TO LOOK FOR PICKPOCKET BECAUSE THERE AM NO CROWDS HERE, RIGHT, DADDY!

COME-- HAVE A PEANUT, BABY KANGAROO!

¡SH-HH.!¡--THAT LADY BESIDE CARRIAGE AM ACTING SUSPICIOUS! ME GOT IDEA! LISTEN...

NEXT MOMENT, THE TWO LOONEY LAWMEN STREAK INTO ACTION...

FASTER THAN MOLASSES, ME BEND CAGE BARS!

MY HEAT VISION GIVING BABY KANGAROO HOT JAB SO HIM HOP IN PAIN TOWARD BECKONING LADY!

4

AND AS THE TINY KANGAROO'S LEAP LANDS HIM IN THE WOMAN'S BUGGY...

YOU UNDER ARREST! YOU LURED BABY KANGAROO INTO JUMPING OUT OF HIS **MOMMY'S POCKET**... YOU AM A PICKPOCKET!

Y!!-!!!

HA, HA! ME GO GET SHACKLES FROM CAR 45!

NEXT MOMENT...

NOW YOU GO TO JAIL!

EEK! THEY'RE...MAD, MAD, MAD!!

MINUTES AFTERWARD, AS CAPTAIN BLOKE LEARNS THE WORST...

OOLP! ACCORDING TO THE **BIZARROS'** MIXED-UP THINKING, THEY MADE GOOD ON THEIR ASSIGNMENT! --BUT I WON'T GIVE UP! SOMEHOW, I'LL MANAGE TO GET RID OF THEM BY **USING MY HEAD**!!

LATER, AS THE **BIZARRO** POLICEMEN REPORT BACK TO THE STATION...

WAIT! WHAT AM I DOING? WHY SHOULD **I** FRISK THIS CROOK, WHEN I'M THE CAPTAIN? TAKE OVER, PATROLMEN! FRISK HIM!

OKAY, BOSS!

OFF TO THE WEAPONS ROOM STREAK THE **BIZARROS**...

WEAPONS ROOM

US HELP OURSELVES!

THEN, AS THEY RETURN...

HERE, NICE MAN! TAKE MACHINE GUN! THAT AM ORDER!

HERE AM HAND GRENADE, TOO! CONSIDER YOURSELF **FRISKED**!

GEE, THANKS, GUYS!

OH, **NO**!!

5

AS THE GANGSTER HURLS THE GRENADE AT THE WALL...

HA, HA! -- STAND BACK, WHILE I ESCAPE THROUGH THE HOLE I MADE!

¡GROAN! STUPID ME! I FORGOT THE MONSTERS WOULD FRISK HIM BIZARRO-STYLE...

BWAMMMM

...AND GIVE HIM, INSTEAD OF TAKING AWAY, WEAPONS! WELL, THIS PROVES MORE THAN EVER THAT I'LL TRIUMPH OVER THESE MONSTERS ONLY BY USING MY HEAD!!

STOP STANDING THERE LOOKING PLEASED WITH YOURSELF! GET BACK ON THE JOB! AND REMEMBER -- IF YOU MUFF EVEN ONE ASSIGNMENT, YOU QUIT -- RIGHT?

RIGHT! LET'S GO, JUNIOR!

US GO, GO, GO!!

SOON... CALLING ALL CARS! THERE'S A BIG CRIME HAPPENING ON CLOVER STREET, AT ITS INTERSECTION WITH 10TH STREET!

US DO OUR DUTY!

BIG CRIME, EH? THIS AM JOB FOR CAR 45!

IN AND OUT OF TRAFFIC TEARS THE STRANGEST POLICE VEHICLE ON EARTH...

FASTER, DADDY!

STOP NAGGING, SON!

POLICE 45

SOON, AT CLOVER AND 10TH STREET...

OH-OH! A POLICE CAR!

HELP, HELP!

AH! US GOT HERE JUST IN TIME!

POLICE 45

6

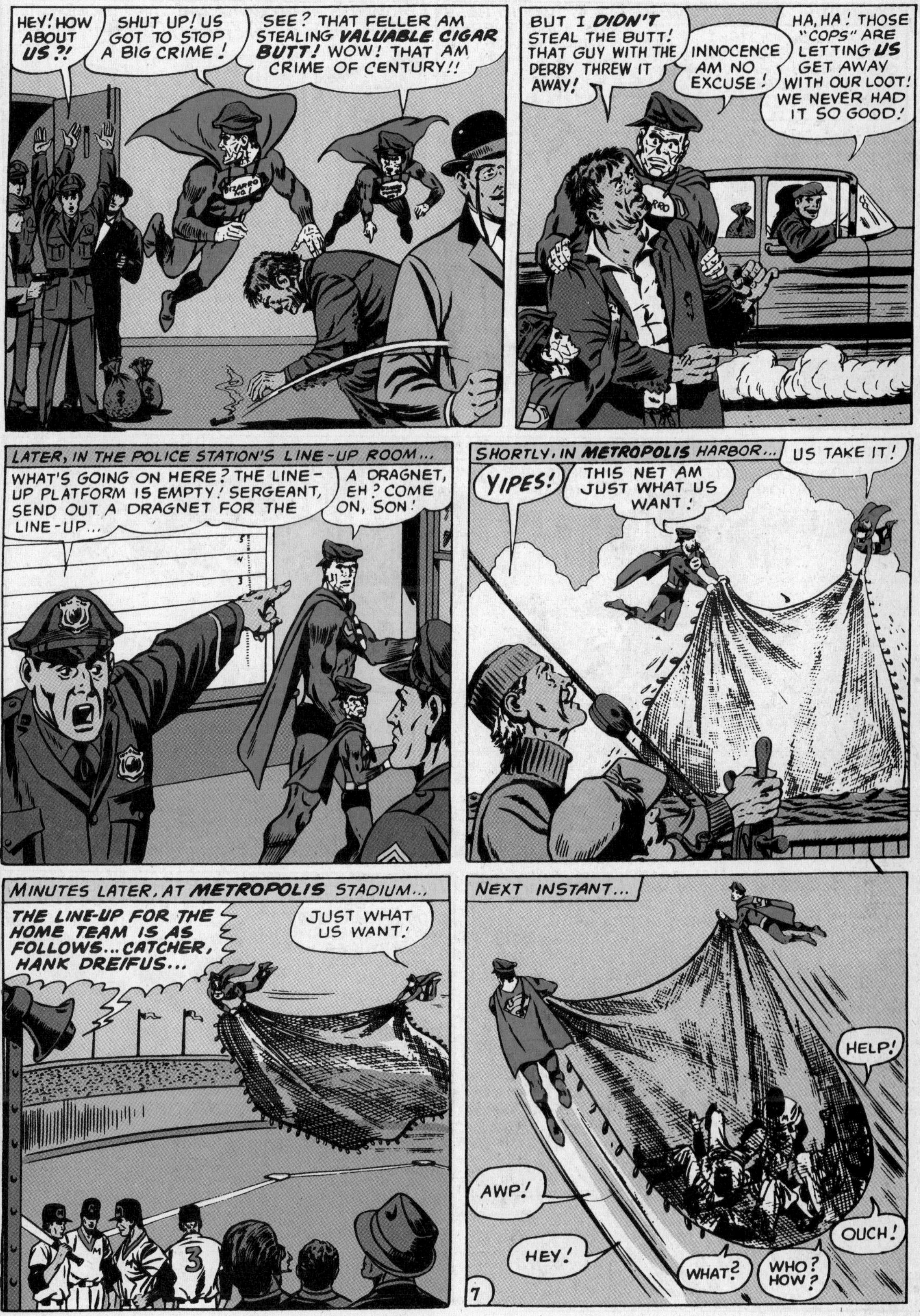
HEY! HOW ABOUT US?!
SHUT UP! US GOT TO STOP A BIG CRIME!
SEE? THAT FELLER AM STEALING VALUABLE CIGAR BUTT! WOW! THAT AM CRIME OF CENTURY!!
BIZARRO NO. 1
BUT I DIDN'T STEAL THE BUTT! THAT GUY WITH THE DERBY THREW IT AWAY!
INNOCENCE AM NO EXCUSE!
HA, HA! THOSE "COPS" ARE LETTING US GET AWAY WITH OUR LOOT! WE NEVER HAD IT SO GOOD!
LATER, IN THE POLICE STATION'S LINE-UP ROOM...
WHAT'S GOING ON HERE? THE LINE-UP PLATFORM IS EMPTY! SERGEANT, SEND OUT A DRAGNET FOR THE LINE-UP...
A DRAGNET, EH? COME ON, SON!
SHORTLY, IN METROPOLIS HARBOR...
YIPES!
THIS NET AM JUST WHAT US WANT!
US TAKE IT!
MINUTES LATER, AT METROPOLIS STADIUM...
THE LINE-UP FOR THE HOME TEAM IS AS FOLLOWS... CATCHER, HANK DREIFUS...
JUST WHAT US WANT!
3
NEXT INSTANT...
HELP!
AWP!
OUCH!
HEY!
WHAT?
WHO? HOW?
7

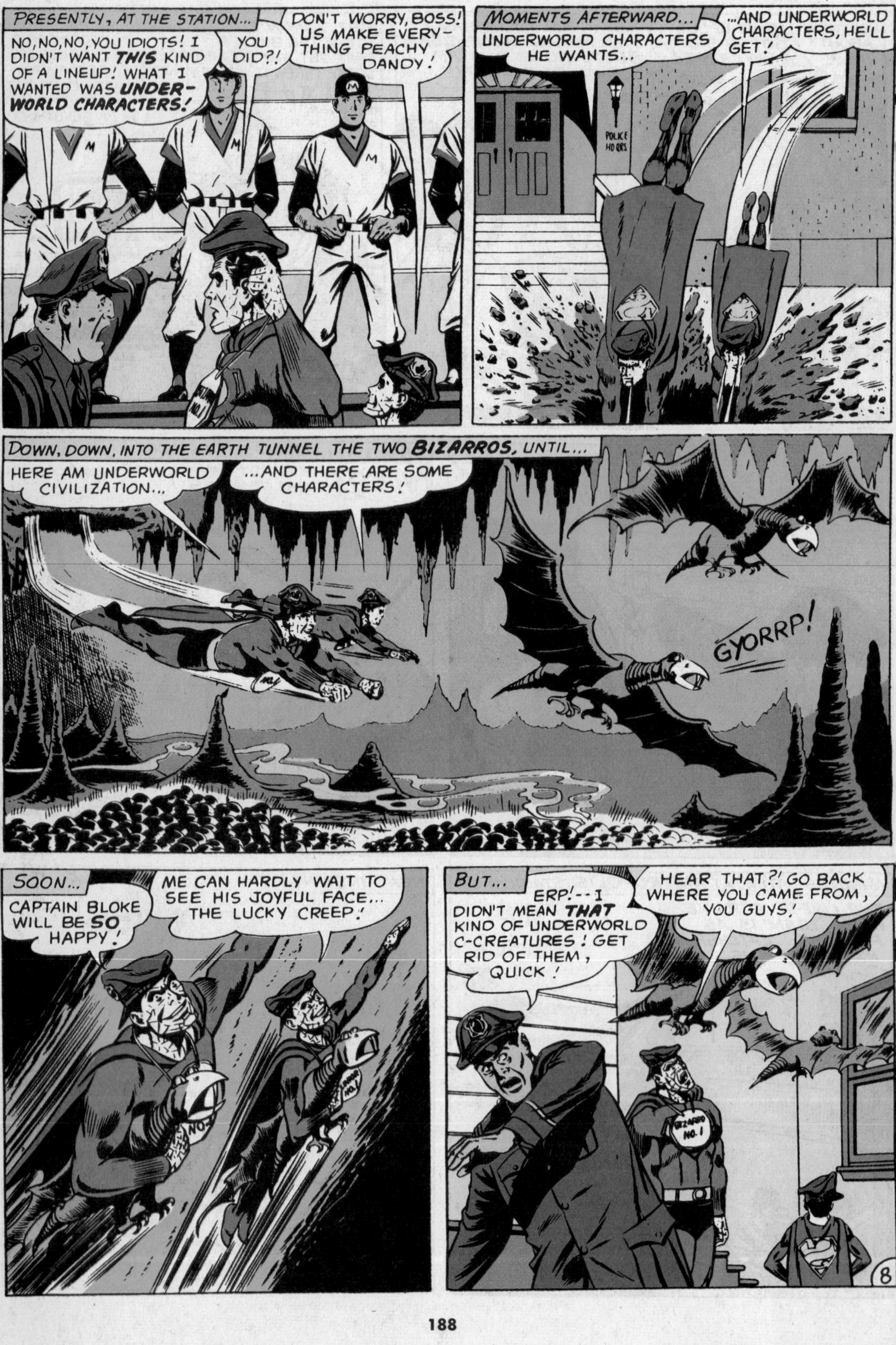

PRESENTLY, AT THE STATION...
NO, NO, NO, YOU IDIOTS! I DIDN'T WANT THIS KIND OF A LINEUP! WHAT I WANTED WAS UNDERWORLD CHARACTERS!
YOU DID?!
DON'T WORRY, BOSS! US MAKE EVERYTHING PEACHY DANDY!
MOMENTS AFTERWARD...
UNDERWORLD CHARACTERS HE WANTS...
...AND UNDERWORLD CHARACTERS, HE'LL GET!
POLICE HDQRS
DOWN, DOWN, INTO THE EARTH TUNNEL THE TWO BIZARROS, UNTIL...
HERE AM UNDERWORLD CIVILIZATION...
...AND THERE ARE SOME CHARACTERS!
GYORRP!
SOON...
CAPTAIN BLOKE WILL BE SO HAPPY!
ME CAN HARDLY WAIT TO SEE HIS JOYFUL FACE... THE LUCKY CREEP!
BUT...
ERP!--I DIDN'T MEAN THAT KIND OF UNDERWORLD C-CREATURES! GET RID OF THEM, QUICK!
HEAR THAT?! GO BACK WHERE YOU CAME FROM, YOU GUYS!
BIZARRO NO. 1
8

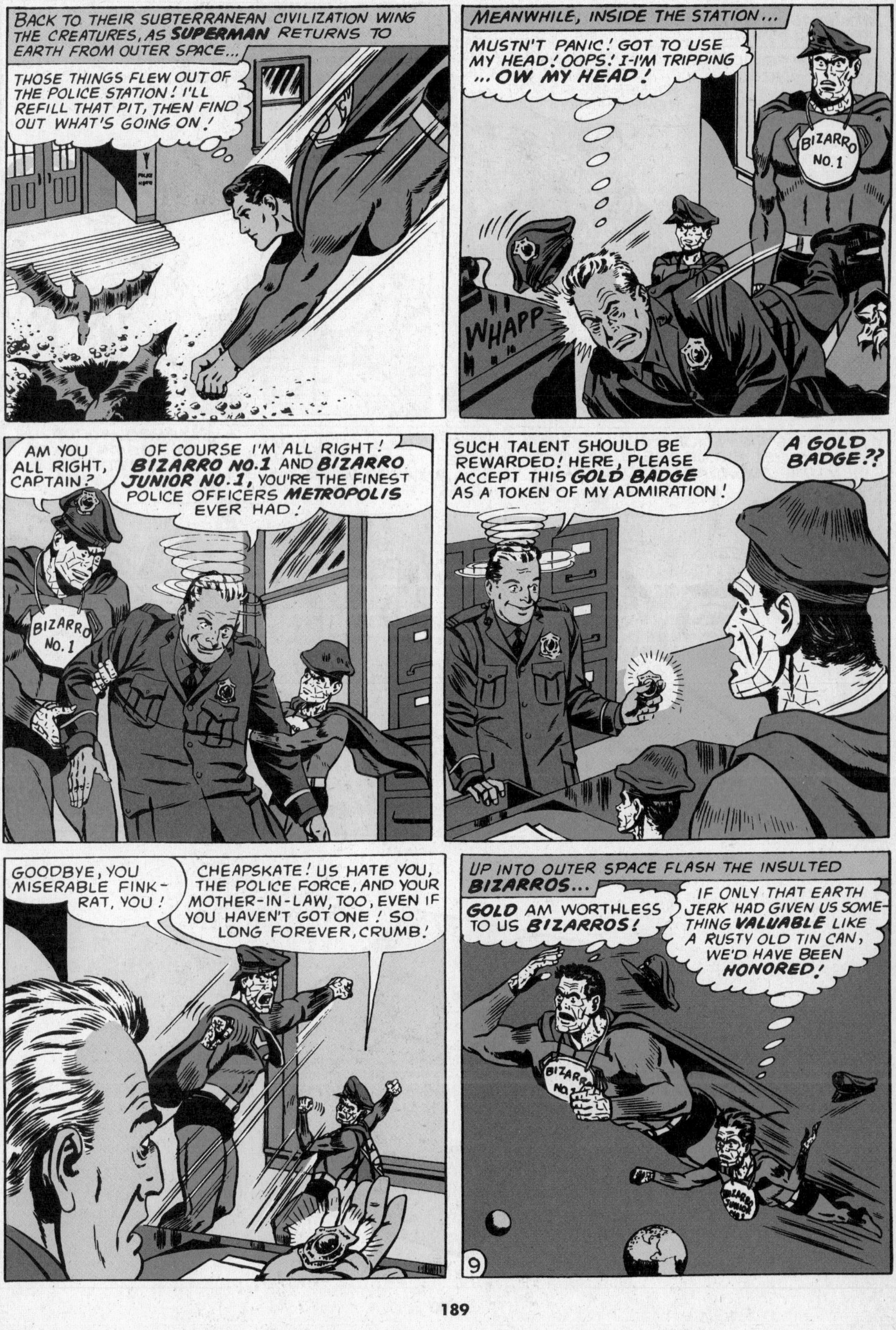

BACK TO THEIR SUBTERRANEAN CIVILIZATION WING THE CREATURES, AS **SUPERMAN** RETURNS TO EARTH FROM OUTER SPACE...
THOSE THINGS FLEW OUT OF THE POLICE STATION! I'LL REFILL THAT PIT, THEN FIND OUT WHAT'S GOING ON!
MEANWHILE, INSIDE THE STATION...
MUSTN'T PANIC! GOT TO USE MY HEAD! OOPS! I-I'M TRIPPING ...**OW MY HEAD!**
BIZARRO NO. 1
WHAPP
AM YOU ALL RIGHT, CAPTAIN?
OF COURSE I'M ALL RIGHT! **BIZARRO NO. 1** AND **BIZARRO JUNIOR NO. 1**, YOU'RE THE FINEST POLICE OFFICERS **METROPOLIS** EVER HAD!
BIZARRO NO. 1
SUCH TALENT SHOULD BE REWARDED! HERE, PLEASE ACCEPT THIS **GOLD BADGE** AS A TOKEN OF MY ADMIRATION!
A GOLD BADGE??
GOODBYE, YOU MISERABLE FINK-RAT, YOU!
CHEAPSKATE! US HATE YOU, THE POLICE FORCE, AND YOUR MOTHER-IN-LAW, TOO, EVEN IF YOU HAVEN'T GOT ONE! SO LONG FOREVER, CRUMB!
UP INTO OUTER SPACE FLASH THE INSULTED **BIZARROS**...
GOLD AM WORTHLESS TO US **BIZARROS!**
IF ONLY THAT EARTH JERK HAD GIVEN US SOMETHING **VALUABLE** LIKE A RUSTY OLD TIN CAN, WE'D HAVE BEEN **HONORED!**
9

MOMENTS LATER, AS **SUPERMAN** CONFRONTS THE POLICE CAPTAIN...

WHAT...HAPPENED? I FEEL --DAZED!

MY SUPER-VISION SAW EVERY-THING, CAPTAIN BLOKE! AN ACCIDENTAL BLOW ON YOUR HEAD DERANGED YOU TEMPORARILY...

YOU'VE RECOVERED NOW, BUT WHILE YOU WERE OUT OF YOUR MIND, YOU OFFENDED THE **BIZARROS!** THEY QUIT THE FORCE AND HAVE RETURNED TO THE **BIZARRO WORLD!**

A BANG ON THE HEAD, EH?

HA! I WAS **RIGHT** ALL ALONG! I **KNEW** THAT I'D GET RID OF THE **BIZARROS** BY **USING MY HEAD!!** AND I **DID!**

⑩

PRESENTLY... GOSH, WHAT GREAT RELIEF TO BE BACK ON **BIZARRO WORLD** WHERE EVERYTHING IS **NORMAL!**

BIZARRO WORLD, US NEVER AGAIN LEAVE YOU FOR COCKEYED PLANET EARTH!

The End

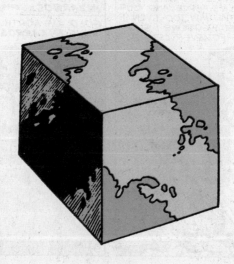

Wayne Boring

Born in 1916, Boring started working in comics on DC's *Slam Bradley* and *Spy*, but by far he is best known as the definitive Superman artist of the 1950s. Having started out as one of Siegel and Shuster's first ghosts, he grew to take over the art chores on the Superman comic strip as well as many of Superman's appearances in comic books. Leaving comics in 1968, he assisted Hal Foster on his comic strip *Prince Valiant* for four years until his brief return to comics to work on a handful of Marvel titles in the 1970s.

Boring passed away on February 20, 1987.

John Forte

Artist John Forte began his comics career at Marvel (then Timely) Comics in 1942 working with Stan Lee on the *Destroyer* backup strip. Throughout the 1940s and 1950s Forte worked for many of the top comics publishers such as Quality and Gleason. After a stint as an artist for ACG's line of horror comics he came to DC Comics to illustrate various stories in GIRLS' ROMANCE and GIRLS' LOVE STORIES.

Brought over to the line of Superman comics by then editor Mort Weisinger, he received his first regular feature in ADVENTURE COMICS, *Tales of the Bizarro World*. The strip lasted just over a year, but Forte then smoothly made the transition into its replacement and produced the work he is best known for: *The Legion of Super-Heroes*. As the Legion's first regular artist, Forte established a definitive look for the characters and the strip, which he drew until his death in 1965.

Stan Kaye

Stan Kaye began his career in comics during World War II, drawing and occasionally writing humor strips such as *Drafty*, about a bumbling soldier whose antics still made it tough on the Axis. He also worked on *Hayfoot Henry*, a backup strip in the early issues of ACTION COMICS. In 1944, as inker, he joined penciller Wayne Boring on the Superman newspaper strip. In 1948 the Boring-Kaye team added their talents to the Superman comic books. Kaye also inked Curt Swan on various stories in the Superman line of comic books for several years.

Kaye retired from comics in 1962 to enter his family's business.

Jerry Siegel

Born in 1914 in Cleveland, Ohio, young writer Jerome Siegel, along with his childhood friend Joe Shuster, created the most influential comic-book character ever: Superman.

Throughout the 1940s Siegel continued to write SUPERMAN while creating such features as *The Spectre*, *Robotman* and the *Star-Spangled Kid* for DC. After a brief attempt at comic strips in the 1950s he returned to DC to write many of the Superman family of books, including *Tales of the Bizarro World* and *Legion of Super-Heroes*.

Siegel died of heart failure on July 30, 1992.

Curt Swan

Fresh out of military service in 1945 where he had been providing illustrations for *Stars and Stripes*, Curt Swan immediately began his long association with DC Comics by pencilling a BOY COMMANDOS story and doing numerous other features. Recruited by editor Mort Weisinger in the 1950s, he moved to the Superman titles in 1955, eventually becoming the most popular Superman artist in the 1960s, working on such titles as WORLD'S FINEST, JIMMY OLSEN, and Superman's own titles for three decades.

Although he retired in 1986, Swan continued to produce work for DC until his death in 1996.

Biographical material researched by Mark Waid, Joe Desris, and Dr. Jerry Bails.

THE NEVER-ENDING BATTLE CONTINUES IN THESE BOOKS FROM DC COMICS:

TO FIND MORE COLLECTED EDITIONS AND MONTHLY COMIC BOOKS FROM DC COMICS,
CALL 1-888-COMIC BOOK FOR THE NEAREST COMICS SHOP
OR GO TO YOUR LOCAL BOOK STORE.

Visit us at www.dccomics.com